Alternative Theories of the State

Alternative Theories of the State

Edited by Steven Pressman

palgrave
macmillan

First published 2006 by
PALGRAVE MACMILLAN
Houndmills, Basingstoke, Hampshire RG21 6XS and
175 Fifth Avenue, New York, N.Y. 10010
Companies and representatives throughout the world

PALGRAVE MACMILLAN is the global academic imprint of the Palgrave Macmillan division of St. Martin's Press, LLC and of Palgrave Macmillan Ltd. Macmillan® is a registered trademark in the United States, United Kingdom and other countries. Palgrave is a registered trademark in the European Union and other countries.

ISBN 13: 978–1–4039–9939–9 hardback
ISBN 10: 1–4039–9939–2 hardback

This book is printed on paper suitable for recycling and made from fully managed and sustained forest sources.

A catalogue record for this book is available from the British Library.

Library of Congress Cataloging-in-Publication Data

Alternative theories of the state / edited by Steven Pressman.
p. cm.
Includes bibliographical references and index.
ISBN 1–4039–9939–2 (cloth)
1. State, The. I. Pressman, Steven.

JC11.A58 2006
320.1–dc22 2006043411

10 9 8 7 6 5 4 3 2 1
15 14 13 12 11 10 09 08 07 06

Printed and bound in Great Britain by
Antony Rowe Ltd, Chippenham and Eastbourne

Contents

List of Figures

List of Tables

Notes on Contributors

Morris Altman is Department Head and Professor in the Department of Economics, University of Saskatchewan, Canada.

Peter Boettke is Deputy Director at the James M. Buchanan Center for Political Economy, Senior Research Fellow at the Mercatus Center, and a Professor in the Economics Department at George Mason University, USA.

Bridget Butkevich is a PhD Candidate at the George Mason University, USA.

Raju Das is Assistant Professor in the Department of Geography, York University, Canada.

Ellen Mutari is Assistant Professor in the General Studies Division, Richard Stockton College, USA.

Phillip Anthony O'Hara is Director at the Global Political Economy Research Unit and Associate Professor, Curtin University, Australia.

Jacqueline Stanfield is Professor of Sociology, University of Northern Colorado, USA.

James Ronald Stanfield is Professor of Economics at Colorado State University, USA.

William Waller is Professor of Economics at Hobart and William Smith Colleges, USA.

1
Alternative Views of the State

Steven Pressman

In the real world, the state plays a significant role in the economy. It establishes the laws and sets the rules by which economic activity takes place. It also protects domestic producers from forces (both domestic and foreign) that threaten domestic production and consumption. Furthermore, for most developed countries in the world the state purchases more than one-fifth of the output produced in the national economy. This gives the state a large say in what gets produced and how goods get produced and sold.

The state also must raise revenues to engage in spending. This too affects economic behavior and economic performance. Taxed items are more expensive, so less of them are bought, and the effort to avoid paying taxes may lead to large inefficiencies.

Tax and spending decisions, taken together, also affect national interest rates. These, in turn, affect consumption and investment decisions as well as the value of the national currency.

Because different groups of people benefit and lose from these decisions about spending, taxation and regulation, government tax and spending policy can have a big impact on the national distribution of income. But perhaps most important of all, state governments can affect economic performance (growth rates, unemployment rates and inflation rates), and so all nations employ economic policies in an attempt to improve macroeconomic performance and stabilize the economy.

Unfortunately, neoclassical economics has very little use for the state and assigns virtually no positive role for the state in the economy. In most incarnations of neoclassical thought, the state is necessary only as a night watchman. Its main function is to protect property rights so that free market economic activity can go forward with minimal outside interference. When the state attempts to do anything beyond this, it is seen as a negative force on the national economy. There are several reasons why this is so according to neoclassical thinking.

First, as noted above, any state activity must be paid for. This requires either imposing taxes on market activities or incurring public debt. The former creates disincentives to engage in productive activities. The latter requires that the government borrow money that otherwise would have been borrowed or spent by the private sector (either consumption or investment). In either case, private economic activity gets crowded out by state activity. Since private economic activity is usually regarded as more desirable than public activity, and since private production is believed to take place more efficiently without any outside interference, the state can only lower economic welfare through its expenditures.

Second, in the market, consumers are assumed to buy and get what they want most, while at the same time business firms have strong incentives to produce goods efficiently. This leads to Pareto Optimal outcomes, states of affairs that cannot be improved upon unless someone is made worse off. Whenever the state enters the economic arena, someone must be made worse off. Moreover, since the state is assumed to operate less efficiently (due to the lack of a profit motive) any activities performed by the state, rather than by for-profit firms, should lower economic output and economic well-being.

Third, the existence of the state is thought to lead to rent-seeking by individuals. Self-interested economic agents will attempt to use the state to alter the distribution of income – either directly through favorable tax and transfer programs, or indirectly through government-granted monopolies (and other benefits that lead to higher incomes for some special interest group). It is for this reason that national governments have traditionally supported farmers through mechanisms such as price support for farm products and even making payments to farmers for not producing more crops.

Rent-seeking behavior also leads to trade restrictions that benefit some domestic industry, such as tariffs and quotas imposed on foreign goods. This leads to higher prices and profits for goods produced within that industry because it faces less competition. The gain for the protected industry, however, is simultaneously a loss for the large number of consumers who have to pay higher prices. More importantly, this loss can be substantial. For example, it has been estimated that restrictions on steel imports in the US during the 1980s cost US consumers around $500,000 for each job saved in the steel industry

(Hufbauer, Berliner & Elliot, 1986). As many economists pointed out, it would have been cheaper to pay steelworkers $100,000 a year (much more than their average pay at the time) and have them do nothing. Likewise, as many economists have pointed out, those who lose (US consumers) do not lose enough individually to make it worth their time and money to organize and demand that the government eliminate trade restrictions.

But the negative impact from protecting the domestic steel industry goes far beyond some gains to the steel industry and some losses to US consumers. There will be additional losses for other domestic industries when one industry receives protection from foreign competition. For example, tariffs on steel imports to help the US steel industry will hurt the domestic US automobile industry that has to pay higher prices for the steel used in making cars. Because foreign automobile producers have access to lower-priced steel, they gain a competitive advantage over US auto manufacturers who will have to charge higher prices for their cars, leading to lost sales and market share in a competitive global economy.

A massive amount of rent-seeking activity is also a big waste of resources. It wastes the time of individuals who lobby politicians and political bodies instead of producing goods and services. And it wastes the time of government officials who have to respond to this pressure and make decisions. These (real) resources could have been used producing things; consequently, the national standard of living is lower.

All these arguments against the state depend on adopting the neoclassical perspective and on making neoclassical assumptions about individual and firm behavior. Neoclassical economics assumes that firms are run by individual entrepreneurs who seek only to maximize profits and that they operate in a perfectly competitive economic environment. Neoclassical economic theory also assumes that individuals are rational and self-interested, as well as knowledgeable agents whose preferences are formed without any outside influences. Thus, by assumption, neoclassical economics ignores the possibility of economic power possessed by the firm and it ignores the possibility that individuals may be influenced by their social environment. It also ignores the possibility of fundamental or Keynesian uncertainty (see Rosser, 2001), a situation in which people do not know the future and cannot rationally calculate what will bring them the greatest utility or what is in their own best interest. Finally, the standard neoclassical position assumes that general equilibrium is readily achieved, bringing with it the full utilization of all resources, including labor. Here the thrust of real world macroeconomic policy to lower unemployment is assumed away.

The numerous heterodox schools of economic thought have rejected one or more of these key assumptions of neoclassical theory, or they have modified some of the more extreme assumptions employed in neoclassical analysis. In so doing, they have adopted some other set of glasses to view the economic world. For example, Post Keynesians and Austrians have stressed that the economic world is characterized by uncertainty, while feminists, behavioral economists, economic sociologists, institutionalists and Marxists have stressed the impact of society and class relations on individual preferences and behavior. For these schools of thought, individual rationality as defined by neoclassical theory does not exist in the real world. Institutionalists, Post Keynesians and most radical economists have focused on the economic power accumulated by large firms and their ability to influence consumption decisions and control markets.

Many heterodox schools have also questioned the assumption of full employment. Post Keynesians and institutionalists have emphasized the persistence of unemployment in the world economy, while Marxists and other radical economists have emphasized the important economic role that a large "reserve army" of unemployed workers plays in a capitalist economy. Feminists, meanwhile, have stressed that the notion of full employment must be reconsidered in a world where many single women have child-rearing responsibilities.

These alternative assumptions and perspectives also give rise to alternative views of the role of the state. For Post Keynesians, uncertainty makes business firms reluctant to invest. This lack of investment, in turn, means that economies may find themselves experiencing prolonged bouts of unemployment, which requires the remedy of government macroeconomic policies. For feminists, government action is needed to enable single women to work at the same time that they are raising a family. For institutionalists and economic sociologists, the state must counter the tendency of economic relations to dominate all of life and thereby leave important social aspects out of the picture. The state must also counter the power of business interests and politically assert the public interest. For radical economists who follow the social structure of accumulation approach, and for public choice and Austrian economists, state institutions must be established that enable business firms to thrive and to accumulate capital and grow.

Unfortunately, the people writing within each of these alternative economic approaches tend to read little of the work written from other heterodox perspectives. One result is that heterodox approaches in economics are fragmented – both intellectually and politically. As a set of diverse dissenting perspectives it presents meager opposition to neoclassical thought. A second result is that people working on the same topic within different heterodox schools do not get the important cross-fertilization from people who are working on similar questions but do not share all the standard neoclassical assumptions. This leads to something akin to reinventing the wheel from different points of view – similar discoveries or arguments are being made in different places, and too many individual authors are working on topics that have already been addressed at length within other schools. A further consequence of this fragmentation is that it stultifies the development of alternative perspectives. When one is working on a specific topic, and has few colleagues with whom one can debate and discuss the issues, an intellectual torpor tends to set in. Moreover, the theories being set forth are narrower and less nuanced due to the absence of stimulation from people with different perspectives.

One purpose of this volume is to get people working in different heterodox traditions to begin to communicate with each other. It contains eight substantive chapters on the role of the state. Each chapter looks at the functions, roles and effects of government activity from a different heterodox perspective. The chapters are written by well-known and knowledgeable people within a particular heterodox perspective, and are written at a level and in a manner so that they can be understood by readers from any heterodox point of view.

In Chapter 2, William Waller discusses the institutionalist view of the state. For institutionalists, the role of the state in modern economies is to mediate conflicts and solve problems that arise from a world with differing interests and power. Two key figures in the history of institutional economics, Commons and Tugwell, saw the state as a means of dealing with these conflicts. Independent regulatory authorities, comprised of people from all power groups, would mitigate monopoly power and help regulate business in the public interest. The state is thus a pragmatic or instrumental force that promotes social and economic stability. It does this by printing money, by establishing legal roles and enforcing them, and by helping to resolve conflicts among various economic groups. It is also pragmatic in that its solutions lead to minimal changes from accepted practice and so minimal social dislocation. However, the state still must be creative in solving the practical problems of the members of a community.

Chapter 3 looks at the views of Karl Polanyi on the state, or what Ronald and Jacqueline Stanfield call "the economic sociology approach." On this approach, economic activity requires a social system that supports it. In order to provide goods and services in any economy, the production and distribution system that gets us these goods needs to operate within a social or cultural setting that sets standards, norms and establishes practices. People must behave in certain ways. They need to go out and work; they need to receive sufficient income; and they must use that income to buy things. These behaviors depend on societal norms and practices and on ethical beliefs (for example, self-interested behavior is desirable and that one should act the way that other people do).

However, when market activity becomes predominant it tends to destroy the sense of community that is necessary for its own survival. For example, the mobile labor force necessary for capitalist production destroys the rootedness of people in community life. Polanyi argued that market economies would result in disruptions to social life, and that society would reassert itself and attempt to protect itself through state legislation. Thus we have government intervention in labor markets to regulate working time, working conditions and wages, as well as government actions to protect the environment and maintain full employment.

In Chapter 4, Raju Das sets forth the Marxist theory of the state. Or, perhaps, it would be best to say Marxist theories of the state. In general, Marxists view the state through the lens of class and class struggle. The state is seen as integral to the struggle between workers and capitalists that is the capitalist production process. But as Das points out, there is no single Marxist view of the state; rather, Marxists have several different theories. These theories all concern the role of the state in mediating conflicts among particular capitalists and in mediating conflicts between labor and capital in general.

Instrumentalists view all state action as being controlled by capital. The state is run by the government officials and the individuals who fund political parties and candidates. These people have been educated and paid to help business. One problem with the instrumental view is that sometimes the state does employ policies, like labor reform, that capital does not want. Also, there may not be single interests of capital; rather, there are interests of individual capitalists that sometimes conflict.

The structuralist view sees the state as an institution attempting to give unity and cohesion to capitalists; it is an arena where they can work out their differences and a place where they can maintain their interests by keeping non-capitalists disorganized. For example, some goods that are necessary for reproduction to take place profitably may not be able to be produced privately. So the state, in the interest of capital, will produce these goods. The limitation of the structural approach, according to Das, is that it ignores the agency or intention of individual actors. For example, how and why do the actions of government bureaucrats result in policies that are compromises among different capitals and that tend to promote their mutual interest? And how does this relate to the class struggle?

Chapter 5 explores the social structure of accumulation (SSA) approach. Phillip O'Hara identifies several salient features of this perspective. Then he examines whether neoliberalism might provide the foundation for a new long-term upswing in economic activity. Neoliberalism, prevalent since the late 1970s in the US and UK, and then catching on through the rest of the world, promotes privatization, deregulation and reduced government spending. Under the banner of promoting free markets and reducing government interference with these markets, state expenditures have been reduced for both infrastructure and for maintaining a social safety net (Keynesian welfare policies). The goal of all these policies is to stimulate private initiatives, increase private investment and spur growth.

O'Hara examines economic data from the end of World War II to the beginning of the 21st century to see whether neoliberal policies of the late 20th century have improved economic performance over the long run. In terms of economic growth, in terms of productivity growth, in terms of financial crises, and in terms of inequality, O'Hara argues that the late 20th century looks bad when compared with the decades immediately following World War II. From this he concludes that the neoliberal policies of the late 20th century have been a failure and have not contributed to a new long-run economic upswing.

In Chapter 6, Steven Pressman presents a Post Keynesian view of the role of the state. One of the fundamental Post Keynesian ideas is that the world is uncertain. This uncertainty differs from risk, the case where people can attach probabilities to future scenarios or states of the world. With true uncertainty, the future is unknown and no probabilities can be attached to the future. Spending under such circumstances requires overcoming the uncertainty of the future. When consumers and firms are willing to do this, economies perform well.

When firms and consumers are so uncertain about the future that they are unwilling to spend, economies experience recessions and Depressions. For Post Keynesians, the state is necessary to reduce uncertainty and to help convert uncertainty into risk. The main way it goes about doing this is to employ fiscal policy to mitigate business cycles. This will make economic agents confident about the future, and so it increases the propensity to spend and improves economic outcomes. By providing a social safety net, the state also mitigates the uncertainty of future incomes. People can be more confident of future incomes at some minimal level, and thus are more likely to spend.

A second important Post Keynesian idea is that individual behavior is not the result of some rational decision regarding maximizing utility among all possible choices. It is not even clear that individuals know what will give them utility or can correctly estimate what choices will more likely maximize their utility because of their inability to assess probabilities correctly. In contrast to neoclassical thought, Post Keynesians see human behavior as determined by institutions, habits, conventions, and by our genetic makeup as it has evolved over hundreds of millions of years. Here the Post Keynesian view of the state dovetails with the work of institutionalist and behavioralist economists. But when individual behavior is determined by something other than neoclassical utility maximization, the state may be able to increase total utility through economic policies that change habits or conventions, or through rules or policies that keep people from making decisions that do not really increase their well-being.

In Chapter 7, Ellen Mutari presents the feminist view of the state. Feminists, according to Mutari, see the state as neither a force for evil (as both neoclassical and Marxist economists tend to do) nor a force for good (as many Post Keynesian and institutional economists think). Rather feminists see the state as either reproducing existing gender relations or transforming those relations. The state is thus an arena in which battles over appropriate gender roles get fought out. But unlike economic activity, where outcomes get determined by those with the most wealth and income, in the political arena and the social arena the general rule is that each person has one vote. This provides the possibility for the state to be a positive force. But with individual habits and prejudices affecting political outcomes, the state can also be a negative force.

As Mutari shows, historically, the state has supported the ideal of the male breadwinner but has also attempted to provide equal opportunities for women, thereby breaking down this mode. Mutari shows how this is true of welfare policy, employment policy, childcare policy and tax policy. In all these cases, feminists call for a more progressive state policy, one that seeks to transform gendered relationships, alleviate gender inequity, and allow women to pursue the same developmental options available to men.

In Chapter 8, Morris Altman presents a behavioralist theory of the role of the state. Building on institutionalist studies (as described in Chapter 2 by William Waller) the behavioral approach focuses on how institutions affect human behavior. Of particular interest for Altman is the impact of institutions on work effort and on the decisions by firms to invest in new technology.

The decision to invest depends on several things. First, there must be private property rights. Firms will not invest unless the owners of the firm are able to reap the benefits of that investment. This is the variable that neoclassical economics focuses on; but this exclusive focus on property rights ignores other important determinants of technological advance. For Altman, the other key variable is the relative bargaining power of labor and capital. It is capital that determines whether or not new investment will take place with the most advanced technology. If labor costs are low, there may be little incentive to invest since there is little to be gained. In contrast, if labor power is greater and wages are higher, firms will have an incentive to invest in new technology that reduces the relative use of labor in the production process.

Altman builds on the work of Harvey Leibenstein and his theory of x-efficiency. For Leibenstein, the efficiency of firms depends not only on whether firms invest in more advanced and up-to-date technology. Also important is how people work. When people work in teams, as in most modern firms, it is impossible to detect slacking and so work effort becomes a variable. And work effort itself will be a function of how much workers get paid and how happy they are. Poorly paid workers, who have little economic power, are likely to put in less effort. This increases unit labor costs for the firm. In contrast, well-paid workers will likely be more productive both because they are happier and because of the additional investment in new technology that will help workers be more productive.

The policy lesson that Altman draws from this analysis is that strengthening the bargaining power of labor will lead firms to engage in behavior that increases efficiency. In this way, the higher wages that result from greater bargaining power do not get translated into higher costs and inflation. Rather, higher wages lead to greater productivity – to the benefit of everyone. Besides generating economic benefits, Altman argues that this also makes the economy more democratic.

Chapter 9 written by Peter Boettke and Bridget Butkevich, provide a public choice perspective on the role of the state. They see two possible roles for the state (player and referee) and also two possible roles for economists (student of the economy and savior). Boettke and Butkewicz argue that only two of the possible four combinations are viable – state as player plus economist as savior, and state as referee plus economist as student. If the state is a player in the market, it needs economic advice about how to play. Economists cannot just study the economy and the way it works. On the other hand if the state is just a referee, enforcing the rules of the market, it has no need for economist-saviors that tell it what needs to be done.

Boettke and Butkewicz then use this framework to examine the transition of the Russian economy from communism to capitalism. The paper explains why the dismantling of the Soviet system of economic command-and-control did not lead to the utopian outcomes predicted by many free market economists. Their answer is that the state is still a player, and that Russians put their hopes in the state as an economic player-savior, to improve their condition, but that given their recent history, Russians themselves prefer the state to merely serve as a referee. This conflict remains to be played out.

There are many areas of agreement in the chapters that follow and many places where one heterodox perspective can gain a lot by listening to other heterodox perspectives. First, most heterodox economists think that the state may be necessary to improve economic performance and to protect people with few rights and little power (such as women and the poor). Yet, as Boettke and Butkewicz note, and as Das and O'Hara note, the state can also make things worse rather than better. Thus, it is important to have some checks and balances. The state must balance the power of the private sector, while firms and especially citizens must monitor the state and make sure it does not abuse its power.

Second, the state needs to provide things that the market economic does not and cannot provide. The Stanfields point to social life and a sense of community as one important human value that we cannot purchase in the market but that we nonetheless desire. Keynes also viewed the socialization of investment along these lines. So do feminist economists when they argue for having the state transform gender relations and allow women the same opportunities as men.

Third, the many different perspectives on the state are mutually supportive in a number of respects. While many schools of thought see the state impacting human behavior, there is a great deal of agreement that it is necessary to worry about *how* the state affects people and firms. Altman, for example, points out that how state policy affects private sector behavior will determine whether we are in a low-wage and low-effort equilibrium or in a high-wage and highly productive economic environment. And while many schools of thought see the state as supporting the economic interests of the rich and powerful against its citizens, they also see the state as a necessary force to counterbalance the power of large firms that dominate the market economy. The market economy may not always generate the best economic outcomes for the citizens of a nation. When the market economy gives us sub-optimal results, then it is the responsibility of the state government to make sure that the economy generates enough jobs and sufficient incomes.

In the final analysis, we may need to follow the advice in the title of Waller's chapter and adopt a pragmatic approach to the role of the state. The state is not to be looked at as a savior and cannot be expected to deal with all the problems that arise from capitalism and that arise in the world. But the state can do things like provide minimum incomes, a minimum level of healthcare, and sufficient police protection so that the lives of many people are extended. On the other hand, we cannot lose our vigilance in monitoring the state. We must make sure that it does not become hostage to firms that want to bribe it for favors or that seek to use it to further its ends rather than the ends of the general populace. For example, we cannot let drug companies gain control of the state and then pedal expensive and useless (and possibly dangerous) drugs to citizens who do not and cannot be expected to know any better than the government scientists and regulators who give these drugs a government "good housekeeping" seal of approval. We must always be on the lookout for, and try our best to prevent, rent-seeking and corruption, while at the same time we must try to prevent firms from exploiting the average citizen, the environment, and government officials. In short, we must walk a fine line, make sure that there are adequate checks and balances on the power of the state, but at the same time we must recognize that the state is an important player in modern economies, not least of which is because of its role in countering the power of the large corporation. If the state is unable to this, there is really no one else to fill the gap. In this case, everyone loses. Thus, there are real and important economic incentives to make the state a real and a powerful economic player, but one that operates for the people whose interests it is supposed to serve.

References

Hufbauer, G., Berliner, D. & Elliott, K. (1986) *Trade Protection in the United States: 31 Case Studies*, Washington, D.C.: Institute for International Economics.

Rosser, J.B., Jr. (2001) "Uncertainty and Expectations," in R. Holt & S. Pressman (eds) *A New Guide to Post Keynesian Economics*, New York & London: Routledge, pp. 52–64.

2

The Pragmatic State: Institutionalist Perspectives on the State

William Waller

In original institutional economics the study of the economy is culturally and historically specific. For institutionalists, economics is about the actual practices and processes of people in their everyday activities that provide the material support for the members of a community. Concepts, generalizations, analyses, and theories are developed from case studies of actual behavior in specific contexts. Individual human behavior is explained within the framework of cultural processes. Ideas and theories are developed and modified as they arise in the culture and are incorporated in the analyses of solving daily problems.

Institutionalists study provisioning processes in order to solve real problems. This motive for inquiry emerges from the roots of institutionalism in the philosophy of American Pragmatism. The problem may be as esoteric as a desire to understand what is going on around us or as simple as the need to fasten the shoes on a child's feet. But all inquiry emerges from such problem situations. Problems are always socially constructed because they are formulated in language, the cultural symbolic system that provides the concepts for organizing thought, and experienced by people who live within a culture at a particular point in time. And the inquiry can be pursued individually or socially; but inquiry is engaging in culturally constructed knowledge creation procedures and behaviors. Since the inquiry is always purposeful – to solve problems – valuation is an integral part of the inquiry process. Solving problems is an improvement over not solving them. A successful society is one that uses culturally constructed knowledge to solve its problems of provisioning and sustaining the culture. Progress means solving more problems and/or solving them better. Thus progress and success are both defined within the context of the culture, which determines what is a problem, and what constitutes a solution or a better solution within that cultural context.

In the institutionalist tradition theorizing about the state takes the form of theorizing about the functioning of particular states at particular points in time. A general or abstract "Institutionalist Theory of the State" would be a methodological contradiction. However, some of the analytic constructs employed, and the terminology in which theories are expressed, will be drawn from earlier attempts to theorize about the state, including prior abstract, non-cultural, ahistorical forms of theorizing. That caveat aside, institutionalists have had a great deal to say about the structure and function of the state. Since original institutional economics developed in response to the neoclassical economic theory emerging from the end of the 19th century and up to today in Western market economies, in particular the US, there are sufficient historical and cultural boundaries on the question of what constitutes the state that we can characterize those efforts and draw some generalizations. We shall see, as we review some important institutionalist theories of the state, that they are always grounded in a historical place and time, and must be reinterpreted as the culture that is being examined evolves.

Early institutionalists on the state

Thorstein Veblen did not explicitly theorize about the state. His popular essays in the *Dial* magazine portrayed the state as a predatory institution serving the vested interests and absentee owners that often pursued dynastic or imperialist policies to the determent of the common man (Veblen, 1965). Similarly, in his interwar book *The Nature of the Peace*, Veblen (1917) characterized jingoistic patriotism as a cultural process used to enlist the aid of the common man in the dangerous pursuit of national aggrandizement popular with the vested interests but contrary to the interests of the commonweal. Like Marx, for Veblen the state was the handmaiden of vested interests or the dominant social group in a culture. But for Veblen all institutional forms of the state were not equally dangerous. In *Imperial Germany and the Industrial Revolution* Veblen [1946] (1990) discusses the imperial ambitions of Germany as a leftover from dynastic politics of the medieval period. He notes Germany borrowed advanced industrial technology very efficiently from England, but neglected to borrow the democratic institutions that the British developed along with that technology. And he found industrial technology and dynastic politics to be a dangerous combination in both Germany and Japan (Veblen, [1946] 1990, [1915] 1964). From this we can only conclude that Veblen disapproved of imperial policies and preferred the evolution of the state in England, but still regarded the state largely as an instrument of powerful vested interests. From a theoretical standpoint, Veblen viewed the state as an instrument of popular mobilization that could be used on behalf of whatever interests managed to hold positions of power within the nation. The ability of the state to act as an instrument of particular vested interests was mitigated and mediated by the positions of power being widely held by various interests and by social institutions that kept office holders accountable to the public interest.

These themes persist in Institutionalist writing on the state. John R. Commons, Veblen's contemporary and co-founder of Institutional Economics, wrote extensively about the state in modern industrial economies. For Commons, the state was a feature of the development of modern industrial growth in Western Europe, particularly the UK. Thus the tradition of classic liberalism, the institution of private property, British Common Law and subsequent developments in jurisprudence, and the evolution of modern liberalism all underlie his work (Commons, 1974: ch. 2). Commons (1990 [1934]: ch. 10) discussed the issues of sovereignty and the police powers of the state. He viewed the state as an instrument to reconcile competing interests in a democratic society. Its role was social mediation in solving problems; this role would lead to his development of standards of reasonable value.

This led Commons to focus on the institution of the independent regulatory commission as a governmental entity. He saw democratic governance structures as forums for the articulation and mediation of different interests in society. But problem solving often required more than just public discourse; expert knowledge of the particular circumstances surrounding a particular social problem was frequently necessary. Commons' solution was to create a commission that would include all interested parties, including the public interest, and that would gather evidence, debate, and compromise and produce reasonable (if not perfect) solutions to pressing problems. This approach has been extensively adopted in the US in the form of independent government regulatory bodies.

Rexford Tugwell, a member of the Roosevelt's "brain-trust," had the most extensive experience in government of any institutionalist. His book *The Economic Basis of the Public Interest* [1922] develops the cultural rationale for government action within the liberal state. Tugwell carefully reviewed theories of public interest and the extant case law that combined to provide the rationale for the regulation of business by governments. The theories are:

> (1) the monopoly theory, (2) the theory that all business is public under the common law, (3) the theory of delegated governmental obligation, (4) the theory of assumpsit and later legislative determination, (5) the theory of complete legislative determination. The first implies that monopoly was the earliest test to be applied and that it is the test which now creates public utilities; the second theory is that all business is and has been always, public under the common law and that distinctions set up between businesses that are private and businesses that are public are artificial distinctions which arose through a series of mistakes and misinterpretations of common law principles; the third regards public callings as essentially governmental functions which, for convenience, private organizations are allowed to perform, but which the government cannot fail to regulate in the interest of the public; and the fourth and fifth would agree in allowing the legislature at present to completely determine social policy in respect of governmental control of business. (Tugwell, [1922] 1968: 46)

Tugwell finds all of these theoretical explanations inadequate. He notes, however, that the courts have been consistent and that the rationale for regulation of business by government and a definition of the public interest can be inferred from the history of regulation. The rationale that accounts for court decisions is "a business is likely to be subjected to regulation if consumers are harmed by it as to prices or standards, in ways not reachable under the other phases of the police powers" (Tugwell, 1968: 78). Tugwell (1968: 78–9) argues for a definition of "the public interest" from the following question:

> is the consumer really having to pay too high rates or to put up with inferior service? And if he is thus harmed, it seems clear that there arises simply by reason of this, a public interest as it is legally meant, and that the implicated business is likely to become at once, when a legislative act is passed and the matter is brought to the attention of the court, subject to regulation of rates and standards of service. This is, of course, presuming the regulation to be made under the police powers. If a definite analogy with an existing public utility can be shown, the courts may be persuaded to permit regulation under the common law and without legislative act. This

> latter type of regulation is however, more and more rarely applied to businesses not heretofore regulated.

Tugwell's position then is based upon a combination of monopoly theory that focuses not on market structure but rather the consumer harm that results. Focusing on consumer harm, Tugwell (1968: 99; italics added) concludes:

> Because a business is big and powerful...it is not necessarily harmful, nor will the courts necessarily permit it to be regulated. But *when the product it deals in becomes a necessity to all of us, or at least to many of us; when we are compelled to resort to it and when at the same time unfair rates are maintained or the service given is inadequate, it then becomes "clothed with the public interest."* It may be regulated. It is the disadvantage of the consumers that makes it so.

No institutional economist has written more extensively on the state than John Kenneth Galbraith. Galbraith (1967) called the modern state *The New Industrial State*. The economy had a dual nature – an administered sector and a market sector. The goal of the administered sector, consisting of large corporations, was to escape the discipline of the market and replace it with planning and coordination. Toward that end, some employees of these corporations evolved into what Galbraith called "the technostructure" – those individuals with the technical knowledge and expertise to manage the affairs of the administered sector. The administered sector needs government for aggregate demand management, funding of infrastructure, and subsidizing important industries. In developing the expertise to address these matters both the executive and legislative branches of government, like the corporations of the administered sector, develop a highly skilled cadre of staff to coordinate planning and implement government policies. What develops, according to J. Ronald Stanfield (1996: 116), is a bureaucratic symbiosis between the technostructure and the government bureaucracy. Coordination and cooperation is the norm rather than the exception – although often obscured by pluralist apologia.

Galbraith expands on this conception of the state in *The Culture of Contentment* (1972). He argues that the US political system is structured to minimize the participation of ordinary working people. Only a minority of the population participates in electoral politics; so winning elections and directing government policy falls to whoever wins the support of a majority of the minority of our society. This minority consists of the largely affluent and content segments of the population. Galbraith argues that there is a "contented majority" within this sector that has a consensus view and that this consensus has dominated US government policy in recent years. This consensus view consists of four beliefs about the appropriate role for the state.

1. The affluence and success of the contented majority result from their efforts and constitute their just desserts.
2. Short-run public inaction is preferred to long-run protective public action.
3. The government should only be involved in a few highly selective activities such as Social Security, providing medical care to the high-income strata, farm income supports, financial guarantees for imperiled financial institutions, and military expenditure.
4. Large income disparities are acceptable and do not require state action.

These four beliefs limit the state to a small and reactive role in society. It seeks to protect the contentment of the "contented majority." This contentment, in turn, provides electoral and financial support to government officials (Galbraith, 1972: 18–26).

For Galbraith, like Veblen, the state is subservient to vested interests. But Galbraith develops more fully the cultural processes that support and perpetuate dominance of the state by vested interests in modern American society. The problems that Galbraith's state attempts to solve are those of the contented majority. Problems of the whole nation get addressed only when crises threaten their contentment. Despite Galbraith's view that the state is passive, he does not believe that the state must necessarily be passive. Indeed, he argues that at different times, US citizens have expected a more activist role for government. Thus the state for Galbraith is a product of the dominant ideological position in a culture at a particular historical juncture. He clearly articulates a more positive and problem-solving view of the state in his policy recommendations that have consistently reflected a progressive and pragmatic role for the state in managing the economy. Galbraith (1996) argues that such a state is possible and desirable if there is a change in public attitudes.

This more optimistic side of Galbraith is clearly consistent with Robert Solo's (1982) *Positive State* that emerged out of necessity from the Keynesian revolution. Charles Whalen (1992) expanded upon this evolving conception of the state by elaborating on the institution-creating and problem-solving functions of what he characterized as "the Creative State." These contributions reject the passive and non-interventionist state envisioned in classic liberalism, and usually move beyond the interventionist state of modern liberalism. Instead, they favor a state with responsibilities to act proactively in the public interest.

This cursory review of institutionalist thought on the state warrants one generalization. Most institutionalists view the state in modern industrial (and post-industrial) economies as having the potential and the responsibility to mediate conflict and to solve social and political problems within its boundaries. A term that reflects this sort of problem-solving state is the "Pragmatic State." This state has several key features.

Characteristics of the pragmatic state

Sovereignty

Sovereignty is the basis of the modern state. In essence sovereignty is about boundaries. Everything within the boundary is the state; everything outside the boundary is not the state. The state then, is an institution that manages the boundary. Those within the boundary expect the state to manage relations with similar states and other groups outside their boundary. At the simplest level the state protects its population from incursions by other states or groups. Thus it is an institution organized around the defense of boundaries.

In protecting the integrity of its boundaries, the state must keep its population from making unauthorized incursions into territory beyond its boundaries because this may create conflicts with other states and groups. Thus the state must maintain a monopoly on the legitimate use of violence across its borders.

Since the emergence of the nation-state in Western European is coincident with the decline of the medieval manorial economy and the emergence of commercial capitalism, the state carries with it the functions developed by medieval sovereigns. States continue the traditional functions of the sovereign through standardizing weights and measures and the judicial function of mediating disputes among those within their borders as cities evolved from the commercial fairs from which commercial capitalism emerged. Since this trade involved outsiders bringing goods across borders it was the responsibility of the sovereign to insure that these commercial activities did not threaten the integrity of borders. These regulatory and judicial functions continue for the modern state.

Police powers

This history gives rise to what is commonly referred to as the "inherent police powers of the state." The state always maintains a monopoly on the legitimate use of violence both within and across its borders. In addition, the regulation of behavior occurring within the state's borders that might impinge on maintaining the integrity of the state is included among those police powers. This includes defining criminal activity, mediating conflicts among parties within its borders, and regulating activities that might impinge on the continuity and stability of the state. Additionally, this includes the regulation of commercial activity.

Of course, in the medieval economy the sovereign was a person who controlled a particular piece of real estate. The integrity of the border was coincident with the security of the holdings of the sovereign. The common folk's well-being, if considered at all, was a by-product of the interest of the sovereign.

The emergence of the modern liberal state out of the medieval context occurs with the secularization of the warrant for the state and the emergence of natural rights doctrine. The sovereign, whose stewardship of land and its populations was legitimated by divine right and thus beyond the question of the common folk, was replaced by the notion of the natural individual endowed with inalienable rights. Consequently any legitimate state would have to incorporate these rights and characteristics into its warrant to be considered legitimate.

This had two consequences of great importance. First, sovereignty would necessarily emerge from this human nature with its inalienable rights thus requiring that the state secure the consent of the governed and respect those individual rights. Second, this agglomeration of individuals would permit the state to exercise sovereignty with respect to its collective interests rather than the interest of a single individual defined as the divine embodiment of the social order. There is an inherent conflict between these two consequences. The legitimacy of state action emerging from individual rights means that the state's authority to act is limited by those rights while at the same time requiring the state to act in the common interest which might impinge upon the exercise of those individual rights.

Thus the modern liberal state must negotiate the limitations of state action and the right of the state to impinge upon individual liberty in protecting and extending the common interests.

Public interest

Fortunately, the functions of the state did not emerge from an abstract discussion of the conflict between individual liberty and the pursuit of the common interest. Instead, the modern national economy emerged out of the conflict created by the heavily regulated commerce of the medieval town as external trade grew. The sharp distinction between internal (within the town) and external trade (between towns) maintained in the medieval town remains today. Mercantilism emerged as the modern state emerged. Those involved in external trade enlisted those building the emerging nation-states to break down trade barriers imposed by the towns. As industrialization spread outside towns, as the population of walled cities spread outside their walls, and as gilds expanded their geographic scope, the power of the towns to regulate commerce broke down. The ability of the nation-state to tax external trade made those engaged in nation-building responsive to the wishes of those participating in external trade (Polanyi, 1944: 60–7, 274–9). The policy of mercantilism was basically the geographic expansion of the highly successful system of trade regulation that had evolved within towns to the larger area encompassed by the new state. Consequently, all of the modern states that emerged already had functioning institutions legitimized by law and tradition.

Towns developed the notion of citizenship. The business people in the town were originally the only citizens. The town was governed to protect their interest against outside merchants. As the governance system of the town expanded to a national level, the citizen, again, was the person to be protected against external threats. The modern liberal state emerges from the expansion of the definition of citizen over the last 300 years. The modern liberal state is similarly charged with protecting the interest of its citizens just as its historical antecedents were.

Locke, Rousseau and Hobbes not withstanding, human beings never came together in a state of nature to create a state by consensus and contract. Human beings are social animals living together in groups and the history of governance of those human groups is coincident with the species. The modern liberal state emerged out of the cultural practice and history of Western European people.

In the UK and the US a great deal of cultural practice and history is codified in English Common Law and development over the last 786 years. This legal tradition recognizes that certain activities fall under the police powers of the state because they inherently are vested with the public interest. In the liberal state these become limitations on the free use of private property. The right of eminent domain limits the right to own and keep secure private property since it involves its forcible alienation of property by the state with compensation. Thus the underlying legal and moral foundation of economic regulation by the state is embodied in our property law and embedded in our legal regulation of business activity and commerce in general.

So while both classic and modern liberal ideology argue for a very limited government role, particularly in economic affairs, the rational for extensive involvement by the state in economic matters is historically co-evolutionary and coincident with the liberal tradition in Western Europe and North America.

The function of the pragmatic state

The pragmatic state is historically and culturally constructed, so the institutionalist view of the ongoing functions of the state includes much of what we associate with the modern liberal state. The state is responsible for maintaining the integrity of its borders, keeping peace within its borders, defending its citizens against external threats, and protecting individual rights. From these responsibilities emerge trade and immigration authority, national defense, police powers, and a system of courts and administrative agencies for resolving conflicts and disputes. As products of modern industrial culture, with its commitment to individual rights and democratic principles, institutionalists accept these tenets of liberalism and extend them. For institutionalists, the pragmatic state has a responsibility to prepare its citizens for full participation in society. It also has a responsibility to create institutions that insure stable, secure, and adequate support to the social provisioning process, including the maintenance of real income, stable employment, and providing education and medical care. Institutionalists see these responsibilities not as an unwarranted intrusion into a natural order or an infringement of individual rights, but as a requirement for democracy. Further, they are logical extensions of the police powers of the liberal state when a stable economy is recognized as a prerequisite for keeping the peace and protecting individual rights.

The activities of the pragmatic state generally fall into two major categories – social stability and continuity, and problem solving.

Social stability and continuity

The concept of sovereignty and its accompanying security concerns extend to economic security. The state must insure that those outside its borders do not engage in activities that harm the ongoing economic activity of people within the state's borders. This extends to regulation of terms, conditions, and character of trade across those borders of course. This may involve negotiating with other sovereign powers.

Within its boundaries the state serves a number of functions that facilitate commerce. Since the state controls customs it can regulate the import and export of goods; its system of record keeping leads to the standardization of weights and measures; and its ability to impose duties and tariffs causes all those involved in international commerce to need whatever means of payment the state accepts for the payment of taxes. The power to tax internally means that whatever the state requires from its citizens to pay their taxes becomes a state currency. Consequently, the state usually provides what we have come to consider modern money (Wray, 1998: 18). The state also maintains a system of conflict resolution through its courts and administrative agencies. Similarly, it maintains social welfare structures, protective legislation and enforcement agencies, and other institutions to insure that economic behavior is carried on in a manner that insures the continuation of provisioning.

Rejecting the assertion of harmonious of interests, institutionalists recognize that capitalism is a terrain of conflicting interests. It is usually incumbent upon individual actors to negotiate a mutually satisfactory resolution of their interests. Because these arrangements are complicated, contract law has evolved. The difference between an agreement between two parties and a contract is that a contract presumes the possibility of the government being called upon to enforce the agreement or mediate the conflict. This is part of the civil judicial process in the United States.

But not all conflict is between discrete parties. Often many people will be affected by economic activity. Again, Commons noted that in a democratic society, regulatory bodies with members representing the major interest groups should be convened to solve the problems of economic coordination and resolve conflicts of interest. This vision ultimately led to the development of independent regulatory agencies in the United States.

This pragmatic solution to the problem of conflict of interest led to the development of Commons' unique value theory (1950: Part IV). Commons thought that the compromise solution of varied interested parties would give rise to an understanding of the commonality of some elements of value. Thus the decisions made by such deliberations would generate what he called "reasonable value." This remains an important value criterion in institutional economics today. It explicitly rejects the supremacy of efficiency (meaning cost efficiency) arguments employed in contemporary neoclassical policy analyses.

Problem solving

The other appropriate function of the pragmatic state is problem solving. The state is not unique in this regard. Indeed, all human activity is directed in some ways at problem solving to the degree that it is intentional. It is not the role of the state to solve all problems. Again the concept of the public interest is essential. A problem that involves the common good or public interest is the proper responsibility of the state. But beyond this we must now talk about the state in less abstract terms. In the US "the State" is an amalgamation of loosely related governmental structures representing different geographical levels of governance as well as different sorts of functions. The level of government ranges from the very local to national in scope, and the appropriate level of government to deal with a particular problem is determined by the character of the problem. A problem involving other sovereign states usually requires national government oversight. A local problem, such as elementary school administration, requires a very local branch of government. But geographic scope is not the only determinate of the level of government for solving a problem. Technology may be important. For example, air traffic control is regulated by national governments and international organizations, while automobile traffic control is usually handled by very local municipal and regional public safety agencies.

In most cases modern industrial market economies will require a multilevel state because the problems to be addressed in the day-to-day business of maintaining the stability and continuity of provisioning behavior will require different levels of government to deal with them.

Suppose the people of a small town determine that their social and economic well-being would be enhanced if more childcare was available. Neoclassical economists would seek to solve this problem by having each person purchase additional childcare. This would result in a price increase for childcare which would encourage providers to supply more childcare. For institutionalist economists, the pragmatic state insures the provisioning of the childcare. A first step would be to determine whether the neoclassical solution was viable. The problem would be studied (a very local function). If people with jobs couldn't find childcare, then the neoclassical solution might be viable. But if people could not accept jobs because childcare was unavailable the neoclassical solution would fail to solve the problem. Second, the pragmatic state might attempt a number of strategies including credits to employers to open childcare facilities, tax credits to parents for childcare expenses, the use of public money to expand existing or create new childcare facilities, the use of public school facilities to provide after-school childcare, the expansion of juvenile recreational programs, etc. These solutions all presume the legitimacy of the pragmatic state using its taxing authority to insure safe childcare and enhance the economic provisioning process. Third, programs and facilities need to be assessed for quality and for the efficiency with which it is meeting its citizen needs. When needs are unaddressed, or if new needs emerge, the institutional structure needs to be adjusted. The process of adjusting policy does not end unless the need for childcare disappears; then the resources used on childcare should be reallocated.

There is a stark contrast here between the institutionalist vision of the pragmatic state and the neoclassical vision of the minimal state as an intrusion into the otherwise stable and desirable natural order.

Institutional adjustment and the state

The state is made up of myriad governmental structures all with institutionalized behaviors. Within each structure new and old behaviors are mixed together to carry out current and past government activities. The resulting behaviors emerge from the unique history of each governmental structure. However some generalizations can be made.

Each governmental structure making up a state at any particular time is the result of some initial discretionary act or choice of some group of people delegated to make the decisions necessary to build the social structure. Thus each governmental structure constitutes a particular historical case of institutional building.

Government structures evolve over time. They acquire additional responsibilities, change the way they act with regard to existing responsibilities, and may even abandon some old responsibilities. Moreover, the behaviors they organize and coordinate may change simply because of variations in practice over time. At any point in time the activities and behaviors organized by a particular government structure are a mix of institutionalized behaviors, some of which are habitual and routine, and others representing discretionary choices that may be new and innovative. This makes the state the most common site of both institutional creation and institutional adjustment.

There is no general theory of institutional creation. People begin new behaviors as a matter of choice and in response to a problem that requires action. Some of these behaviors are repeated and become habituated. However, repetition and habituation is not an indication of functionality or instrumentality. People repeat ineffective behaviors and develop bad habits all the time. There is no necessary connection between habituation and efficiency or effectiveness. Human beings have an amazing capacity to construct useless behaviors to fill a void where because of lack of useful alternatives or adequate knowledge nothing effective can be done. And the phenomenon of path dependency may lead the useless actions to impede the adoption of useful behavior at a later date.

Consequently, all institutions and all elements of the state constantly need reassessment and reevaluation. This has led institutionalists to focus on the process of institutional adjustment. Marc Tool (2000) has presented a general framework for addressing the process of institutional adjustment. Much of the following discussion draws from this body of work.

Technology

The technology and techniques available for addressing a problem limit the ability of the state to solve certain problems. At the simplest level, if we lack the knowledge and ability to solve a particular problem, there is little to be done except to learn more. Also, when we have the technology to solve a problem, the technology may render the state ineffective for implementing the technology.

Environmental compatibility

Solutions to problems must address the reality that problems occur in a particular environment and problem-solving behavior will impact that environment. Thus all solutions must take account of their consequences on the environment.

Democracy

Problems are culturally defined; human beings analyze the way things are and the way they ought to be. Consequently, effective problem solving and institutional adjustment require social processes for their implementation. Institutionalists usually prefer democratic decision-making processes for problem solving. The reasons for this preference are both ideological and functional.

The ideological component is straightforward. Since human beings are all products and producers of their cultures, all should participate fully in that culture. Moreover, human beings are active, curious, tool-using animals with the capacity to reason and choose and find their fullest expression of their capacities and experience their lives most richly when fully participating in all aspects of their social and cultural existence.

The functional component to democracy is equally straightforward. People are more likely to help make a particular policy work when they are both affected by the problem and vested in the process of finding a solution. Also, a policy achieves legitimacy, and thus the ability to move people to action, when those affected by a policy have a hand in creating or approving it. In addition, the state apparatus is likely to be more responsible to the needs of citizens when it is held accountable and democratic structures have the potential to hold public officials accountable.

Tolerance for change

All change creates the need for further adjustment; and some cultures and groups tolerate change better than others. Consequently the capacity for change may be limited by the willingness of the participants to accept change and to handle the disruption that change may bring. Additionally, all change involves the likelihood of unintended consequences that people must subsequently address.

Minimum dislocation

The solution to any social problem may disrupt the integrated web of social activities. Thus solutions that create the least social dislocation are preferable to those that impact them more widely. This leads to congruence between institutional thought and the general liberal preference for a limited state.

Non-invidiousness

A state limited by rule of law means that all its citizens must be equal before the law. Non-invidiousness, the refusal to injure, limit or disadvantage the participation of people in cultural activities, has been a major theme running through the institutional literature. Whether equality before the law is non-invidious or not will be a consequence of the particular public policy problem being addressed. We cannot know in the abstract whether equality of action or equality of effect will meet the criterion of non-invidiousness. For example, providing every child with identical educational experiences may enhance invidiousness because of the different needs of individual children.

Some corollary issues:

1. *Beware of complexity*. Social processes are notoriously complex. Thus social problems are likely to be complex. This suggests that simple solutions will be inadequate. At the same time complex solutions are fraught with uncertainty and the danger of social disruption. Step-by-step problem solving allows us to experiment with program design without running the risk of large-scale disintegrative disruptions of cultural systems.
2. *Problem solving is a process*. Problems change and evolve; thus solutions must be provisional and subject to reevaluation and replacement. The step-by-step approach recommended above coincides with this notion of evolving problems. We cannot become so vested in a particular solution to a problem that we cannot contemplate altering our behavior as the problem changes. It is also the case that problems rarely disappear. Thus it is useful to think of the pragmatic state as requiring an ongoing dialogue between problem definition and problem solving. The pragmatic state should be engaged in a dialectical relationship in its problem-solving behavior, constantly reassessing its programs for the purpose of improvement, replacement and, on happy occasions where problems are solved, retirement.
3. *Bureaucracy grows*. Max Weber (1946) was right. Over time bureaucracies seem to grow and expand their reach and influence. Rarely does this growth benefit the public interest. Oversight and accountability are thus crucial.
4. *If it is not broke don't fix it*. This is really an extension of the principle of minimal dislocation. It also extends the previous point regarding the growth of bureaucracy and the growth of the state in general. Put simply, it is not necessary for the pragmatic state to get involved in problem solving until the problem is identified as one that requires collective action.
5. *Urgency and irreversibility*. Some problems require quick action because the consequences of the problem are irreversible. This is where reasonable value must come to the forefront of public policy decision-making and state action. Vested interests may wish to block certain kinds of problem-solving behaviors. They may do this at a stage where solutions are still manageable. A good example of this is the issue of global warming. Vested interests wish to wait until "all or better scientific information" is available. This simply uses the problem of induction in the service of the vested interest. There is no objective resolution to this problem coming in the future since all knowledge is provisional. Thus the state must have a

mechanism for assessing problems where the power of vested interests is countered by other interests and creates some structure that is charged and held accountable for that vague, imperfect, abstract conception of the public interest.

Contrasting views of the state

The institutional conception of the pragmatic state differs fundamentally from the view of the state associated with neoclassical economics. First and foremost, institutional economists believe neoclassical economists largely ignore the state or assign it a minimal role. The state's actions *vis-à-vis* the economy are seen as unwelcome intrusions in market processes – disturbances to be avoided whenever possible in the normal and natural functioning of a market economy. Institutionalist do not argue that neoclassical economists have no theory of the state; rather, in the majority of neoclassical analysis no particular theory of the state is expressedly put forth to ground that analysis. Second, when theories of the state are proffered in neoclassical economics they tend to be ahistorical and non-cultural in character. Two examples of theories of the state consistent with neoclassical economics will illustrate these differences.

In his classic, *A Theory of Justice*, John Rawls (1971) puts forward a theory of the state built on utilitarian foundations. His is a social contract theory in the tradition of Locke and Rousseau. His theory presumes a state of nature occupied by individuals who come together to form a social contract from which society is formed. Individuals in a state of nature are non-historical, pre-social, abstract, self-interest agents making rational decisions in an original position behind a "veil of ignorance". This parallels the methodological individualism and the high-level of abstraction typically employed in neoclassical economics. The "veil of ignorance" consists of the following assumptions about rational agents:

> They do not know how the various alternatives will affect their own particular case and they are obliged to evaluate principles solely on the basis of general considerations.
>
> It is assumed, then, that the parties do not know certain kinds of particular facts. First of all, no one knows his place in society, his class position or social status; nor does he know his fortune in the distribution of natural assets and abilities, his intelligence and strength, and the like. Nor, again, does anyone know his conception

> of the good, the particulars of his rational plan of life, or even the special features of his psychology such as his aversion to risk or liability to optimism or pessimism. More that this, I assume that the parties do not know the particular circumstances of their own society. That is, they do not know its economic or political situation, or the level of civilization and culture it has been able to achieve. The persons in the original position have no information as to which generation they belong. (Rawls, 1971: 137)

Such theorizing is clearly inconsistent with the historical and cultural approach to understanding the state in the original institutional economics.

This utilitarian approach also finds expression in the work of Robert Nozick. In *Anarchy, State, and Utopia*, Nozick (1974: 10) writes: "Individuals in Locke's state of nature are in 'a state of perfect freedom to order their actions and dispose of their possessions and persons as they think fit, within the bounds of the law of nature, without asking leave or dependency upon the will of any other man.'" Quoting Locke's *Second Treatise on Government*, Nozick contends that the bounds of the law of nature require that "no one ought to harm another in his life, health, liberty, or possessions."

Nozick, like Rawls, argues from an abstract, methodologically individualistic, ahistorical, non-cultural, pre-social, conception of human agency. Unlike Rawls, Nozick is explicitly concerned with theorizing about the character of the good and morally imperative forms the state must take. Nozick argues that if we assume individuals act in a moral way, these rights are sufficient to provide an invisible hand explanation of how the state becomes the sole wielder of the power. This monopoly power can legitimately be used to prohibit behavior that violates the rights of others, to use force in order to protect individuals from violations of their rights, and to punish those who violate the rights of others. Since the state is morally required to compensate each individual for any intrusion on their individual rights that occurs as a result of state activities, this creates a moral necessity for a minimal state, one that carries out no functions beyond protecting individual rights. (Nozick, 1974: 118–19)

From the same methodological foundations employed in the construction of neoclassical economics, Nozick provides a moral argument for the minimal state that is consistent with most of neoclassical economics. Little ground is available for original institutionalists and the adherents to various permutations of neoclassical economics regarding the appropriate theory, role, or functions of the state.

Conclusions

The pragmatic state of institutional economists is not an ideal type. It has no ideologically preconceived structures that are necessary components of it. There is no particular form it should take. It consists of structures designed to address the ongoing functions of social provisioning and problem solving. A particular state evolves from its unique cultural, social, and political history.

Although this may seem hopelessly vague, it should be noted that institutional economics did not emerge in a cultural, social, or political vacuum. Rather, it arose out of the Western European intellectual and political history of the last 150 years. Consequently, most institutionalists take the liberal tradition, and the existing Western European and North American states, as a provisional foundation or context for their analyses and theories.

The need for collective problem solving does not necessarily imply state action. However, many institutional economists, for example Commons (1950), see institutional economics as concerned with collective action of various types. One area where the institutionalist approach to the state needs extension is in determining the appropriateness of government problem solving versus other forms of collective action.

This question should not be conceived of in terms of a public-private dualism. The long, sordid history of political corruption at every level of government in the US argues forcefully for considering non-governmental collective action. The similarly sordid history of the activities of US businesses, labor unions, and other non-governmental organizations argues strongly for public accountability of all manner of private, quasi-governmental, and pseudo-governmental agencies as well. The interconnectedness among different problem-solving institutions is a major area where more empirical research is necessary before any sort of generalization or theorizing is appropriate. Of particular concern are the issues of coordination among institutions, oversight and assessment of problem-solving programs, and the accountability of people and institutions engaged in problem solving activities.

Additionally, globalization of the world economy means supra-governmental and non-governmental organizations will become increasingly immersed in global problem-solving processes. These global matters seem likely to exceed in scale and complexity the global problem-solving experience and expertise of transnational corporations and international organizations. The problems of coordination, assessment, and accountability must be addressed in this global context.

The problematic that needs to be addressed by institutional economists interested in the state will be the character of inter-institutional coordination of collective problem solving. It seems that as long as the concept of sovereignty remains an essential component of our definition of the state, the problems of coordination, assessment, and accountability will functionally be located with the nation-state for global matters and many different levels of government within the sovereign state. A theory of coordination of collective action in service of the common good and public interest seems eminently necessary.

References

Commons, J.R. [1924] *The Legal Foundations of Capitalism*, Clifton: Augustus M. Kelley, 1974.

Commons, J.R. [1934] *Institutional Economics*, New Brunswick: Transactions Press, 1990.

Commons, J.R. (1950) *The Economics of Collective Action*, New York: Macmillan.

Galbraith, J.K. (1967) *The New Industrial State*, Boston: Houghton Mifflin.

Galbraith, J.K. (1973) *Economics and the Public Purpose*, Boston: Houghton Mifflin.

Galbraith, J.K. (1972) *The Culture of Contentment*, Boston: Houghton Mifflin.

Galbraith, J.K. (1996) *The Good Society: The Humane Agenda*, Boston: Houghton Mifflin.

Nozick, R. (1974) *Anarchy, State, and Utopia*, Oxford: Basil Blackwell.

Polanyi, K. (1944) *The Great Transformation*, Boston: Beacon Press.

Rawls, J. (1971) *A Theory of Justice*, Cambridge: Harvard University Press.

Solo, R. (1982) *The Positive State*, Cincinnati: South-Western Publishing.

Stanfield, J.R. (1996) *John Kenneth Galbraith*, New York: St. Martins Press.

Tool, M.R. (2000) *Value Theory and Economic Progress: The Institutional Economics of J. Fagg Foster*, Kluwer Academic Publishers.

Tugwell, R. [1922] *The Economic Basis of the Public Interest*, New York: Augustus M. Kelley, 1968.

Veblen, T. [1915] "The Case of Japan" in *Essays in Our Changing Order*, ed. Ardzrooni, Clinton: Augustus M. Kelley, 1964, pp. 248–66.

Veblen, T. (1917) *An Inquiry into The Nature of Peace and the Terms of Its Perpetuation*, New York: B.W. Huebsch.

Veblen, T. [1946] *Imperial Germany and the Industrial Revolution*, New Brunswick: Transactions Press, 1990.

Veblen, T. (1965) *The Vested Interests and the Common Man*, Clinton: Augustus M. Kelley.

Weber, M. (1946) "Bureaucracy" in *From Max Weber*, ed. and trans. Gerth and Mills, New York: Oxford University Press, pp. 196–8.

Whalen, C.J. (1992) "Schools of Thought and Theories of the State" in *The Stratified State*, ed. W. Dugger and W. Waller, Armonk, N.Y.: M.E. Sharpe, pp. 55–85.

Wray, L.R. (1998) *Understanding Modern Money*, Northhampton, MA: Edward Elgar.

3

The Protective Response and the Evolution of the Capitalist State

James Ronald Stanfield and Jacqueline B. Stanfield

> *[Polanyi's] arguments – and his concerns – are consonant with the issues raised by the rioters and marchers who took to the streets in Seattle and Prague in 1999 and 2000 to oppose the international financial institutions.*
>
> — *Joseph E. Stiglitz, 2001*

Introduction

In his foreword to the new edition of Polanyi's *The Great Transformation*, from which we excerpted the epigraph above, Stiglitz asserts that:

> economic science and economic history have come to recognize the validity of Polanyi's key contentions. But public policy – particularly as reflected in the Washington consensus doctrines concerning how the developing world and the economies in transition should make *their* great transformations – seems all too often not to have done so.

One may share Stiglitz's scorn for the Washington consensus policy regime without accepting his confidence that economic science has come to accept Polanyi's arguments in key regards. We share Stiglitz's enthusiasm with regard to the continuing relevance of Polanyi's work, indeed its mounting relevance in this era of the neoliberal Great Capitalist Restoration.

This essay utilizes Karl Polanyi's concept of the protective response to address the evolution of the role of the capitalist state, with some comparison to the views of other heterodox economists. We frequently use the compound expression, corporate-welfare state, to indicate that the evolution of the capitalist state is intertwined with that of other institutions, notably corporate enterprises and labor organizations (see also Stanfield, 1995: ch. 9). The basis of this compound expression will become clear as we review Polanyi's protective response, which encompasses private as well as public institutional changes.

The first section provides an overview of Polanyi's analysis of the nature of market capitalism and its characteristic social and political economic dynamic, to which Polanyi applied the term the "double movement" to indicate the spontaneous protective response that accompanies the extension of commodity production. The second section emphasizes the importance of distinguishing industrialism from market capitalism and considers the problem of freedom in a complex society in the work of Polanyi and other heterodox economists.

The political economy of market capitalism

Polanyi insisted that market capitalism comprises a "double movement" in which extension of the sphere of the market leads to a countervailing socially protective response. It is this protective response that accounts for the increasing role of the state and private organizational power despite the market cultural celebration of individual action in voluntary exchanges and its pronounced anti-state bias. This contrasts sharply with explanations of the rise of the state and private power in terms of a leftward ideological drift (see Hayek, 1944) because Polanyi insisted that the protective response is spontaneous and not supported by any coherent ideological scheme. Indeed, those seeking protection from the ravages of the spot market are more often than not adherents to the market ideology, which should occasion no surprise since the market mentality continues to be the dominant ideology

Polanyi also contested the notion that the market economy rose spontaneously from social life. In so doing he separated the market elements of trade, money, and market places from the market economy *per se* and argued that, even in the mercantilist era, there was no inherent impetus for these long-standing institutional elements to evolve into the market economy. The dramatic change was ideological: the notion of a self-regulating market system was the institutional "innovation which gave rise to a specific civilization" (Polanyi, 1944: 3) and led to the "utopian endeavor of economic liberalism to set up a self-regulating market system" (Polanyi, 1944: 29). This attempt foundered in the tumultous period before and after World War I. Polanyi was convinced that comprehension of this turmoil and subsequent institutional reform required a focus upon the socially unrealistic notion of a self-regulating market economy. In our view, the corporate-welfare state is best viewed as having emerged from this spontaneous social activity to resolve the market economy's inherent conflicts between lives and livelihood.

In distinguishing the market economy from all its historical predecessors, Polanyi referred to it as a "disembedded economy," which he sharply contrasted to earlier socio-economic formations.

> The outstanding discovery of recent historical and anthropological research is that man's economy, as a rule, is submerged in his social relationships. He does not act so as to safeguard his individual interest in the possession of material goods; he acts so as to safeguard his social standing, his social claims, his social assets. He values material goods only insofar as they serve this end. Neither the process of production nor that of distribution is linked to specific economic interests attached to the possession of goods; but every single step in that process is geared to a number of social interests which eventually ensure that the required step be taken. These interests will be very different in a small hunting or fishing community from those in a vast despotic society, but in either case the economic [substantive] system will be run on noneconomic [non-calculative] motives (Polanyi, 1944: 46).

It is necessary to be very clear in this regard. Any process of economic integration requires a correspondent social system which supports it and surrounds it with meaning in order to maintain the continuity of material or substantive provisioning. Hence the objection might be that in the modern social economy, people still pursue economic activity in order to sustain their way of life or social situs. The economy is always instituted by a socialization process that molds individual character toward the ethical, aesthetical, and instrumental norms, standards, and practices which are needed to participate in the economy. This much is true of all social economies in that all must integrate economic activity by means of systems of communication and sanction. These systems inform individuals as to the behavior expected of them and of others, and of the rewards and penalties that they can apply to others or expect to be applied to themselves in cases where expected behavior is or is not forthcoming. So, the objection might go, the market economy is no different from earlier societies in that it too is placed within society by socio-cultural interaction.

But the modern economy is different because its rules and norms are shaped by the requirements of the economy. The predominant line of causation is reversed. The economy was previously subordinate to the other social realms which constrained economic activity and set the hue and temper of social life. The modern economy is, by contrast, superordinate to social life in general and economic desiderata are necessarily prescriptive and influence family life, friendships, leisure, and mythology, actively so, in a way totally different from the more proscriptively limiting influence of the economy in previous eras.

Of particular importance is the subordinate position of the motive of self-gain in earlier societies (see Polanyi, 1968: 66; Polanyi, 1944: 47). This motive is the hallmark of the modern disembedded economy. Calculated self-gain is the market economic logic *sui generis*. In contrast, the embedded economy has no inherent logic of its own; there is no distinctive behavior which can be labeled economic in terms of its motivation and guiding principles. There is, of course, an objective substantive function, nature's decreed technological interaction of humanity with the rest of nature. But the subjective meaning of substantive economic activity is not implicit in that objective function. The provisioning function may be latent, inexplicit and the necessity of provisioning carried out in the context of social life in general.

> As long as [the redistribution and reciprocity] forms of integration prevail, no concept of an economy need arise. The elements of the economy are here embedded in non-economic institutions, the economic process itself being instituted through kinship, marriage, age-groups, secret societies, totemic associations, and public solemnities. The term "economic life" would have no obvious meaning. (Polanyi, 1968: 84)

In other words, the economy was anonymous in pre-modern societies. Polanyi developed the concept of the disembedded economy in order to uncover the reversal of this anonymity in recent history (Polanyi, 1968: 81), and to get rid of the modern "ingrained notion that the economy is a field of experience of which human beings have necessarily always been conscious" (Polanyi, 1968: 119). In earlier societies, the problem of livelihood was given less conscious attention and there was generally no term for the economy, even in the substantive sense (Polanyi, 1968: 85). The contrast could not be sharper between this and the fetishistic preoccupation with matters economic in modern society. Modern calculativeness is combined with individual gainsmanship and this combination of the intellect and the ego is a protean, combustible institutional compound, the source of the success and failure of the modern era.

None of this is to say that pre-modern society consisted of people who were intrinsically more altruistic, less selfish than modern man. "The human passions, good or bad, [were] merely directed towards noneconomic ends" (Polanyi, 1944: 47). The motive of self-gain may well have been present but it was constrained and held in check by its interweaving with religious, familial, and political motivations. Self-gain was but one thread in the social fabric such that no whole cloth could ever be made from it. The economic motive is rarely paramount to the individual in pre-modern society because his livelihood is guaranteed by virtue of his belonging to the community, unless, of course, that community were to face an aggregate interruption in its means of livelihood. The social motives of maintaining one's status by fulfilling one's obligations (such as regard for others) and observing social taboos (such as avoiding an unseemly concern for material gain), however, is clearly of crucial concern to the individual. His social ties guarantee his livelihood and it is those social ties which are subjectively meaningful for him (Polanyi, 1944: 46). From the social point of view, reciprocal concern for others is important because it secures cooperation in the substantive function which is vitally necessary to social reproduction. This is in sharp contrast to the modern economy in which gain is promoted to a pillar institution. The peculiarity of the social economy which came to maturity in the 19th century

> was precisely that it rested on economic foundations. Other societies and other civilizations, too, were limited by the material conditions of their existence.... All types of societies are limited by economic factors. Nineteenth century civilization alone was economic in a different and distinctive sense, for it chose to base itself on a motive only rarely acknowledged as valid in the history of human societies, and certainly never before raised to the level of a justification of action and behavior in everyday life, namely, gain. The self-regulating market system was uniquely derived from this principle (Polanyi, 1944: 30).

The institutionalization of gain is manifested by economic growth, i.e., the pay-off at the social level for the new economic organization was the steady improvement in aggregate output.

> Mankind was in the grip, not of new motives, but of new mechanisms. Briefly, the strain sprang from the zone of the market; from there it spread..., [eventually] comprising the whole of society.... [A]

> civilization was being disrupted by the blind action of soulless institutions the only purpose of which was the automatic increase of material welfare (Polanyi, 1944: 219).

The self-regulating market economy must be an economy guided by the variations in relative prices that are established by the supply-demand-process. Note that even an economy driven by relative prices is not a market economy if these prices are administered by political authority, negotiated by political leaders, or established by a dominant kinship system. The division of labor in such settings is accomplished by the political authority or social obligation that sets the prices, not by self-guided markets operating upon calculated self-interest.

The market economy therefore requires a market society and it is in the market society, required for the functioning of a market economy, that one finds many of the characteristic stresses and strains of market capitalism. The socialization necessary for the operation of a market economy requires a legitimation, even a moral imperative, of self-interested bargaining behavior, and this socialization is itself destructive of the community and kinship bonds by which the social fabric has been traditionally woven. The point then is that the market economy is placed in society in an entirely different way from the other two processes for integrating the division of labor, reciprocity and redistribution, which may operate within various patterns of social and political mores. The necessary market society is largely subservient to the economy.

> [O]nce man's everyday activities have been organized through markets of various kinds, based on profit motives, determined by competitive attitudes, and governed by a utilitarian value scale, his society becomes an organism that is, in all essential regards, subservient to gainful purposes. Having thus absolutized the motive of economic gain in practice, he loses the capacity of mentally relativizing it again. His imagination is bounded by stultifying limits. The very word economy evokes in him not the picture of man's livelihood and the technology that helps to secure it, but recalls instead a set of particular motives, peculiar attitudes, and highly specific purposes, all of which he is used to calling economic... (Polanyi, 1977: xlvi).

The motive of gain and the institutional complex of the supply-demand-price system came to be viewed as comprising an autonomous sphere of human activity, "the economic system, governed by economic motives, and subject to the economic principle of formal rationality (i.e. economizing)" (Polanyi, 1968: 132). The "sociological situations which make individuals partake in economic life" were created by "specifically economic institutions." These institutions "are activated by economic motives and governed by laws that are specifically economic." The economy is conceived to be "working without the conscious intervention of human authority" (Polanyi, 1968: 82). This is the disembedded economy: an autonomous sphere of human activity, self-motivating by greed or the threat of hunger and self-governing through a system of price-making markets. Adam Smith seized order from apparent chaos by insisting that an invisible hand was at work.

For the market economy to exert such control over society, it is necessary that land, labor, and capital be organized through the supply-demand-price process. Traditional or political allocation of land or obligatory labor relationships cannot be predominant in the integration of the division of labor. Hence the commodification of the factors of production is the *sine qua non* of the rise of the market economy. For such economy to be fathomable, the business firm must be able to buy, with considerable stability and predictability, the factors of production which it transforms and sells for its income. Short of this, the risk attendant to the construction and operation of a machine-intensive plant would be too great (Polanyi, 1944: 41). Saddled with such a plant, the firm bears considerable fixed or overhead costs which must be met over the short term irrespective of the level of output. If raw materials and labor supplies cannot be confidently expected to be available, such overhead costs would prevent large-scale, machine production. The predictable availability of these supplies requires that factor owners be dependent upon market exchange for their livelihood, i.e. hunger and similar needs must elicit the response on the part of the individual to earn an income (Polanyi, 1968: 64). This response is a matter of socialization in a general sense, but most important is the crude cudgel of economic necessity. The creation of the home market for substantive subsistence requirements involved the dissolution of traditional social relationships and patterns of provisioning. The domestic mode of production, largely self-sufficient production for direct use, was destroyed and commodity production, production for exchange, took its place. "No market economy was conceivable that did not include a market for labor; but to establish such a market, especially in England's rural civilization, implied no less than the wholesale destruction of the traditional fabric of society" (Polanyi, 1944: 77). The feudal serfs first became independent peasant farmers, later their land tenure was dissolved and they became the urban proletariat, of necessity selling their labor power on the market. In the same process, land too became alienable, i.e. saleable on the market.

Thus, the industrialist's markets were secured in a double sense. First, as mentioned, the factors of production were for sale on the market, reliably so because their owners were dependent on the market to earn an income with which to provision their substantive requirements. Second, the industrialist secured a reliable market for his output, the effective demand to fulfill these same requirements. We are not, of course, contending that market capitalism is stable in the sense of the modern concern for economic stabilization. This social economy is patently unstable in the sense of periodic fluctuations and business risk is inherently present. But it is one thing for an industrialist to face higher or lower prices than he expects but quite another for the industrialists as a whole to face laborers or raw materials suppliers who produce their own subsistence and market only a surplus not related to their self-sufficiency. Without their direct production to meet their requirements, laborers must sell their labor power to someone and buy commodities to meet their needs from someone (Polanyi, 1968: 57). Land ownership, once land was marketable, became capitalized and raw materials supply became a production goods industry.

Historically, then, the economy is first stripped of the anonymity in which it existed in earlier forms of society. This began in Archaic Greece and was completed in the mercantilist era. Consciousness of the emerging commercial economy was first met by political administration. In the liberal era, this response was done away with and the social purpose of provisioning was again obscured but in a much different way than in its previous submergence in the cultural patterns of group existence. The consciousness of the market economy was so great that the reality of society and its need for substantive provisioning was obscured. The social provisioning function was to be secured automatically through the market economy's integration of the division of labor. From the social point of view, this conception embodies the achievement of the purpose of provisioning without any institutional consciousness of that purposive activity *per se*. This is of course the notion of unintended consequences or the invisible hand that is central to market culture. As already noted, Polanyi argued that this conception is utopian and that it brings forth an experiment that necessarily fails with disastrous consequences, threatening the continuity of the social order. The economic instability of the market economy along with its requisite factor mobility and bargaining orientation are severely disruptive of social existence. Family and community life and the political process become hollowed out in their subservience not to the requisites of social life but to the stringent requirements of the market economy.

The market economy's institutionalization of socially irresponsible self-seeking is destructive of community because the latter has much to do with reciprocal obligation, responsiveness to each other's needs, and commitment to give-and-take. This antipathy between the market economy and community is evident in the externalities that are so prevalent in the market economy. In a community setting, people are aware of their impacts on each other, responsive to each other, and anything but indifferent to each other.

The erosion of community life is also evident in the exalted mobility of labor, a factor Schumacher links to footlooseness. The importance of the mobility factor and its inconsistency with community roots was made clear by Frank Knight in his classic description of the market economy (Knight, 1971: 77). Among the assumptions he cited for perfect competition was that there be "no exercise of constraint over any individual by another individual or 'society'; each controls his own activities with a view to results which accrue to him individually." There must also be "complete absence of physical obstacles to the making, execution, and changing of plans at will; that is, there must be 'perfect mobility'." Even more clearly to the point, Knight continues:

> Every member of the society is to act as an individual only, in entire independence of all other persons. To complete his independence he must be free from social wants, prejudices, preferences, or repulsions, or any values which are not completely manifested in market dealing. Exchange of finished goods is the only form of relation between individuals, or at least there is no other form which influences economic conduct. And in exchanges between individuals, no interest of persons not parties to the exchange are to be concerned, either for good or ill (Knight, 1971: 78).

In a footnote, Knight qualifies this formulation to allow for families – somewhat: "dependent members of the society must be *completely* dependent on some particular individual in it. The wants of any dependent person will then operate only through wants on his behalf felt by his sponsor.... We simply regard the independent members of the society as having normal solicitudes in regard to families, etc..." We say somewhat because this description could only apply to a narrow, nuclear family and not to an extended family of any significant degree. It certainly would not befit a situation of extensive community relationships.

Of course, Knight was making an idealized typology, using "'heroic abstraction' with regard to an 'imaginary society'." Nonetheless, he did contend that the "assumptions... are idealizations or purifications of tendencies which hold good more or less in reality." Undeniably, the mobility of labor is very important to the functioning of an actual market economy. Von Mises did not have an ideal construct in mind when he remarked that if workers "did not act as trade unionists, but reduced their demands and changed their locations and occupations according to the requirements of the labor market, they could eventually find work" (quoted in Polanyi, 1944: 176). The qualification that only the agent's economic behavior is being addressed does not obviate the damage done to interpersonal relationships. A worker cannot, after all, relocate his employment geographically without moving himself and his family as well. Nor can a movement from one economic sector to another fail to sever interpersonal ties of one kind and other. As Neale observed: "On the social side family unity and community life are put in a constant state of flux since the personnel are so easily forced into movement" (Polanyi *et al.*, 1971: 365).

Polanyi referred to the "economistic transformation" to designate the elevation of the market economy to universal status. Without this naturalization of commercial activity it is unlikely that history would have witnessed the intentional creation of a competitive market economy, the regulation of which is to be left to its own internal devices. This transformation, in its blindness to the delicate interaction between economy and society, disembedded the economy and literally imperiled society itself. As noted above, the gauge of the embeddedness or disembeddedness of an economy is the place occupied by land, labor, and capital. As the market economy was instituted and the factors of production treated as commodities, the traditional social ties linking human beings to each other and the rest of nature were dissolved and replaced with the new linkages of the commodity production economy or "cash nexus".

The institutionalization of the labor market required reversing the historically ubiquitous relationships of individual human beings, society, and subsistence. In general, earlier societies, short of social famine, guaranteed the individual a livelihood by virtue of membership in the group or society and demanded some more or less definite participation in industrial activity by the same virtue. The labor market, in contrast, operates upon the threat of deprivation or appeal to invidious distinction to motivate industrial activity. The implications of the commoditization of labor are far reaching. Within the market economy and society, the wage is set by market forces, and there is no social entity with the responsibility to assure that the wage is sufficient for a minimally decent livelihood. Laborers and their families must be prepared to relocate geographically and occupationally either to find employment or succeed in terms of invidious distinction. This is nothing so much as a prescription for social dislocation. If workers must move their families when the market dictates, it becomes difficult for them to put down roots and sustain a way of life which is structured and meaningful. It is also difficult to maintain professional standards and tradition or moral communities under such occupational flux. The wider identification and self-authentication functions of the work process beyond mere utilitarian production of output and earning an income are mangled.

> The case is similar for land, i.e. the natural environment.
> The economic function is but one of many vital functions of land. It invests man's life with stability; it is the site of his habitation; it is a condition of his physical safety; it is the landscape and the seasons. We might as well imagine his being born without hands and feet as carrying on his life without land. And yet to separate land from man and organize society in such a way as to satisfy the requirements of a real-estate market was a vital part of the utopian concept of a market economy (Polanyi, 1944: 178).

The commercialization of land, then and now, gives the control of land to mere owners who can evict or exact recompense from those who would use the land. In the American 1930s, families whose lineages for a century or more were born and buried on the land were cast off by the financial interests. The same process has long been at work along the interface between traditional and market economies.

Capital markets likewise endangered social cohesion. Technological change, swings in the business cycle, and the ongoing competition in product and factor markets, Marx's "battle among capitals," involve incessant capital restructuring. Schumpeter (1962) captures this well with his notion of "creative destruction" by which he describes change as the essential character of capitalism. Schumpeterian competition, as opposed to Marshallian competition, is the battle between old and new structures of business product and methods, not the Marshallian competition among given and homogeneous structures. Schumpeterian competition accounts for the progressive thrust of capitalism but it also reveals erosion of social and community life that concerned Polanyi. Incessant change in products, production methods, and the relocation of production to serve new market areas necessarily involves the restructuring of social life. Given the requisite mobility of the factors of production, this incessant restructuring drives factor owners in new directions sectorally and geographically. Hence the destruction and reallocation of existing values and income bases which pave the way for new values and income bases cannot be separated from the destruction of existing "social capital" as it is now called. Rebuilding social capital or social relationships is a time-consuming and uncertain process. At the very least some methodology is needed for deducting this social cost from social benefit of economic progress as we struggle with the whole notion of "redefining progress."

Clearly then, left to its own devices, the market economy would threaten social continuity in cultural and ecological terms. Accordingly, Polanyi argued that the effort to establish a self-regulating market economy was necessarily accompanied by a contrary effort to protect society from the disruption which otherwise would have occurred. The market imperative toward extending commoditization generated a protective imperative to safeguard social organization from the effects of commoditization. "Human society would have been annihilated but for protective countermoves which blunted the action of this self-destructive mechanism" (Polanyi, 1944: 76). The protective countermoves are many and diverse. Governments intervened to protect labor with legislation regulating child and women labor, working conditions, and work time lengths. The welfare states of the last century adopted far-reaching income maintenance programs. Legislation was enacted on land-use planning, resource conservation, pollution control, and modern comprehensive environmental protection. Central banking, capital market regulations, and aggregate demand management emerged as policies to combat macroeconomic instability. If factory legislation and social laws were required to protect industrial man from the implications of the commodity fiction in regard to labor power, if land laws and agrarian tariffs were called into being by the necessity of protecting natural resources and the culture of the countryside against the implications of the commodity fiction in respect to them, it was equally true that central banking and the management of the monetary system were needed to keep manufacturers and other productive enterprises safe from the harm involved in the commodity fiction as applied to money. Paradoxically enough, not only social life and natural resources but also the organization of capitalistic production itself had to be sheltered from the devastating effects of the self-regulating market economy (Polanyi, 1944: 132).

Two points deserve particular emphasis. First, it is not valid to present the protective state interventions as resulting from a leftward ideological shift or the increasing political power of labor. There is no universal ideological stance or political statism which can encompass the breadth of intervention involved. Very often the programs were enacted by those quite enamored with a pro-market ideology. The comprehensive feature is not ideology or political interest groups, but the necessity of countering the disruptions of the market process. As already noted, for Polanyi, the installation of the self-regulating market economy was a matter of conscious design, not spontaneous historical forces, it is the subsequent trend away from the self-regulating market that is spontaneous (Polanyi, 1944: 141–9). This contrasts with the usual notions that the market arose from spontaneous social order and has been eroded by a leftward ideological drift, guided perhaps by a "German ideology" (Hayek, 1944).

The second additional point reinforces the first. The protective response is by no means limited to action through the state apparata. The attempted default of the state on the vital area of protecting the social basis of the lives of its members, left this protective function to organizational measures of the populace, in and out of government. Imperialism and nationalism are banners of protective ideology, their practice is the political, diplomatic, and military administration of economy. Combinations, trusts, and cartels are protectively motivated and operated. Even the modern corporation, the central economic organization complex of modern capitalism, can be viewed as part of the protective response. The principal animus behind the corporate revolution is the urge to stabilize and control the exigencies of the corporate environment, and these exigencies are largely the uncertainties concomitant to the operation of the market mechanism. We are convinced that economic and business historians will eventually view the modern corporation in this light, and that corporate officials will do likewise, notwithstanding the free enterprise ideology which remains strong to this time. After all, the image of the corporation as an institutional reform to ensure the orderly operation of the vital provisioning function is not only more correct but also far more salutary than the traditional typification of the corporation as a profit-mongering monopolist.

Much is learned about the nature of the corporate-welfare state when it is viewed as the culmination of what Polanyi referred to as the double movement of the 19th century. The blending of the two institutional impetuses, the self-regulating market and the protective response, underscores the spontaneous character of the latter. The one universal factor behind this response is the necessity of protecting society against the disruption inherent in the automatic market economy. The double movement also uncovers the principal institutional dynamic of the 20th-century democratic industrial social economy. Indeed not only the corporate-welfare state but also various experiments in socialism, even fascism, are founded upon the need to resolve the inconsistencies between the market economy and the continuity of social life.

Polanyi's view of the protective response involves a view of class relations that is more in tune with that of historicists or original institutionalists than Marxists (Polanyi, 1944: 151–4). Polanyi stresses sectional economic interests drawn along geographic or industrial divisions more than class interests *per se*. Presumably opposed class interests within a region or sector often have reason to cooperate with one another in ways that cut across lines. Hence divisions and conflicts within the classes may be as prominent as those between the classes.

This point is important and may be generalized. Polanyi contended that Marxian class analysis contained its own economistic fallacy. Economic determinism is a tendency of the market economy but this tendency is checked in part by the protective response. The implication of the protective response is that the clarification of social conflict into the sharply hewn class lines envisaged by Classical Marxism does not occur. Social conflict and socially structured inequality are not reduced to the structural battle between capital and labor. Capital versus capital and labor versus labor conflicts persist and work themselves out within the protective response. The inequalities and conflicts associated with sexism and patriarchy, racism and bigotry, and nationalism and patriotism do not disappear to be neatly subsumed under the all-embracing rubric of class struggle. In essence, culture, including political ideology, has to be regarded as having a degree of autonomy and as fully interactive with the forces and social relations of production. Western Marxian scholars following the lead of Engels have long recognized these concerns, and in so doing have moved toward the analyses of Polanyi and the American institutionalists.

Industrialism versus market capitalism

Consideration of Polanyi's distinction between industrialism and market capitalism will enable us to further compare and contrast Polanyi to other dissenting views from the conventional economics of the 20th century. The Industrial Revolution and the rise of market capitalism are not only historically contemporaneous but interdependent in myriad and complicated ways. Nonetheless, they must be distinguished because the lasting importance of each to the livelihood of man is radically different. "The 19th century gave birth to two sets of events of a very different order of magnitude: the machine age, a development of millennial range; and the market system, an initial adjustment to that development" (Polanyi, 1977: xlviii). The machine age, or better, *industrialism,* ushered in by the Industrial Revolution, is a radical and most likely permanent change in the way mankind makes its living. It is centered in the technological locus which is the core of the substantive economy, and it is a change of epochal magnitude. Market capitalism, on the other hand, is merely the "initial response to the challenge of the Industrial Revolution" (Polanyi, 1968: 59). Not surprisingly, it was Polanyi's considered judgment that it was the wrong response, or at least one that is long since obsolete. The social disaster of the 19th century, a disaster which continues to be inherited by every generation, was not, and is not, a product of industrialism *per se* but of industrialism as instituted through means of market capitalism. *"The congenital weakness of nineteenth century society was not that it was industrial but that it was a market society"* (Polanyi, 1944: 250).

The point should be stressed: it is not to machine industrial technology but to its situs in market capitalism that one must look for many of the obstacles that impede social life in industrial civilization. This view aligns Polanyi with those like Marx and the American institutionalists who sought to turn industrialism toward a more humane existence via institutional revolution or reform, and it separates Polanyi from social conservative views that the technology itself dehumanizes existence. At several points in *Capital* Marx distinguishes capitalist social relations from machine production. For example, in the discussion of the origin of capitalism, he emphasized that capitalist labor relations arose first in a setting of traditional tools. Thereafter there has been a continuing revolution in the technology of production, but these changes have occurred within capitalism and hence in response to the social relations and characteristic antagonism of capitalist class relationships. Marx's use of derogatory terms in reference to traditional production methods and his call for a global communist movement also reflect his distinction of industrialism from capitalism. He clearly advocated a revolution in social relations and not any sort of reversion to earlier technologic structures. The point is underscored by Marx's discussion of the capitalist reorganization of agriculture and the subsequent mechanization of agriculture under the impetus of capitalist farming.

For Marx then, it is clearly capitalist social relations that generate alienated labor and erosion of community life. Social conservatives, while they have long mistrusted the market system with its individualist license, often seem to emphasize technological change to an even greater extent. Recently, the technology of video broadcasting seems to be singled out in this regard by writers such as Malcolm Muggeridge and Robert Putnam and the volume of television viewing has been held to account for the decline of such community activities as volunteering.

Even E.F. Schumacher (1973) seems at times to implicate technological change for the destruction of a sense of community and the concomitant rootless, structureless psyches of individuals: "A highly developed transport and communications system has one immensely powerful effect: it makes people *footloose.*" Prior to the advent of that technology "the structure was simply there, because people were relatively immobile." Polanyi would say that at most the role of technology is permissive only and that it does not explain the profound and essentially *sociological* phenomena in question. And to be sure Schumacher suggests at other places that the real cause of the erosion of community lies in the market economy and society that determine the selection and deployment of the technology, as when he observes that "the market is the institutionalization of individualism and non-responsibility" and that it "is propelled by a frenzy of greed and indulges in an orgy of envy, and these are not accidental features but the very causes of its expansionist success." This seems to be in substantial agreement with Polanyi's insistence upon distinguishing the social effects of industrialism from those of the market economy.

By the way, a similar distinction should be made today in the discussion of globalization. One very often hears that globalization is inevitable because the revolution in telecommunications has lowered transactions costs, in effect, bringing the world closer together by diminishing in many respects the factor of geographic distance. Such a view neglects the complex and ultimately social and discretionary causes of globalization. Myriad ideological, legal, and political changes have underwritten the pattern of increasing global economic integration that is known as globalization. These changes are the result of powerful individuals and organizations inveighing their resources to rewrite social contracts. Even the development of the new telecommunications technology is the result of discretionary behavior (For excellent analyses of this recently exercised social discretion, see Blau (1999); James Galbraith, 1998; and Palley (1998)).

The key aspect of the erosion of social and community life is the displacement of reciprocity or morally obligatory interpersonal obligation. The widely discussed phenomena of cost-shifting and externalities are evidence of diminished reciprocity. As noted above, the mobility of labor is an all-important requisite to the operation of a self-regulating market economy, and this mobility, enforced by unemployment and other market considerations, cannot but erode the community rootedness of workers. This is a matter of market capitalism, not industrialism. There is nothing in the nature of machine industrial technology that requires this mobility of labor. The salient issues involved are not explicable in terms of technological considerations. They are instead questions of price, cost, and profitability answered by those whose power and interest are vested in the scarcity price system. To be sure, the crucial decisions made are about how technology is employed, and there is some truth behind the common notion that the requirements of machinery are superior to social and human needs. But it would be more correct to say that the interests of those who control the technology are superior to the interests of those who do not. Power and discretion are essential themes of heterodox economics.

As Knight makes clear, it is to the requirements of the market economy that one must look to explain the necessity that independent action exists such that social considerations and non-market relations do not interfere with exchange behavior. In practice, Knight's assumption was expressed in the institutionalization of the freedom of contract, and "this meant that the non-contractual organizations of kinship, neighborhood, profession, and creed were liquidated since they claimed the allegiance of the individual and thus restrained his freedom" (Polanyi, 1944: 163).

The footloose, almost nomadic character of wage-labor is mirrored in the effects of the market economy on agriculture. But land, like labor, is far more than a mere factor of production, it is nature itself; it is the habitat of man and other species. It is not a mere utilitarian fount but is instead saturated with numerous other social and cultural functions and meanings (see Polanyi, 1944: 178, 184). After all, wars are fought for territory that make little sense insofar as real estate values are concerned. The organization of farming has profound consequences beyond the production and distribution of foodstuffs and fibers. The agriculture of a society is intimately connected with the character of its people, and a civilization's social and ecological stability is rooted in its agrarian culture.

As noted above, the market economy is at odds not only with the social and ecological needs of labor and land but also with industrial production itself through the important matter of purchasing power. A system fueled by profits must have a high degree of monetary stability and yet have a monetary system capable of expanding along with industrial output. "This is the easily understandable reason why a system of commodity money, such as the market mechanism tends to produce without outside interference, is incompatible with industrial production" (Polanyi, 1944: 193). Commodity money, usually gold or silver, simply cannot be relied upon to expand apace with industrial output. If it does not, a deflation ensues which is ruinous to profits and economic calculation. Token monetary systems result but these in turn conflict with the need for commodity money in international trade. In the 19th century, "in its simplest form, the problem was this: commodity money was vital to the existence of foreign trade; token money, to the existence of domestic trade" (Polanyi, 1944: 193). Central banking, part of the protective response, largely mitigated this conflict, but it did not do so entirely and remnants of the problem still bedevil the managed economies of today.

Polanyi's point is that the true defect of the age was that the market economy required that the development and application of industrial technology be subordinated to the commercial principle of profit rather than to the character of social and human needs. This echoes the socialist plaint that production should be for human needs and not profit and the social structure of accumulation models emphasized by contemporary radical economists. It is also reminiscent of Veblen's dichotomous analysis of the conflict between commerce and industry. It is not difficult to find in the institutionalist literature agreement with Polanyi that the root problem is not industrialism *per se* but industrial market capitalism. Veblen's celebrated dichotomy between industrial and pecuniary interests is to the point and requires no comment. Mitchell (1913: 25) too emphasized the warping of personalities by the pecuniary culture and emphasized that although "for the well being of the community efficient industry and commerce [distributive services] are vastly more important than successful money-making... , in practice, [they] are thoroughly subordinated to business."

Certainly no one has excelled Veblen in making the case that sharp practice and irresponsible action are not incidental but the heart and core of the market capitalist economy. The freedom of free enterprise – the "rule of self-help and free bargaining" – is the right to wreck matters at large in the pursuit of one's self-interest. The essential power of private property in such a setting is not to hold for personal use but rather to withhold from social use if one is dissatisfied with the terms of the bargain.

> [A]ny person who has a legal right to withhold any part of the necessary industrial apparatus or materials from current use will be in a position to impose terms and exact obedience, on pain of rendering the community's joint stock of technology inoperative to that extent. Ownership of industrial equipment and natural resources confers such a right legally to enforce unemployment, and so to make the community's workmanship useless to that extent (Veblen, 1967: 65–6).

It follows that one's power to command income in the normal operation of market capitalism is directly related to the mayhem one can wreak by refusing to cooperate, i.e., by the derangement of the social process of production that one can cause.

> The common good, so far as it is a question of material welfare, is evidently best served by an unhampered working of the industrial system... without interruption or dislocation. But it is equally evident that the owner or manager of any given concern or section of this industrial system may be in a position to gain something for himself at the cost of the rest by obstructing, retarding or dislocating this working system at some critical point in such a way as will enable him to get the best of the bargain in his dealings with the rest. This appears constantly in the altogether usual, and altogether legitimate, practice of holding out for a better price. So also in the scarcely less usual, and no less legitimate, practice of withholding needed ground or right of way, or needed materials or information, from a business rival.... All these things are usual and a matter of course, because business management under [present] conditions... is in great part made up of these things. Sabotage of this kind is

indispensable to any large success in industrial business (Veblen, 1969: 93).

As a result, a radical disjuncture exists between the interests of society and those practicing businesslike management of their property, a point which Veblen had emphasized in his earlier work, *The Theory of Business Enterprise*, in which he emphasized the transition to profit-seeking business management in capitalism, in contrast to the "pre-capitalistic business situation [in which] business...was customarily managed with a view to earning a livelihood rather than with a view to profit on investment." This seems to echo Aristotle's distinction between natural and unnatural exchange, upon which Polanyi placed so much emphasis.

According to Gruchy (1967: 435), Tugwell also spoke very clearly on this point, arguing that industrialism has brought forth great technical capacity but that this capacity has yet to be institutionally implemented to serve the general welfare. Instead, in Tugwell's view, the prevailing institutional climate assures the dominance of the business interest without regard to the costs to the general interest. Clark's analysis was even closer to Polanyi's than the other institutionalists. Gruchy (1967: 372–3), summarizing the final section of Clark's *Studies in the Economics of Overhead Costs*, attributes to Clark the view that "the industrial system has evolved along lines which may be regarded more as adjustments to the requirements of the machine than as adjustments to the needs of decent human living" owing to the fact that "the making of the policies that dominate the machine process is restricted to the select few who own or control the machines." In general, then, for the institutionalists, the key problem with industrialism to date has been that "pecuniary considerations are more decisive with respect to the working of the economy than are technological considerations," and the challenge posed by industrialism to a humane civilization cannot be met without first throwing off the mental shackles of the market myth.

This is as well a key theme of the work of Kenneth Galbraith's, who is sharply critical of the power exercised by the large corporations over individual and public sector choices. Unwittingly abetted by the "imagery of choice" presented by conventional economics (see Stanfield, 1996), powerful corporate interests administer a system in which the needs of commodity production and consumption are paramount and non-market, non-commodity needs are neglected.

These concerns echo Polanyi's point that the market economy requires a market society which in turn maintains a market personality through a market culture. The personality and character of individuals have been subordinated to the logic of industrial market capitalism.

> The first century of the Machine Age is drawing to a close.... Its fabulous material success was due to the willing, indeed the enthusiastic, subordination of man to the needs of the machine. Liberal capitalism was in effect man's initial response to the challenge of the Industrial Revolution. In order to allow scope to the use of elaborate, powerful machinery, we transformed human economy into a self-adjusting system of markets, and cast our thoughts and values in the mold of this unique innovation (Polanyi, 1968: 59).

Of course, in Polanyi's view, this initial market economic response to industrialism must be, and largely if unconsciously has been, abandoned with the growth of the protective response. Polanyi recognized that the struggle was first and foremost ideological, the necessity of overcoming the obsolete market mentality so that the protective response may be accurately comprehended and social and individual action reformed on the basis of that insight.

A theme very similar to Polanyi's protective response forms a main current in original institutionalism, which insists that industrialism contains within itself a logic of reform. This theme was imported to America by the precursors and founders of Institutionalism, men such as Richard T. Ely, Edwin R.A. Seligman, and Henry Carter Adams, who studied in Germany with the German Historicists. The Historicists, in a wide-ranging break with classical economics over method and the nature of economic science, rejected *laissez-faire* and emphasized the potential for state economic action and social reform. In his classic restatement of institutionalism, Gruchy (1967: 620–1) has emphasized this point:

> The logic of economic development shows that modern industrial technology is throwing economic activity into a mold which is becoming increasingly collective in nature. This technology, if not interrupted in its development, will continue its work of transforming the competitive economy into a system in which collective economic action is of major importance. The logic of this economic development necessarily leads to some form of intervention by forces which operate outside private markets, since the modern

> economy cannot function smoothly and efficiently under the direction of private enterprise alone.

Moreover, the institutionalists, as did Polanyi, took a broad view of the political or administrative process that emerged to displace the self-regulating market economy, insisting that governance must be viewed broadly to include non-state organizations. This was emphasized by Walton Hamilton (1957: 6–7):

> The thesis here is that the market which of old was sovereign to the whole economy has been deposed, and that the mandate of supply and demand which rigidly it enforced has ceased to be an 'iron law.' It is not that the market is no longer of importance.... It is rather that the throne has had to be shared... ; and that the stream of judgments by which the vast network of productive activities is kept going no longer emerges from the automatic play of economic forces. A host of procedures and arrangements – political and character – have invaded the domain of business. As a result there has arisen, quite apart from the ordinary operations of state, a government of industry which in its own distinctive way has its constitution and its statutes, its administrative and judicial processes, and its own manner of dealing with those who do not abide by the law of industry.

Hamilton also emphasized the spontaneous nature of the governance reform and the key role played therein by business personnel: "Corporate decisions involve discretion, and where there is discretion there is the making of policy, and policy is a political phenomenon" (Hamilton, 1957: 7). Accordingly, in the revolutionary deposition of the market economy, it was "the businessman who among them all was the greatest of radicals" (Hamilton, 1957: 34). Moreover,

> The old order was never abolished. No law, statute, mandate, or decree brought it to an end. There was no intent on anyone's part to set down a period and formally to proclaim a new era. The great transformation – the word is more exact than revolution – came at a headlong pace, and yet was gradual...
>
> The new order of things emerged unplanned, unsaluted and unsung. It is not a response to a call for an economic order which is fresh and different.... Instead it is a by-product of the everyday concern of a host of individuals with their own problems (Hamilton, 1957: 33).

Similar views are found in the work of Kenneth Galbraith who stresses the blurring of the dichotomy between public and private and the integral relationship between the private and public governments: "the industrial system will not long be regarded as something apart from government. Rather it will increasingly be seen as part of a much larger complex which embraces both the industrial system and the state" (Galbraith, 1967: 399). Galbraith also insists upon the non-ideological nature of the supersession of the market and follows Hamilton in citing business as "the greatest of radicals" in this great transformation.

It should be noted that these views of the corporation and the evolving nature of capitalism are not at odds with Marx's analysis. In Volume III of *Capital*, he insists that the corporation, or "joint stock company," would prove to be the major institutional conduit from capitalism to socialism. He anticipated the separation of ownership of control and referred to the corporation as socialism growing within the womb of capitalism. Michael Harrington's (1966) *Accidental Century* exemplifies the similarity of Marxian and institutionalist analyses of modern corporate capitalism.

All of this is, of course, similar to Polanyi's insistence that the protective response was spontaneous and not the result of a leftist conspiracy or ideological shift. Explanation of the spontaneous character of the protective does not mean it is a matter of indifference on how it is done. Far from it. The manner in which the transformation is finally completed and the market economy cast away, in fact and principle, is absolutely crucial with respect to the continuation of a humane and civilized way of life. The collapse of the market economy can be replaced with an administered economy placed anywhere along the spectrum between democracy and totalitarianism. The issues come down to retaining and revitalizing the liberal ideals of personal freedom and responsibility while administering the economy to safeguard the reproduction and stability of society. Social control of economic activity will shift from markets to reciprocity and redistribution and not just any form of control is adequate to the task. Mere intervention is not planning, and the mere accumulation of rules and regulations and politicized economic relationships will not achieve an administered economy in which personal liberties and other human values are safeguarded. Nor is just any form of planning acceptable; it must be participatory, institutionalized in such a way as to encourage the widest possible popular input and understanding. Planning must be a learning process in which people are moved to learn about the economy, its place in society, and its relation to their lives. It was this "bottom up" planning that Polanyi desired; he rejected any "topdown" scenario (Polanyi, 1968: 74–7).

To accomplish this, it will be necessary to escape the myopia of the market mentality and review the place of economy in society. This will turn upon a reviewing of the spontaneous protective response and a renewed understanding of the nature of the corporate-welfare state (see Stanfield, 1995: ch. 9). The institutionalist literature on industrialism and the logic of reform is the major intellectual effort to provide a *positive* interpretation of the corporate-welfare state. As noted above, the logic of reform theme runs throughout Gruchy's examination of the major Institutionalists in *Modern Economic Thought* and has been emphasized by later writers in the tradition as well, notably Galbraith. The logic of reform is essentially the same as the protective response; the institutional logic at work is the necessity of protecting society against the vagaries of the self-regulating market by reembedding economic decisions in the social and political fabric.

These myriad reembedding actions expand in the history of market capitalism because the market mechanism extends its reach and because the growth of scale and complexity of machine industrial technology increases the mayhem wrought by irresponsible market-oriented actions. "The more comprehensive the market system became, the more it revealed its incapacity to satisfy the requirements of a stable society" (Polanyi, 1977: 1). The tendency of the market toward extension of its reach is commonplace. Market capitalism grew by reaching into and destroying the traditional economy and replacing production for direct use with commodity production. This is an ongoing process. Early in this century, as more of the fabrication and processing of drugs, foodstuffs, and the like were removed from the household to the commodity sphere, regulatory measures were required to protect consumers. More recently, care for children and the elderly have been in process of commoditization. Predictably, it has been necessary to provide protection through regulation of daycare centers and nursing homes. Provision of these services on a commodity basis is far different from their provision through the extended family because in the latter the element of embeddedness remains in the form of the familial relationship. No matter the means employed, the upshot of the protective response to reembed the market in society is, of course, the demise of the self-regulating market economy.

The transformation away from the market economy to a politically mandated increase in reciprocity and redistribution need not undermine individual freedom. But care must be taken and it must be based upon the reviewing of the place of economy in society to which allusion has already been made. It is necessary to overcome the narrow view of freedom as the absence of state intervention in the market. Preoccupation with this narrow conception has confined the liberal tradition to the conclusion that any expansion in the role of the state is necessarily a decrease in freedom. This myopic perspective is rooted historically in the liberal conception of the market economy as a natural order of some sort which emerged spontaneously due to its superior consonance with human nature. Polanyi gave a detailed rebuttal of this view, arguing in effect, that the market economy was a conscious political creation and did not and would not have emerged spontaneously (Stanfield, 1986: ch. 4). The importance of this recognition that the market economy resulted from political action, albeit virtually suicidal action for the polity, is to demystify or denaturalize the market economy and take away the aura of inevitability which is its predominant ideological defense. Thus viewed, market capitalism has no pride of place and the political action of human beings to install it can be examined on equal footing with like action to dismantle it.

This point is crucial and deserves emphasis. There is too much discourse on the so-called market solution versus political intervention. It must be recognized that there is no market solution in any useful sense. There is only one political-economic solution versus another political-economic solution. Every market outcome is structured by a complex set of political, legal, and social rules and norms (Stanfield, 1995: ch. 1). Such iconic terms as free trade and free competition are fatally incomplete and should be abolished in favor of terminology that emphasizes the alternative political and social regimes that may structure market economic activity. A capitalist economy has some substance because it specifies a regime in which the residual of enterprise revenue over cost is the property of the owners of the enterprise's equity and not of labor or other elements of society. But even then, further specification is needed as to whether or not collective bargaining or corporate profits taxation is legally mandated. Only by improved terminology will we come to emphasize the social *discretion* that is the essential thrust of heterodox economics (Tool, 1979).

Once this intellectual clarification is completed, the problem of freedom must be examined in an altogether different light. Polanyi spoke of "freedom in a complex society" (Polanyi, 1944: ch. 21) to underscore the necessity of going beyond the simplism of the market myth. It is simplistic to see freedom primarily in terms of the state's noninterference in market activities and this simplism follows from the image of economy and society contained in the market myth. It is grossly simplistic – not simpleminded since the market myth has been given very sophisticated and artful promulgation – to reduce the economy to a process of calculation and exchange operating to establish relative prices which determine production and distribution, and then to cordon off this sphere as the economy, a thing apart from the polity, family, religion, etc. In reality, the interaction involved is continuous, complex, and commanding so that holistic economic thought is required if the primacy of society is not to be neglected. Because this neglect of society is a threat to freedom, the simplistic market view of freedom is in fact a threat to freedom. Therefore, "we cannot achieve the freedom we seek, unless we comprehend the true significance of freedom in a complex society" (Polanyi, 1944: 254).

The first step toward treating freedom as a vastly more complicated problem than that envisaged by the market myth is to recognize that there are many different kinds of freedom, some having good effects, some bad. The interaction between the various freedoms are complex. Some freedoms reinforce and strengthen other freedoms while some undermine and threaten other freedoms. Polanyi argued that the future society would have to distinguish between desirable and undesirable freedoms, ensure the first and suppress the latter (Polanyi, 1944: 254–5). Irresponsible self-seeking which embodies no regard for the public good fosters the erosion of social and community life which in turn brings forth the protective response.

A society whose freedoms are purchased at the cost of injustice and insecurity is neither enduring nor good. The problem of democratic control of the economy to protect society is to separate the two kinds of freedoms in order to eliminate the one and preserve the other. This can only be done if the complexity of freedom is recognized and the distinctions among freedoms accepted. Polanyi conceded to the liberal's insistence that the market economy is linked historically with social and political freedoms, but he sharply dissented from the logical extension that the demise of the market economy must necessarily extinguish all freedom in its wake, i.e., that the evil freedoms are the necessary costs of the cherished ones. There is no necessary abnegation of freedom in a planned economy. "In truth, we will have just as much freedom as we will desire to create and to safeguard. There is no *one* determinant in human society. Institutional guarantees of personal freedom are compatible with any economic system" (Polanyi, 1968: 76).

The market economy is not a necessary condition for the cherished freedoms. Indeed generations of Marxian scholars have insisted that the social relations of market capitalism are profoundly inconsistent with individual freedom in an ultimate sense. Subordination to the requisites of capitalist commodity production generates alienated, one-dimensional personalities who lack the institutional means to achieve authentic self-actualization (Stanfield, 1995: ch. 13).

J.M. Clark wrote in passionate terms in substantial agreement with Polanyi's point when he contrasted the reality of the 20th century economy to the market conception.

> We have inherited an economics of irresponsibility. We are in an economy of control with which our intellectual inheritance fits but awkwardly. To make control really tolerable we need something more; something which is still in its infancy. We need an economics of responsibility, developed and embodied in our working business ethics (Clark, 1967: 67).

In contrast to the responsibility needed for a controlled economy,

> ... the *laissez-faire* economics may well be characterized as the economics of irresponsibility, and the business system of free contract is also a system of irresponsibility when judged by the same standard.... Liberal economics... [neglects the responsibility problem] by separating business sharply off from the rest of life (Clark, 1967: 77).

Clark goes on to denounce the socialization pattern which induces people in business or politics to subscribe to "the law of getting all they can." For Clark, "the economics of control is at war with the economics of irresponsibility."

The freedoms of irresponsible self-seeking and sharp practice threaten all freedoms because they threaten society. By creating injustice, insecurity, and disorder, they leave the way open to an authoritarian, totalitarian resolution. The primacy of society exists, it is reality, and social reproduction, i.e., the continuation of society, will be achieved by measures as extreme and dire as deemed necessary. Without a viable resolution of the problem of freedom and order in a free society, the issue will be settled all on the side of order. The fascistic regimes of the early 20th century arose from just such disorder created by a stalemate of irresponsible forces clashing in industry and government in a polarized political economy (Polanyi, 1944: 235–6).

Conclusion

We insist that Polanyi's work along with original institutionalism and neo-Marxism should be viewed as one research program: that of economic sociology or evolutionary economics. Schumpeter (1950: 21) defines economic sociology as the effort to account for how people have come to behave as they do. We would add inquiry as to how this behavior is evolving, the implications of this evolution, and what if any programmatic change should be attempted in this regard. The new or not-so-original institutionalists as well as the neo-Austrians have research programs that are in many ways complementary and no doubt have valuable insights to contribute, especially with regard to individual agency and the care that must be taken upon embarking on a journey of programming change in the way people behave.

Marx is widely credited with having founded the sociology of knowledge. In doing so, he also laid the foundations for an evolutionary economics or economic sociology. Of particular interest in this regard are his discussion of the evolution of economic institutions in the *Grundrisse*, his theme in several works of the one-dimensional character of capitalist culture, and of course the analysis of the capitalist laws of motion. Polanyi's work shows the influence of these themes from Marx. He emphasizes the place of economy in society, criticizes the shallow interpretation of pre-modern economies, and writes powerfully of the disembedded character and dominant role of the market complex in capitalism. With the concept of the protective response, Polanyi departs from Marx and, indeed, criticizes Marx for having an economistic fallacy of his own. Of particular significance is Marx's expectation that the objective conditions of capitalism would clarify the class struggle and more or less resolve social conflict into capital versus labor. Polanyi's analysis suggests that the protective response interferes with the laws of motion of capitalism in this regard, preventing the realization of the logical tendencies of capitalism that Marx anticipated. Polanyi's argument supports the Cultural Marxism of his acquaintance, Lukacs, and provides a fresh perspective on left wing political strategy.

Polanyi's emphasis upon economic anthropology and the protective response also links his work to original institutional economics. Like Polanyi, the institutionalists insist upon a logic of reform in democratic industrial society which has less to do with ideology and more to do with the realities of socio-economic life in complex modern societies. Like many of the original institutionalists, Polanyi saw that the greatest threat to freedom lies in a poorly instituted administered economy, such as must exist so long as democratic industrial society labors under the influence of the market mentality. In practice, society has rejected Hayek's call for submission to the organic process of uncontrolled market forces with its attendant windfall gains and losses, insecurity, instability, and unmanaged change. Conscious social control of the forces which shape life's chances and their realization is a powerful popular commitment. The task ahead is to throw off the ideological remnant of the 19th century, the market mentality, so to be able to construct a theory with which to inform and guide the practice to which democratic industrial society is committed.

Heterodox economists should sound the alarm that freedom's frustration in authoritarian reaction is an ever-present possibility in a poorly instituted managed or regulated capitalist economy. Social and ecological continuity will be maintained at the expense of freedom unless freedom is consciously preserved within a regime that also ensures continuity (Heilbroner, 1974; Lowe, 1988). In the present era of corporate-dominated globalization, this admonition is being neglected. The threat is very real that identity politics will surge onto a powerful reactionary force as it did in the interwar period of the last century. In this context, the development of a viable heterodox economics is mandatory.

References

Blau, J. (1999) *Illusions of Prosperity: America's Working Families in an Age of Economic Insecurity*, New York: Oxford University Press.

Clark, J.M. (1967) *Preface to Social Economics*, New York: A.M. Kelley.

Galbraith, J. Kenneth (1967) *The New Industrial State*, Boston: Houghton Mifflin.

Galbraith, James K. (1998) *Created Unequal*, New York: Free Press.

Gruchy, A.G. (1967) *Modern Economic Thought*, New York: A.M. Kelley.

Hamilton, W.H. (1957) *The Politics of Industry*, New York: A.A. Knopf.

Harrington, M. (1966) *The Accidental Century*, Baltimore MD: Penquin.

Hayek, F.A. (1944) *The Road To Serfdom*, Chicago: University of Chicago.

Heilbroner, R.L. (1974) *An Inquiry Into the Human Prospect*, New York: Norton.

Knight, Frank (1971) *Risk, Uncertainty and Profit*, Chicago: University of Chicago Press.

Lowe, A. (1988) *Has Freedom a Future?*, New York: Praeger.

Mitchell, W.C. (1913) *Business Cycles*, Berkeley: University of California Press.

Palley, T. (1998) *Plenty of Nothing*, Princeton: Princeton University Press.

Polanyi, K. (1944) *The Great Transformation*, New York: Rinehart. 1957, Boston: Beacon.

Polanyi, K. (1968) *Primitive, Archaic, and Modern Economies*, ed. G. Dalton, Garden City, NY: Doubleday.

Polanyi, K. (1977) *The Livelihood of Man*, ed. H.W. Pearson, New York: Academic Press.

Polanyi, K., Arensberg, C.M. & Pearson, H.W. (eds) (1971) *Trade and Market in the Early Empires*, Chicago: Henry Regnery.

Schumacher, E.F. (1973) *Small is Beautiful*, New York: Harper & Row.

Schumpeter, J.A. (1950) *History of Economic Analysis*, New York: Oxford University Press.

Schumpeter, J.A. (1962) *Capitalism, Socialism, and Democracy*, 3rd edn., New York: Harper & Row.

Stanfield, J.R. (1986) *The Economic Thought of Karl Polanyi*, London: Macmillan Press and New York: St. Martin's Press.

Stanfield, J.R. (1995) *Economics, Power, and Culture: Essays in the Development of Radical Institutionalism*, London: Macmillan.

Stanfield, J.R. (1996) *John Kenneth Galbraith*, London: Macmillan.

Tool, M.R. (1979) *The Discretionary Economy*, Santa Monica, CA: Goodyear Press.

Veblen, T.B. (1967) *Absentee Ownership and Business Enterprise in Recent Times*, Boston: Beacon Press.

Veblen, T.B. (1969) *The Vested Interests and the Common Man*, New York: Capricorn.

4
Marxist Theories of the State

Raju J. Das

Marxist theories of the capitalist state deal with questions about the role of the state in society, and more specifically its relation to class and class struggle. This chapter critically examines some of these theories. In discussing these I will indicate their links to classical Marxism, and also pay attention to the tensions within and among the different Marxian approaches. In the discussion I will try to highlight contributions of scholars to state theory working in different disciplines including economics, sociology, human geography and political science.

This chapter is divided into five sections. The first section presents a Marxist instrumentalist theory, and the second discusses Marxist structuralist theories of the state. Both instrumentalism and structuralism underemphasize the agency of dominated classes and state actors. Sections III and IV deal with these aspects in greater detail – theories of class struggle and state autonomy respectively. The concluding section indicates some gaps in the Marxist literature on the state.

I. Dominant class instrumentalist theory of the state

According to the instrumentalist theory of the state, the state is merely an instrument in the hands of the dominant class. The origin of this theory can be traced to Marx and Engels, who characterized the state in the *Communist Manifesto* as "a committee for managing the common affairs of the whole bourgeoisie" (1953: 44) and in *German Ideology* as "the form in which the individuals of a ruling class assert their common interests" (1970: 80).[1] These statements have been taken to mean that state *action* is under the *direct control* of capitalists and is utilized to *maximize* their *long-term* and *common* interests and/or the *special interests* of specific groups of capitalists (Meckstroth, 2000: 56, 60; Ollman, 1982: 42).

There are several mechanisms through which the state works as an instrument of capital. According to Miliband, whose early work popularized the instrumentalist theory, personnel at the height of the state system (including the government, legislature, bureaucracy, army and judiciary) "have tended to belong to the economically dominant class" – the bourgeoisie (1977: 69). Another way of saying this is that the bourgeoisie directly control the state: they have legislative seats,[2] they advise the government, sit on commissions and regulatory boards, make decisions on behalf of the state, present (even write) actual bills for legislative consideration, fund political parties, and so on.[3]

High-level state actors, including those who are bourgeois by class origin and those who *become* bourgeois by virtue of their "education, connections, and way of life" (Miliband, 1977: 69), share bourgeois ideology. That is, they share a commitment to the rationality of capitalism and a "belief that the national interest is inextricably bound up with the wealth and strength of capitalist enterprise". It is natural, therefore, that they seek to help business and businesspersons (Miliband, 1969: 76–7).[4]

A special form of the instrumentalist theory is the theory of State Monopoly Capitalism. According to this theory, competition between capitalists leads to the centralization and concentration of capital, and hence to the development of monopoly capital. Monopoly capitalism becomes state monopoly capitalism as monopolies and the state are fused together. Because of the tendency for the rate of profit to fall in capitalism, state intervention (e.g., the creation of markets for commodities) is necessary to offset this tendency. State intervention is possible because it is an instrument of dominant monopolies (for a discussion of State Monopoly Capitalism theory, see Jessop, 1982).

Instrumentalist theory reveals how capitalists control the state in order to promote their own common and/or special interests. It thus helps demystify the liberal view of a class-neutral state (Ollman, 1982). However, the theory has several conceptual and empirical flaws.

For one thing, it does not recognize that to act in the general interest of *capital*, the state must be able to act *against* the interests of particular *capitalists*.[5] This means that the state should have more autonomy from direct capitalist control than the instrumentalist theory allows (Block, 1987a). Another, and perhaps more important, problem with this theory is that the use of state power cannot be decisively determined by the class background and affiliation of state elite. The reason for this is that "state power reflects the interaction between state elite and the circumstances in which it must act" (Jessop, 1990: 150). More specifically, the theory ignores structural constraints on the state (elite).

The theory is also open to empirical criticism. To begin with, the social backgrounds of state personnel vary widely. The bourgeoisie may not occupy important positions in the state. For example, throughout most of the 19th century, in capitalist Britain "the whole business of government. remained the guaranteed domain of the landed aristocracy," not the bourgeoisie (Marx in Miliband, 1977: 70).[6] So any coherent policy in the long-term interest of the capitalist class emerging through the instrumental use of the state seems unlikely. Further, bourgeois-led states have pursued policies that capital has approved of, including pro-labor reforms (Miliband, 1977: 71). This shows that the state cannot just be a tool of capital, acting "at its behest." One could argue that such reforms are mere concessions that capital gives to labor in order to co-opt it. But as Gold *et al.* (1975: 35) rightly note, "even when such reforms are ultimately cooptive, to treat all reforms as the result of an instrumentalist use of the state is to deny the possibility of struggle over reforms."[7]

II. The structuralist theory of the state

In the structuralist theory, the state's class character and functions are examined not in terms of who runs and controls the state (as in instrumentalist theory), but in terms of the constraints on state actions imposed by the capitalist class structure. Miliband (1970: 57) admits that he perhaps should have stressed more on the structural constraints on the state in his early work. In his classic *Marxism and Politics* (Miliband, 1977) he goes even further, arguing that "The question is not one of purpose or attitude [of the state elite] but of 'structural constraints'." He adds, the socio-economic system provides the contexts for the political system and state action, and the purpose and the attitude of state elites "are themselves greatly affected by that socio-economic context, so that what appears 'reasonable' by way of state action (or non-action) to power-holders [i.e. state elites] will normally be in tune with the 'rationality' and requirements of the socio-economic system itself" (Miliband, 1977: 93).

State functions, broadly speaking, can be either political or economic. So, structuralist/functionalist theory can be of two types: political structuralism (e.g. early Poulantzas) *or* economic structuralism (e.g.

Altvater, 1978; Offe, 1984). These two strands emphasize the political and the economic functions of the state respectively.[8]

A. Political structuralism

Political structuralism views the state as "the factor of cohesion of a social formation" (Poulantzas, 1969: 73). Its "global role" is maintaining the unity of a social formation divided into classes. This role "corresponds to the political interest of the dominant class" (Poulantzas, 1968: 54) and conditions its other functions including its economic functions (e.g. creating conditions to counter the falling rate of profit) (Poulantzas, 1978: 44; 1968: 54, 187).

Poulantzas says that the state functions differently for different classes. For the dominated classes, its function "is to prevent their political organization" (Poulantzas, 1968: 188; 1978: 127). It performs this function by presenting itself to the working class as representing the general interests (of juridically-created citizens, *not class* members) (Poulantzas, 1968: 133).[9] This notion of the general interest is not trickery, but a real fact: the state "gives to the economic interest of certain dominated classes guarantees which may even be contrary to the short-term economic interests of dominant classes, but which are compatible with their political interests and their hegemonic domination" (Poulantzas, 1968: 190–1). Making this guarantee, says Poulantzas, the state aims precisely at the political disorganization of the dominated classes, in that the *economic* concessions help prevent the dominated classes from attacking the *political* basis of exploitation by the dominant class, i.e. state power.[10]

With regard to the dominant classes the state plays a different role. The bourgeoisie cannot realize its hegemony over the dominated classes because of its internal divisions, and the lack of political unity and organized political struggle of dominated classes. So "the state takes charge of the bourgeoisie's political interest" (Poulantzas, 1968: 284) and tries to organize its different fractions into a power bloc "under the protection of the hegemonic fraction" (Poulantzas, 1968: 137, 190, 239).

To perform these two different roles, the state has to be relatively autonomous from dominant classes and factions. Relative autonomy "allows the state to intervene not only to arrange compromises..., but also to intervene against the long term economic interest of one or other fraction of the dominant class: for such compromises and sacrifices are sometimes necessary for the realization of their *political* class interests" (Poulantzas, 1968: 284–5; emphasis added).[11] Such interventions can be useful for the long-run *economic* interest of the dominant classes as well (e.g. absorption of the surplus of monopoly production).[12]

But where does this relative autonomy come from? Poulantzas says that relative autonomy has two foundations. One is in the structure; another is in class struggle. In terms of the former, the separation of the state from society (particularly, from the economic relations), which exists by virtue of the nature of the capitalist structure, is crucial. Capitalism is characterized by the "separation of direct producers from the means of production" (Poulantzas, 1968: 129), which means that direct political power does not have to be exercised in order to appropriate surplus labor from producers, a point originally made by Marx (1977). This "produces the specific autonomy of the political and the economic" (Poulantzas, 1968: 129).[13] The capitalist state, in the long run, can only correspond to the political interest of the dominant class(es). This is the negative limit to state autonomy. But within this limit, the degree and the form of relative autonomy (i.e. "*how* relative, *how* it is relative") depends on the precise conjuncture of the class struggle (e.g. configuration of the power bloc, degree of hegemony of the power bloc, relation between capital and labor) (Poulantzas, 1976: 10; 1968: 289).

Poulantzas sheds considerable light on the class nature of the capitalist state in terms of its functions with respect to different classes, and he shows that the state may not necessarily be a tool of any specific class. But his theory has several problems.[14] First, Poulantzas (1968: 284) seems to subscribe to a structural-functionalist explanation of the state – capital needs something to maintain the unity of the social formation, and particularly, of different fractions of the bourgeoisie. A relatively autonomous state comes into being to perform that function. But it is not clear why a state that is relatively autonomous must perform the functions Poulantzas says it does (i.e. organizing the ruling classes and disorganizing the dominated classes). For him, structural constraints on the state derive from the *place* of the state in the social structure; the state is constrained to be a *class*-state. His (political) structuralist theory is most succinctly put forth in his 1969 article (Poulantzas, 1969: 73): "[I]f the *function* of the State...and the *interests* of the dominant class...coincide, it is by reason of the system itself: the direct participation of members of the ruling class in the State apparatus is not the *cause* but the *effect*, and moreover a chance and a contingent one, of this objective coincidence." If instrumental control by "members of the ruling class" is ruled out, then it is not clear what mechanisms constrain state actions.

Second, Poulantzas *under*emphasizes the economic functions of the state. Although he discusses some economic functions in his 1978 book, Poulantzas (1978: 52) notes: they "are not the primary functions" of the state. In addition, he overemphasizes the political role of the state and its separation from society. Like instrumentalism, political structuralism underplays the relationship between the economic and the political as discrete forms of capitalist social relations (Holloway & Picciotto, 1978). So there needs to be an adequate theory of this relation. Economic structuralism has two variants that seek to specify the nature of this relation as well as the mechanisms forcing the state to act in the interest of capital.

B. Economic structuralism: the derivationist theory

Inspired by Marx's *Capital*, and also by the work of Engels, economic structuralism is a reaction to instrumentalism. It denies any autonomy to the state; it is also a critique of the politicist tendency of Poulantzas. It derives the needs for, and the limits to, state functions from the laws of motion of capitalism (Holloway & Picciotto, 1978: 19).

According to Muller and Neususs (1978), and Altvater (1978), the necessity of the state as a separate institution is derived from the nature of the relations among capitalists. Altvater (1978) views the state as an ideal collective capitalist that furthers the general interests of capital. First, competing with each other in pursuit of surplus value, capitalists will not produce certain things (e.g., labor power) because such production is not profitable (also see Muller & Neususs, 1978: 38). So, the state must socialize the production of these things if accumulation is to take place. Second, capitalist production, driven by competition for maximum value, might threaten the existence of society – for example by destroying natural resources or the reserve army of labor. As Marx (1977a: 348) says in his discussion of the working class struggle over the reduction of the working day in England, the state had to "curb capital's drive towards a limitless draining away of labor-power," otherwise, the blind desire for profit would seize "hold of the vital force of the nation at its roots." In this way, the state creates general, long term conditions for capitalist accumulation.

Since capital cannot reproduce the conditions of its own reproduction for the reasons stated above, the state performs four *functions* to preserve capitalism, according to Altvater (1977a: 42). These functions are: (i) providing for general material conditions (e.g. fixed capital in the environment in the form of physical infrastructure); (ii) establishing and guaranteeing general legal relations; (iii) regulating capital-labor relations, if necessary by repression; and (iv) safeguarding the existence and expansion of national capital on the world market. The last function, an explicitly geographical one, entails various strategies, three of which seem very important (Callinicos, 1987a: 99–102). One is that "*Every* capitalist state requires a military establishment in order to maintain control over its territory and enforce its interests *vis-à-vis* other states" (Callinicos, 1987a: 100). Here military expenditure is crucial in that "a substantial portion of every national economy is regulated by...direct (and often very cosy) relations between the state concerned, and either local defence contractors or other states" (Callinicos, 1987a: 100). Military expenditure by the state (defense contracts to the military-industrial capitalists) plays a crucial role in the recovery of national economies and in economic restructuring. Of still greater importance is the role of the state as a guarantor of the "stability of exchanges – and therefore of the form of value" (Callinicos, 1987a: 100), especially the fact that the state's role as a lender of last resort which has prevented the collapse of the monetary order and banking systems. Thirdly, the state protects its national markets (protectionism). What Callinicos – and derivationists – do not (sufficiently) stress is the connection between the capitalist state and imperialism. As Harvey (1978) argues:

> In response to the organized power of labor within its borders, a particular nation-state may seek to export the worst elements of capitalist exploitation through imperialist domination of other countries. Imperialist domination has other functions also – facilitating capital export, preserving markets, maintaining access to an industrial reserve army, and the like. By these means a nation-state may purchase the allegiance of elements of the working class within its borders at the expense of labor in dependent countries (p. 178).

Hirsch (1978) takes a different approach. For him, the particular state form comes not from the necessity of realizing the general interest in an anarchic society marked by *relations of competition* between capitalists (as in the work of Altvater), but from the nature of the social *relations of domination* – the exploitation of labor. Capitalism ("free" and "equal" exchange) requires that the means of force be separated from the production process (all barriers to free and equal exchange be destroyed). To achieve this end, some outside authority (the state) needs to be established and given a monopoly on the use of force (Hirsch, 1978: 61). It is possible for the state to carry out some general functions because it is separate from society. And it is necessary because general conditions for accumulation cannot be created by individual capitals (Hirsch, 1978: 66).

State functions, of course, vary. The falling rate of profit, which manifests the contradictory character of capitalism and the need for counter-measures, is the key to analyzing state functions (Hirsch, 1978: 97). Profit rates not only tend to fall, they also tend to equalize given the dynamics of competition, and this is something Hirsch does not pay much attention. And, 'if the profit rate is to be equalised then both capital and labor must be highly mobile which means that the State must actively remove barriers to mobility when necessary' (Harvey, 1978: 176).

But unlike other state derivationists, Hirsch doubts whether the state can act in the interest of capital at all; for capitalist contradictions cannot be resolved in the long run and are only represented in the state. Since the state is separate from the sphere of production, it only *reacts* to accumulation crisis. Thus, Hirsch shows that there are limits to the method of deriving state functions from the needs of capital.

By emphasizing the economic role played by the state, derivationism complements Poulantzas' structuralism, which confines itself largely to the state's political role. As we saw above, Poulantzas also failed to explain what the state does. In the derivationist theory, since the state is outside the sphere of productive activity, it is forced to depend on the bourgeoisie for its survival. This explains one of its most important functions – it has to create conditions for accumulation and capitalist profit.[15] The material concessions to the dominated classes, without which liberal-democracy will be difficult, the salaries of state officials, and the generation of employment without which there will be a political crisis, all depend on accumulation. So the state has a structurally mandated need not to disrupt capitalist accumulation (Hirsch, 1978).[16]

Yet, derivationism suffers from several problems. It assumes that there is only one logic of capital and one set of imperatives at a given point in time. It also assumes that the state can somehow know and meet the needs of capital. But the interests of capital are not wholly given. Rather, they must be articulated in and through what Jessop (1990) calls "accumulation strategies". These must advance the immediate interests of the different factions of capital (located in different territories) and must secure the long-term interests of the hegemonic faction which must, in turn, sacrifice some of its short term economic interests. Economic structuralism not only ignores the scope for different accumulation strategies but also the room for maneuver available to state managers and to capitalists (Jessop, 1990: 253–4). Second, state functions (and forms) are directly explained only in terms of the needs of capital. This implies economic reductionism.

There is also the fact that the institutional separation of the state from the economy limits the state's ability to intervene in the interest of capital. This is ignored by everyone except Hirsch. More generally, a major problem with structuralists, including many derivationists (as well as instrumentalists), is that they too readily assume that the state does and can satisfy capital's economic interest. What tends to be ignored is that the state, like capital, is contradiction-ridden. A large body of work within economic structuralism addresses this problem using the method of systems analysis. The next section discusses Offe's work as representative of this genre.

C. Economic structuralism: systems-theoretic analysis

For Offe, the most important characteristic of the state is that it is enmeshed in the contradictions of advanced capitalism. Capitalism suffers from a tendency towards the paralysis of the commodity form of value. Labor itself is a fictitious commodity; what Marx called "dull economic compulsions" are not enough to transform labor power into wage labor. Labor power has to become actively commodified. Capital, in certain situations, also fails to be involved in exchange relations.[17] The state has to recommodify capital and labor (i.e. it has to ensure conditions for accumulation). And it is in the self-interest of the state to do this: '[T]he *institutional self-interest* of the state in accumulation is conditioned by the fact that the state is denied the power to control the flow of those resources which are nevertheless indispensable for the control of state power" (Offe, 1984: 120).[18]

Two forms of state intervention aim at recommodifying capital and labor – allocative and productive.[19] Allocative policies refer to state distribution of resources which it itself controls. In the allocative mode, the state uses taxes, sovereign control over land (and other natural resources), and repressive force to shape the condition under which accumulation occurs. But these policies can lead to disincentives to invest and to work. In the productive mode, the state produces inputs that are not produced by private firms – things such as education, skills, physical infrastructure and housing. It also stimulates demand through forced consumption (for example, defense expenditures). The state thus produces the conditions of production in the *general interest* of the *capitalist* society, not just of capital or labor, to ensure that individuals of both classes can enter into exchange relations.

Three political consequences of these new tasks, however, limit the success of the state in performing these tasks. First, more intense demands on the state threaten to overburden it. To counter this, the state resorts to corporatism as a strategy.[20] But corporatism fails because including groups with veto power in decision-making, and parceling out state functions, can undermine the state's steering capacity, while what is needed is autonomy for the state in the face of the greater demands placed upon it. The second political consequence of the new tasks of the state is the emergence of rationality problems in public administration. States have to invent decisions and production rules to maintain accumulation, for no capitalist faction knows exactly what policies are needed. But the bureaucratic state is not structurally equipped to invent such rules, as bureaucracy is designed to follow fixed legal structures in processing certain inputs and cannot be creative enough. In addition, state policies pose a threat to the dominance of the capitalist in exchange relations. Finally, when market success depends less on taking risks in the market and more on state policies, commodification of labor and capital is seen as an artefact of politics. This weakens normative and moral fibres of capitalism and threatens to produce a crisis of legitimacy.

Thus capitalism needs an interventionist welfare state to create conditions for accumulation, but the welfare state undermines the capacity of the state to create these conditions. This leads to what Jessop (2002: 275) calls 'Offe's paradox'.[21] As Offe himself puts it: while "capitalism cannot coexist *with*, neither can it exist *without*, the welfare state" (Offe, 1984: 153).

Taken as a whole, the structuralist analysis of the state (including Poulantzas's work, state derivationism, and Offe's systems analysis of capitalism) has much to recommend it. It provides a rich discussion of how the relative autonomy of the state protects the interests of the dominant class and contributes to the reproduction of capitalist society. It also emphasizes the functional necessity of such a state, and the constraints under which any party in power or state bureaucracy (no matter how sympathetic it is to the dominated classes) must act (Gold *et al.* 1975: 38; Ollman, 1982. 45).

Yet, the structuralist approach suffers from several weaknesses. For one thing, it tends to under-emphasize agency, both of the dominated classes and of state actors. Miliband (1977: 73; also see 1970: 57) argued that the structuralism of the early Poulantzas deprived "'agents' of any freedom of choice and maneuver." Although the state is considered relatively autonomous, the emphasis is on *relative* rather than on *autonomous*. The state is relatively autonomous[22] but it does have to function according to capital's political (Poulantzas) or economic (Altvater) needs, leaving no space for autonomous actions by state actors. Structuralists, such as Poulantzas, fail to specify *how* constraining the constraints are (Miliband, 1977: 73; Block, 1987b: 83) and tend to abstract from the possibility that "governments can and do press against the 'structural constraints' by which they are beset" (Miliband, 1977) and from the fact state actors can be more autonomous in one place than in another. Structuralists not only downplay the agency of state actors, but also of dominated classes. Poulantzas, especially in his early works, wrongly assumes that welfare, labor rights and franchise are automatically given by the separation of the political from the economic, thus making class struggle over these citizenship rights inconsequential. In fact, given this separation, whether these rights exist is an open question; if they are to exist, they have had to be fought for. Offe also underestimates "the ability of political representatives and administrators to be effective agents of political strategy" by focusing on the "functional imperatives (the necessity to satisfy capital and labor, accumulation and legitimation)" (Held, 1984: 73).[23] The state, Offe says, has displaced the capital-labor struggle as the dominant conflict (the dominated classes are fragmented by state policies in terms of age, gender and race, etc.).[24] As far as derivationists are concerned, their original aim was to integrate class struggle and the functional logic of the state, but they failed to achieve this (hence my preference to call their theory "economic structuralist"). I next discuss two views of the state that take agency more seriously: class struggle and state-centered theories.

III. Class struggle theories

The relation between the state and class struggle can be looked at in different ways. Political class struggle theory emphasizes the political importance of class struggle for the state; structural class struggle theory takes into account the relationship between class struggle on the one hand and economic and state structures on the other.

A. Political class struggle theory

For political class struggle theory the changing balance of class forces determines the role of the state over space and time. In turn, the changing balance of class forces is usually considered in isolation from the constraints imposed by the laws of accumulation (Jessop, 1990: 88–9). Class interests are assumed to be transformed into corresponding political outputs of the neutral state in a relatively undistorted fashion and an automatic way. Poulantzas, who in his 1976 work admitted that he *under*emphasized class struggle in his early work, offers a version of this class struggle theory.

For him, state functions reflect a complex parallelogram of economic, political and ideological forces rather than the immediate economic interests of the dominant class (Poulantzas, 1968: 190). Crucial to his class struggle theory is his discussion of how state policy is established to favor the long-term interest of the bourgeoisie. The state is always divided by class contradictions. This means two things. On the one hand, different branches of the state "are often the pre-eminent representatives of the diverging interests of one or several fractions of the power bloc," although subject to the unity of the state power of the hegemonic fraction" (Poulantzas, 1978: 133, 142), so that state policy emerges out of the collision of many micro-policies representing the different fractions. On the other hand, state policy also depends on the relation between the state and the dominated classes because state power is "founded on an unstable equilibrium of compromise". Compromise means that state power can take into account the economic interests of some dominated classes; equilibrium means that while economic sacrifices are real and provide the ground for an equilibrium they do not challenge the political power which sets precise limits to that equilibrium; unstable means that the limits of the equilibrium are set by the political conjuncture, including class struggle (Poulantzas, 1968: 192; see Gramsci, 1971: 182). And the state itself is a terrain of class struggle in that dominated classes are present in the state "in the form of centers of opposition to the power of the dominant classes" (Poulantzas, 1978: 142). The state is therefore neither an instrument nor a subject, but a relation. More precisely, the state embodies a power relationship between classes and among class factions (Poulantzas, 1978: 128–9; 1976: 12–13).

Poulantzas (1968: 191; 1978: 140) argues that the political and economic struggles of capitalism require the state to set forth reforms. Frequent hostility between the state and capitalists show this to be true. Hence "the state is not a class instrument, but rather the state of a society divided into classes" (Poulantzas, 1968: 285).

One merit of Poulantzas' class struggle theory is that it helps us see that state policy has a contradictory character and that this stems from the "contradictory measures that different classes and fractions, through their specific presence in the state, manage to have integrated into state policy" (Poulantzas, 1978: 135).[25] Another merit is that class struggle over state policies implies that there can be a gradation of *classness* in state policies. Esping-Anderson *et al.* (1976) say that the object of working class struggle is not policies that are either pro-worker or anti-worker; rather, the policies that the working class struggles over have varying degrees of *classness*. For example, while both minimum-wage law and adequate guaranteed income for all workers are "commodified circulation" policies, the former causes minimum disturbance to commodity relations, but the latter poses a greater threat to the interests of capital since it threatens labor's separation from the means of subsistence.

This approach to the relationship between class struggle and the state is not without its problems, however. First, Clarke (1978) has criticized Poulantzas and his followers for emphasizing particular capitals and neglecting capital-as-a-whole. Particular capitals cannot exist independent of capital-in-general or of the exploitative class relation between capital and labor. Clarke (1978: 46) complains that Poulantzas has "no concept of capital-in-general independent of the state". That is, capital-as-a-whole exists only politically, only through the state which organizes different fractions of capital into a bloc. Overemphasis on capitalist class fractions, in turn, leads to an under-emphasis on class struggle between capital and labor at the level of the state. Indeed, Poulantzas writes, "The contradictions. reflected within the state are those among the dominant classes and fractions and between these and their supporting classes, far more than the contradictions between the power bloc and the working class. The latter are basically expressed in the bourgeois state 'at a distance'" (in Clarke, 1978: 47–8).

Also, Poulantzas' structuralism colors his view of class struggle, in that class struggle is seen as constrained by, and confined within, the structure. As a result there is little indication that class struggle also can influence the structure that constrains it (Holloway, 1991: 97; Wright, 1978: 21). I will discuss the structural class struggle theory to shed light on this point.

B. Structural class struggle theory

In attempting to develop what they call a "materialist (not economic, not political) theory of the state,"[26] Holloway & Picciotto (1977) note that the separation of the political from the economic (i.e., the autonomy of the state) is both real and illusory. It is real in that it has a material foundation: extra-economic coercion in the sphere of capitalist exploitation makes state autonomy possible (this point is also made by Hirsch and Poulantzas, as we have seen). It is illusory because of its ideological character: state autonomy from the economy masks the class character of social relations between capital and labor.[27] This is so in the sense that the inequality between capital and labor is transformed into political equality between citizens before the state (Holloway & Picciotto, 1977: 80). In turn, the survival of the state (and therefore of capital), and the separation of the political from the economic, depends on the outcomes of class struggle. On the one hand, the ruling class struggles to maintain the separation of the political from the economic by channeling the conflicts arising from the sphere of production into the political processes. On the other hand, the working class struggles to challenge capital politically (for example, by opposing the property rights that the state protects) and economically (by pushing for higher wages).

Since the state is a form of capitalist relation, the history of the development of the state must be rooted in the history of capitalist development. The state has to be seen as creating conditions for the establishment of capitalism (primitive accumulation[28]) and caught up in the history of capitalist contradictions (Holloway & Picciotto, 1977: 81, 86). This history, of course, is the history of class struggle.[29] The major problem with the Holloway-Picciotto argument is that it tends to dilute the importance of class struggle by looking at the state only in terms of an economic contradiction in the reproduction of capitalism.

Simon Clarke moves class struggle theory even further. For Clarke (1983: 119) the *raison d'être* of the state is in class struggle: "If there were no class struggle...there would be no state.... Thus it is the class struggle that is the mediating term between the abstract analysis of capitalist reproduction and the concept of the state." This relation between the state and class struggle, as posited by Clarke, is rooted in classical Marxism. In *Origin of the Family, Private Property and State*, Engels says "in order that...classes with conflicting economic interests...might not consume themselves and society in fruitless struggle, it became necessary to have a power seemingly standing above society that would alleviate the conflict..., and this power is the state" (Marx & Engels, 1969c: 327).

For Clarke class struggle not only helped create the state, but it was also responsible for the continued reproduction of the state as an entity separate from the economy. Based on studies of tenants' struggles in Britain in the 1970s, and on Holloway and Picciotto's theoretical work,

Clarke argues that property rights of the ruling class are enshrined in the law and enforced by the state; the political power of the ruling class is derived from these property rights. When the dominated class struggles against economic exploitation, it also struggles against the state that defends property rights. "The tenant experiences his or her exploitation not simply as economic, but as inseparably economic and political, with the threat of the bailiff and eviction standing behind the landlord" (Clarke, 1983: 32). This means that the economic and the political are combined in the immediate experience of exploitation and class struggle. The state responds to class struggles by reinforcing the separation of the economic from the political. For example, when tenants struggle against exploitation, "[T]he state seeks to enforce the rights of property on the dominated classes "individually through the courts, fragmenting collective resistance to the social power of property and ensuring that such power will be imposed on dominated classes individually through the 'market', decomposing class forces, and recomposing them as 'interest groups' based on tenure categories" (Clarke, 1991: 33), so that tenants are prevented from struggling as a *class*. Whenever class struggle tends to overstep the constitutional boundaries of politics and law, and to challenge the rights of property, the state makes economic concessions in an attempt to reestablish the rule of money and law and to restore the separation of the two spheres. This is how the state as separate from the economic is reproduced. It means that class struggle takes place not just over policies (e.g. some economic benefits). It also takes place over: (i) the fact of the separation of the political (i.e. the very existence of the capitalist state); and (ii) the form of that separation (e.g. how much separation – the extent to which it intervenes in the economic). Both of these are not constant features of the state, as structuralists wrongly think. While the state reinforces and imposes the separation of the political from the economic, the dominated classes tend to fuse them together in the manner suggested above (Clarke, 1991; see also Rothstein, 1990). It is true that capital and the state constrain class struggle. But Clarke, unlike Poulantzas and other structuralists, does not think that these structures are permanent. Rather they are subject to, and reproduced through, class struggle.

> The wage contract between individual worker and capitalist is a very solid reality if the capitalist has the power to enforce that contract, but dissolves into pure illusion if the workers are able to counterpose their collective power to that of capital. [Similarly] The 'majesty of the law' can inspire awe when it confronts the isolated

individual, while becoming an object of ridicule in the face of collective resistance. (Clarke, 1991: 45)

One important point that emerges from the above is that the state as relatively autonomous of the economic is not automatically reproduced; separation of workers from means of production, and correspondingly the separation of the state from the economy, is not a one-time event. This separation is contingent on, and is reproduced in and through, class struggle. Thus there is a dialectical relation between the state and class struggle. In my view, this is a definite advance on more structuralist approaches to the state.

IV. State-centered theories of the state

Class struggle theories emphasize the agency of the dominated classes, but they do not deal with the agency of state actors. The latter is the subject of state-centered theories, which view the state as an autonomous actor and where state functions are given more importance than the power of capital in specific circumstances. There are at least two state-centered theories.

A. Marxist state centric theory

In *Eighteenth Brummaire*, Marx talks about the executive power of the Bonapartist state as an "enormous bureaucratic and military organization, with its ingenious state machinery," and an army of half a million officials alongside the actual army; the state was a "parasitic body, which enmeshes the body of French society like a net and chokes all its pores." Further, the state seemed to become "completely independent of society" (Marx & Engels, 1969a: 477f.). Bureaucratic apparatuses, Marx says, can act in their own interests but represent these as public interests.

Marx says that it is periodic class equilibrium that explains this sort of extra-ordinary autonomy of the state. In the French Civil War, he says, Bonapartism "was the only form of government possible at a time when the bourgeoisie had already lost, and the working class had not yet acquired, the faculty of ruling the nation" (Marx & Engels, 1969b: 219). Sometimes, the explanation takes the form of a more general view of society, as in *the German Ideology*: out of the "contradiction between the interest of the individual and that of the community the latter takes an independent form as the *State*, divorced from the real interests of the individual and community" (Marx & Engels, 1970: 53).

Miliband and Marx have consistent approaches to state autonomy. Miliband (1983a) says that there are two sets of impulses to state action: external (class interests) and internal (those generated within the state). Internal impulses are of two types: the self-interest of state managers and their conception of the national interest. Since the capitalist state is a source of power, prestige and high salaries, it can serve the self-interest of state managers. Further, those who seek state power persuade themselves that achieving it and holding on to it are synonymous with the national interest, whose service is their paramount interest. Internal and external impulses to state action are related in that state managers have been imbued with the belief that the national interest is bound up with the well-being of the capitalist enterprise. Hence, state managers have been attentive to capitalist interests (Miliband, 1983a: 70f.). Consequently the relation between state managers and capitalists is one of "*partnership between two different, separate forces,* linked to each other by many threads, yet each having its separate spheres of action" (Miliband, 1983a: 72).[30]

The state is never a junior partner, however; the contradictions of capitalism, and class pressures and social tensions, necessitate a more pronounced role for the state. But it has to act in the class context: "So long as a government works within it [i.e. the capitalist limit], so long does the partnership hold" (Miliband, 1983a: 73). Against post-Marxist state autonomists, Miliband (1983a: 74) argues that there cannot be a state for itself, a state which is not a partner of anyone. It is difficult to see, he says, how there can be a state whose interests conflict with *all* classes or groups in society, as Skocpol (1979, 1985) and Meckstroth (2000) claim. The partnership does not mean a merger of state agents and dominant class agents but that the state is able to act with considerable independence in regulating class conflict and maintaining and defending the social order of which the ruling class is the main beneficiary. As Wood (1997: 2) says, "actions of the state in partnership with capital certainly reflect an adverse distribution of power between capital and labor".[31]

B. Post-Marxist state centric theories

A common feature of the post-Marxist theories is their belief in the non-correspondence between the economic and the political. This means that there is no necessary relation between the class character of society and the nature of the state (Wood, 1996: 52).

Carter develops a theory which has more in common with the anarchist Bakunin than with Marx.[32] In this theory, which, it must be said, rightly sees the state in its geo-political context, a state (as in post-Revolution Russia) selects economic relations which promote technological development because it is functional for the state to do so. It helps increase the surplus that is needed for developing its defensive capacity. This is important not just because it helps the state compete militarily with other states, but also because it enables the state to protect the economic relations which it has chosen to preserve. Given that states compete militarily with one another, and that each state is interested in having as productive an economy as possible in order to remain militarily competitive, state elites will tend to support economic class relations which they regard as most appropriate for furthering technological development (Carter, 1997: 173–5).

Like Carter, Block (1987c) also recognizes that state actors have their independent interests and powers. But Block claims that the exercise of state power takes place in class contexts. State managers are collectively interested in maximizing their power, prestige, and wealth, but within political rules of the game given by a set of political institutions. For example, in a democracy, if state managers maximize their self-interest too much, that may jeopardize their chances of returning to power. On the other hand, the bourgeoisie or any other propertied class cannot survive without the state, so they have to seek a *modus vivendi* with state managers. This *modus vivendi* has been favorable to capital: state managers have been restrained from attacking private property and have implemented pro-capital policies.

Block's writings have influenced Skocpol (1979: 301) who draws on both Marx and Weber in her theory of state autonomy. For Skocpol (1979: 31) "states are...organizations controlling (or attempting to control) territories and people." State organizations work within a national and international context. They "must operate within the context of class-based socio-economic relations" which condition and influence these organizations and the activities of state rulers (Skocpol, 1979: 29–30). Geopolitical conditions also create tasks and opportunities for states, and place limits on their ability to cope with external and internal tasks. "The state, in short, is fundamentally Janus-faced, with an intrinsically dual anchorage in class-divided socioeconomic structures and an international system of states" (Skocpol, 1979: 32).

All states are potentially autonomous, in the sense that they "may formulate and pursue goals that are not simply reflective of the demand or interest of social groups, classes, or society" (Skocpol, 1985: 9). However, the degree to which they actually are autonomous, and to what effect, varies from case to case" (Skocpol, 1979: 29–30). The state has interests of its own, which are "not necessarily equivalent to, or fused with, the interests of dominant class" (Skocpol, 1979: 27); indeed, "fundamental conflicts of interest might arise between the existing dominant class...and the state rulers" (Skocpol, 1979: 27). They may compete over appropriating resources from the economic reproduction process. Further, the ways these appropriated resources are used may be "at variance with existing dominant class interests" (Skocpol, 1979: 30). For example, these resources may indeed be used to enhance state autonomy and potentially threaten the dominant class(es).

The basic and necessary task of the state is not to serve the long-term interest of the dominant class, Skocpol says. In contrast to classical Marxism, she says that state power is not inevitably used for dominant class interests. Instead, the two basic tasks of the state are to maintain order and to compete with other actual or potential states. True, states usually function to preserve the existing class relations. But that is because doing so "is normally the smoothest way to enforce order" (Skocpol, 1979: 30). It is this task of maintaining order that defines its autonomous relation with subordinate classes. "Although both the state and dominant class(es) share a broad interest in keeping the subordinate classes in place in society and at work in the existing economy, the state's own fundamental interest in maintaining sheer physical order and political peace may lead it...to enforce concessions" to the subordinate classes (Skocpol, 1979: 30).[33] These concessions may come at the expense of the interest of the dominant class(es), but they are not contrary to the state's interest in maintaining order.

The statist approach of Skocpol and others is useful in countering the society-centrism of many state theories. It is also important because it stresses that state actors can act autonomously. But the theory ends up presenting state and society (especially, the economy) as separate and polar opposites, whereas they are "interdependent and [they] interpenetrate in a multitude of different ways" (Block, 1987c: 21; Das, 2000). Statists also deny the existence of classes and class struggles within the state (Cammack, 1989: 263–4) and outside it. Further, Carter, Skocpol, and others stress that the state's geopolitical military activities are independent of class processes. But, as Callinicos (1987b: 160–71) shows, war-making can be a class process (for example, military competition can be a mechanism of feudal accumulation) and, in contemporary times, war-making is an important part of military-industrial capitalism. Besides, why is the state interested in maintaining order, who benefits from it, who is a threat to order and why? What is it about class relations that makes the state maintaining order and the state keeping the class relations intact coincide? What is problematic in the post-Marxist autonomist theories is the idea that maintaining order and military competition have no necessary connection to class antagonisms.

V. Conclusion

The various theories discussed in this chapter, each rooted in one or more Marxian classics, indicate the vibrancy of Marxist discourse on the state.[34] In addition, they shed light on the state as a complex social entity with multiple aspects. Each theory focuses on one aspect of the state, and offers a more or less distinct perspective on it. Arguably, the apparently contradictory views of the state can be more or less equally true. The Ten Hours Bill was a victory for labor from the standpoint of the class struggle theory (Miliband, 1983b: 16), but a higher order victory for capital in that it helped maintain the conditions for reproducing capital if seen from structuralist standpoint. As Ollman (1982: 43) notes, "Dialectical truth does not fit together like the pieces of a puzzle," but allows for a multiple one-sidedness and an apparent contradictoriness suggested in my discussion of the multiple aspects of the state.

There are many interesting aspects of Marxist state theory that cannot be dealt with in this short review. I can only indicate briefly some areas which I have had to ignore or develop less than completely.

First, the vast majority of countries are not solely capitalist but a combination of capitalist and other modes of production. In peripheral capitalist countries, capitalism coexists with various forms of pre- or non-capitalist social relations. This implies that there can be more than one dominant class in these countries and a coalition of dominant classes "controlling" state power (Alavi, 1982; Bardhan, 1998; Das, 1998). In these countries, class relations are also inevitably influenced by imperialism, which, itself, is a form of class relations at the international scale. Therefore, the nature of state power in peripheral countries cannot be determined from abstract ideas about state theory, but has to be determined at a more concrete level. It must also be said that the nature of the state in 'advanced' capitalist countries cannot be fully appreciated in isolation from imperialism, i.e. in isolation from the geographical contexts in which states operate.

Second, in many societies, especially peripheral capitalist societies, differentiating the political from the economic (leading to the relative autonomy of the state as under capitalism) cannot be easily accomplished (see Wood, 1996). States themselves may be class-like, and may be engaged in appropriating the surplus, as were states under European feudalism.

Third, state theorizing, like social theorizing as a whole, has under-emphasized spatiality. State theorizing must take into account the fact that the nation-state is a scaled entity; that is, it has a scaled division of labor within it (central state, regional and local state) (Cox, 1990), an issue Poulantzas (1978) briefly touches on. State theorizing has also assumed more or less a closed economic system, which is increasingly problematic in the face of the capitalist globalization. An important part of state theory must address the relationship between *globalizing* capital and the *nation*-state. The prevalent idea on the right and even much of the left is that globalization leads to powerless nation-states. But this view is too simplistic. As Wood (1999: 11–12) argues, 'global capitalism is nationally organized and irreducibly dependent on national state. It is necessary to examine how states are complicit in the globalization process, in making national capitalist economies more competitive (Weiss, 1997) and the political implications of this – how anti-capitalism resistance and anti-state resistance can be one; how collusion of the state with capital has become more transparent. One significant recent development is the work of Robinson and Harris (2000) on the emergence of the transnational capitalist state. The nature of this emerging state form needs to be examined in more detail.

Finally, capitalism exists in a concrete context, which is defined not only by unequal distribution of material resources and relations of material exploitation, but also other forms of oppression such as gender and race. The extent to which *capitalist* states are also inherently patriarchal and/or racist (Holloway, 1994: 32; Hoffman, 1998) needs serious attention.

Notes

1 Bukharin, a classical Marxist says that in capitalism "the bourgeoisie is in control of production and therefore also of the state" (Bukharin, 1988: 242). He also says that: "the structure of the State itself reflects the economic structure, i.e. the same classes occupy relatively the same positions," meaning that higher positions in the state are filled by people from the bourgeoisie.

2 From 1889 to 1949, in the United States more than 60% of cabinet members were businessmen. The corresponding figure for Britain for the 1886–1950 period was a third (Miliband, 1969: 56–7).

3 That "the dominant economic interests in capitalist society can normally count on the active goodwill and support of those in whose hands state power lies...does not remove the need for...[capitalists] to exert their own pressure for the achievement of their immediate and specific goals...[And capitalists] bring to the task resources far greater...than those of any other interest in capitalist society" (Miliband, 1969: 145).

4 "By virtue of its ideological dispositions, reinforced by its own interests,...bureaucracy...is a crucially important and committed element in the maintenance and defense of the structure of power and privilege in advanced capitalism" (Miliband, 1969: 128–9).

5 Or more generally, it cannot explain how is it that the state, which may be controlled by a faction/factions of the dominant class, can simultaneously represent the whole capitalist class in opposition to the working class, the non-capitalist sections of the ruling class, and fragments of the capitalist class itself including the section that may be temporarily most powerful in the intra-class conflict (Ollman, 1982: 42).

6 Indeed, the bourgeoisie "have never constituted...more than a relatively small minority of the state elites as whole. It is in this sense that the economic elites of advanced capitalist countries are not...a governing class" (Miliband 1969: 59). But as if to counter criticisms of instrumentalism, Miliband argues that "the significance of this relative distance of businessmen from the state system is markedly reduced" by the fact that the members of the state elite are predominantly drawn from upper and middle classes who share a bourgeois ideology (Miliband, 1969: 59).

7 Poulantzas says, the state's reforms in the interest of the dominated class often lead to (1968: 191; also 1978: 140) "hostility between the state and the dominant class", which cannot be explained by the instrumentalist theory. Hence "the state is not a class instrument, but rather the state of a society divided into classes" (1968: 285).

8 This means that the early Poulantzas, contrary to what most discussions of state theory suggest, does not exhaust structuralist analysis.

9 One implication of the state being separate from the economic is "the institutionalized fixing of the agents as juridical objects" (Poulantzas, 1978: 128). For example, an employee of a factory is decomposed politically into a "citizen" and economically into a "worker". This makes it possible for the state to present itself as protector of the general interest of all citizens, conceals from the *juridical* agents their *class* character in their economic struggle, and thus helps in the disorganization of the dominated classes.

10 Sweezy (1970: 249) says that "the state may be used to make concessions to the working class provided that the consequences of not doing so are sufficiently dangerous to the stability and functioning of the system as a whole."

11 For example, while leaders of the large monopoly-sector corporations cooperated with the Roosevelt administration to formulate the Social Security Act, those of the small competitive sector corporations opposed it in Congress (Allen, 1991: 580). Yet the Act was passed at least in part keeping the long-term interest of the dominant class as a whole, to avoid the "industrial warfare" (Miller, 1991: 68).

12 Thus, relative autonomy does not reduce the classness of the state. Rather, it allows the state to play its class role in an appropriately flexible way (Miliband, 1977: 87), to work on *behalf* of capitalists, though not at their *behest*.
13 This idea of state's relative autonomous form is based on Marx's more social-theoretical comments as in *Capital* Vol. 3 where he says that "The specific economic form, in which unpaid surplus labor is pumped out of direct producers, [i.e. whether or not extra-economic coercion at the point of production is necessary] determines the relationship between rulers and ruled...[and] the specific form of the state" (Marx & Engels, 1998: 777–8). Thus the nature and action of the state are conditioned by relations of production.
14 These problems have, partly, got to do with the nature of the Poulantzas' project itself aimed at explaining how the state works under *constraints* but is relatively *autonomous*.
15 It may be stressed here that for Poulantzas, the relation between the state and the hegemonic class or fraction does *not* derive "from a direct dependence of the state 'machine' on this class or fraction" (1968: 297).
16 In *German Ideology*, Marx and Engels (1970: 79f; italics added) say, "[T]he modern State, which purchased gradually..., by the owners of property by means of taxation, has fallen entirely into their hands through the national debt, and its existence has become *wholly dependent on* the commercial credit which the owners of property, the bourgeois, extend to it." But, as Marx asks, will the bourgeoisie pay the state just for nothing? He answers, "the bourgeoisie pay their state well...in order to be able *without danger to pay* (laborers) poorly." (in Draper, 1977: 192; italics added).
17 This happens due to several problems, including the saturation of the demand for durable goods, prior state policies in the form of Keynesian intervention which lead to disincentive to work and invest, etc.
18 Then, it may be argued, when/where the state itself is an owner of the means of production, as in many peripheral-capitalist (India) and "transitional" economies (China) then the effectivity of its autonomy may be increased (see Hamilton, 1982: 27–8).
19 This and the next paragraph are based on a discussion of Offe's state theory in Sitton (1996: Ch. 5).
20 Effectiveness of policies is a function of cooperation of the various groups, including capital and labor but also other organizations, who not only possess a monopoly of information relevant to public policy and who have the power to control their respective constituencies. Indeed, corporatism is sought to be used to restrain demands on the state rather than delegation of power.
21 See Jessop (2002: 275–6) for a discussion of how he seeks to solve this paradox.
22 Further, the concept of autonomy of the state, which is what is stressed in Poulantzas, is not exactly the same as autonomy of state officials, just as the concept of capital-in-general and that of capitals are not the same.
23 Of course, another problem with Offe is that if capitalist state form is so problematic for capital, as he thinks, how would he explain the fact that capitalist relations have been reproduced for the last few hundred years?

24 Offe prioritizes non-class conflicts and non-class social actors/movements as more important in shaping state policies.

25 Note that Offe also says that state policy is contradictory but for a different reason: administrative commodification by the state undermines conditions for exchange relations.

26 It may be noted that Jessop (1990) *wrongly* considers their work as structural-functionalist work similar to Hirsch.

27 In the Marxist view, "All class power masks itself", but "capitalist power, however, raises the art of the masquerade to new heights" (Laibman, 2001/2002: 424). The state is one of the most important masks. More precisely, "the delegation of capitalist power to state officials and institutions" is a major mask. The task of the Marxist state theory is to try to remove the mask in the form of the state, understand how the state-mask is related to other masks, such as market, and so on.

28 In *Capital* vol 3, Marx says, "The bourgeoisie, at its rise, wants and uses the power of the state...to force...[wages] within the limits suitable for surplus-value making, to lengthen the working day and to keep the labourer himself in the normal degree of dependence [on capital]. This is an essential element of the so-called primitive accumulation" (Marx & Engels, 1969b: 121–2).

29 For example, consider the early stage of capitalism where appropriation of absolute surplus value was the dominant form of exploitation. Contradiction in this stage of capitalism is indicated by the fact that the inequality in the sphere of production continually undermines the appearance of equality in the sphere of circulation (capital and labor as commodity owners are equal); and this is exposed by the struggle over the length of the working day by labor. The state in response to the struggle tries to resolve the conflict within the sphere of *exchange;* hence some social legislations.

30 In his classic work, Miliband says, "state intervention in economic life entails a constant relationship between businessmen and civil servants...as partners in the service of a 'national interest' which civil servants , like politicians, are most likely to define in terms congruent with the long-term interests of private capitalism" (1968: 125).

31 The partnership idea exemplifies state monopoly capitalism in advanced capitalism, and also the dominant coalition theory of the state in some post-colonial societies where state power is said to be in the hands of a coalition of large landowners, urban-industrial classes and state elites, whose interests the state serves (Das, 1998; Bardhan, 1999).

32 Engels wrote to T. Cuno that "Bakunin maintains that it is the state which has created capital" (Marx & Engels, 1969b: 425).

33 This is quite similar to Hoffman's (1995: 45) idea that the state exists because "rebels and criminals" oppose the state, or more generally, because state's monopoly over coercion "is continually being challenged." For a critique of Hoffman's post-Marxist state theory which understresses the class character of the state, see Das (1999). Much of that critique will apply to the Skocpolian work.

34 Elsewhere, I have shown that there is a tendency towards a convergence among various state theories (Das, 1996).

References

Alavi, H. (1982) "State and Class under Peripheral Capitalism" in H. Alavi & T. Shanin (eds), *Introduction to the Sociology of "Developing Societies*, London: Macmillan, pp. 289–307.

Allen, M. (1991) "Capitalist Response to State Intervention: Theories of the State and Political Finance in the New Deal," *American Sociological Review*, 56: 679–89.

Altvater, E. (1978) "Some Problems of State Interventionism" in J. Holloway & S. Picciotto (eds), *State and Capital: A Marxist Debate*, Austin: University of Texas Press, pp. 40–2.

Bardhan, P. (1998) *The Political Economy of Development in India,* 2nd edition, Delhi: Oxford University Press.

Block, F. (1987a) [1977] "The Ruling Class Does Not Rule: Notes On the Marxist Theory of the State" in F. Block, *Revising State Theory: Essays in Politics and Post-industrialism,* Philadelphia: Temple University Press, pp. 51–68.

Block, F. (1987b) [1980] "Beyond Relative Autonomy: State Managers as Historical Subjects" in F. Block, *Revising State Theory: Essays in Politics and Post-industrialism,* Philadelphia: Temple University Press, pp. 81–96.

Block, F. (1987c) "State Theory in Context" in F. Block, *Revising State Theory: Essays in Politics a Post-industrialism,* Philadelphia: Temple University Press, pp. 3–35.

Bukharin, N. (1988) "Dialectics and Revolution" in D. McLellan (ed.), *Marxism: Essential Writings*, Oxford: Oxford University Press, pp. 226–45.

Callinicos, A. (1987a) "Imperialism, Capitalism and the State Today," *International Socialism*, 2: 35.

Callinicos, A. (1987b) *Making History: Agency, Structure and Change in Social Theory*, Cambridge: Polity Press.

Cammack, P. (1989) "Review Article: Bringing the State Back In," *British Journal of Political Science*, 19: 261–190.

Carter, A. (1998) "Fettering, Development and Revolution," *The Heythrop Journal,* 39: 170–88.

Clarke, S. (1978) "Capital, Fractions of Capital and The State: 'Neo-Marxists' Analysis of the South African State," *Capital and Class*, No. 5: 33–77.

Clarke, S. (1983) "State, Class Struggle, and the Reproduction of Capital," *Kapitalistate, No. 10*, 11: 113–33.

Clarke, S. (1991) "The State Debate" in S. Clarke (ed.) *The State Debate,* New York: St. Martin's Press, pp. 1–69.

Das, R. (1996) "State Theories: A Critical Analysis," *Science and Society*, 60 (1): 27–57.

Das, R. (1998) "The Social and Spatial Character of the Indian State," *Political Geography*, 17(7): 787–808.

Das, R. (1999) "Politicism and Idealism in State Theory," *Science and Society*, 63(1): 97–104.

Das, R. (2000) "The State-Society Relation: The Case of an Anti-poverty Policy," *Environment and Planning C: Government and Policy*, 18(6): 631–50.

Draper, H. (1977) *Karl Marx's Theory of Revolution*, New York: Monthly Review Press.

Gold, A.D. *et al.* (1975) "Recent Developments in Marxist Theories of the Capitalist State" *Monthly Review*, 27: 5, 29–43.

Gramsci, A. (1971) *Selections from the Prison Notebooks*, New York: International Publishers.
Harvey, D. (1978) 'The Marxian theory of the state', *Antipode*, 8: 2, 80–9.
Hamilton, N. (1982) *The Limits of State Autonomy: Post-Revolutionary Mexico*, Princeton: Princeton University Press.
Held, D. (1984) *Political Theory and the Modern State*, Cambridge: Polity Press.
Hirsch, J. (1978) "The State Apparatus and Social Reproduction: Elements of a Theory of the Bourgeois State" in J. Holloway & S. Picciotto (eds), *State and Capital: A Marxist Debate*, London: Arnold, pp. 57–107.
Hoffman, J. (1995) *Beyond the State: An Introductory Critique*, Cambridge: Polity Press.
Hoffman, J. (1998) "Is There a Case for a Feminist Critique of the State?," Contemporary Politics, 4, No. 2: 161–76.
Holloway, J. (1991) "The Great Bear: Post-Fordism and Class Struggle. A Comment on Bonefeld and Jessop" in W. Bonefeld & J. Holloway (eds), *Post-Fordism and Social Form: A Marxist Debate on the Post-Fordist State*, London: Macmillan, pp. 92–102.
Holloway, J. (1994) "Global Capital and the Nation-state," *Capital and Class*, 52: 23–49.
Holloway, J. & Picciotto, S. (1977). "Capital, Crisis and The State," *Capital and Class, 2*, 77–101.
Holloway, J. & Picciotto, S. (1978) "Introduction: Towards a Materialist Theory of the State", in J. Holloway & S. Picciotto (eds), *State and Capital: A Marxist Debate*, London: Arnold, pp. 1–31.
Jessop, B. (1982) *The Capitalist State: Marxist Theories and Methods*, Oxford: Oxford University Press.
Jessop, B. (1990) *The State Theory: Putting the Capitalist State in Its Place*, Cambridge: Polity Press.
Jessop, B. (2002) *The Future of the Capitalist state*, Cambridge: Polity Press.
Laibman, D. (2001/2002) "Anarchism, Marxism, and the Cunning of Capitalism," *Science and Society*, 65(4): 421–7.
Marx, K. (1977) *Capital, Vol. 1*, New York: Vintage.
Marx, K. & Engels, F. (1953) *Communist Manifesto*, Moscow: Progress Publishers.
Marx, K. & Engels, F. (1969a) *Selected Writings*, Vol 1, Moscow: Progress Publishers.
Marx, K. & Engels, F. (1969b) *Selected Writings*, Vol 2, Moscow: Progress Publishers.
Marx, K. & Engels, F. (1969c) *Selected Writings*, Vol 3, Moscow: Progress Publishers.
Marx, K. & Engels, F. (1970) *The German Ideology*, New York: International Publishers.
Marx, K. & Engels, F. (1998) *Collected Works, Vol. 37, Capital, Volume 3*. London: Lawrence & Wishart.
Miliband, R. (1969) *The State in Capitalist Society*, New York: Basic Books.
Miliband, R. (1970) "The Capitalist State: Reply to Nicos Poulantzas," *New Left Review*, No. 59, pp. 53–60.
Miliband, R. (1973) "Poulantzas and the Capitalist State," *New Left Review*, No. 82, pp. 83–92.
Miliband, R. (1977) *Marxism and Politics*, Oxford: Oxford University Press.

Miliband, R. (1983a) "State Power Class Interests", R. Miliband, *Class Power and State Power,* London: Verso, pp. 63–78.

Miliband, R. (1983b) [1965] "Marx and The State" in R. Miliband, *Class Power and State Power,* London: Verso, pp. 3–25.

Miller, R. (1991) "Social and Political Theory: Class, State and Revolution" in T. Carver (ed.) *The Cambridge Companion to Marx,* Cambridge: Cambridge University Press, pp. 92–102.

Muller, W. & Neususs, C. (1978) "The 'Welfare State Illusion' and the Contradiction Between Wage Labor and Capital" in J. Holloway & S. Picciotto (eds), *State and Capital: A Marxist debate,* London: Arnold, pp. 32–9.

Offe, C. (1984) *Contradictions of the Welfare State,* ed. J. Keane, Cambridge: MIT Press.

Ollman, B. (1982) "Theses on the State," *Monthly Review,* 34(7), pp. 41–6.

Poulantzas, N. (1968) *Political Power and Social Classes,* London: New Left Books.

Poulantzas, N. (1969) "The Problem of the Capitalist State," *New Left Review,* No. 58: 67–78.

Poulantzas, N. (1976) "The Capitalist State: A Reply to Miliband and Laclau," *New Left Review,* No. 95: pp. 63–83.

Poulantzas, N. (1978) *State, Power, Socialism,* London: New Left Books.

Robinson, W. & Harris, J. (2000) "Towards a Global Ruling Class: Globalization and the Transnational Capitalist Class," *Science and Society,* 64(1): pp. 11–54.

Rothstein, B. (1990) "Marxism, Institutional Analysis, and Working-Class Power: The Swedish Case," *Politics and Society,* 18(3): 317–45.

Sitton, J. (1996). *Recent Marxian Theory,* Albany: SUNY Press.

Skocpol, T. (1979) *States and Revolution,* Cambridge: Cambridge University Press.

Skocpol, T. (1985) "Bringing the State Back In: Strategies of Analysis in Current Research" in P. Evans *et al.* (eds), *Bringing the State Back In,* New York: Cambridge University Press, pp. 3–43.

Sweezy, P. (1970). *The Theory of Capitalist Development,* New York: Monthly Review Press.

Weiss, L. (1997) "Globalization and the Myth of the Powerless State," *New Left Review,* No. 225: 3–27.

Wood, E. (1996). *Democracy Against Capitalism: Renewing Historical Materialism,* Cambridge: Cambridge University Press.

Wood, E. (1997) "Labor, the State, and Class Struggle," *Monthly Review,* 49 (3): 1–14.

Wood, E. (1999) "Unhappy Families: Global Capitalism in a World of Nation-States," *Monthly Review,* 51: 1–12.

Wright, E. (1978) *Class, Crisis and the State,* London: New Left Books.

5

A New Neoliberal Social Structure of Accumulation for Sustainable Global Growth and Development?

Phillip Anthony O'Hara

Introduction

According to adherents of the social structure of accumulation (SSA) view, Western nations experienced a long-wave upswing in the 1950s and 1960s. Deep recessions and major financial crises were absent, and growth was quite strong for the two or three decades after World War II. These results were thought to be the result of a number of social institutional structures, including a capital-labor accord, a system of US hegemony, reduced inter-capitalist rivalry, and the Keynesian welfare state.

However, these institutional arrangements are said to have faltered from the 1970s to the 1990s as contradictions within these structures led to greater uncertainty, conflict and instability. A long-wave downswing thus emerged, with periodic deep recessions, financial crises, and much slower economic growth.

The Keynesian welfare state, for instance, was implicated in the downswing by negatively affecting productivity growth and profits through a host of regulations and schemes that increased business costs and dampened the work ethic. Starting in the late 1970s, the Thatcher and Reagan revolutions questioned the welfare state as a way of regulating and moderating economic fluctuations. This led to the rise of neoliberalism, a conservative form of economic policy and governance that relies on the free market and individual initiative. Neoliberalism advocates the sale of state enterprises, less government spending, reduced taxes and moderate regulations on business. During the 1990s, and continuing into the new millennium, the ideology and practices of neoliberalism became dominant worldwide, although many challenges emerged during this time.

Much recent debate has centered on whether a long-wave upswing is emerging due to neoliberalism, and also about how to generate a new long-wave upswing. The next section provides some background on the nature of long waves and the institutions underlying long-term economic performance. The third section sets out the main principles of neoliberalism. Section four examines how neoliberal policies and practices have affected economic activity, particularly economic growth, productivity, financial stability, and inequality. The last main section explores the impact of neoliberal fiscal and monetary policies.

Long waves and SSAs

The main SSA hypothesis is that sustainable growth and accumulation requires a set of suitable structures for promoting public goods that transcend market or individual activities. These long-wave functions are carried out, according to Martin Wolfson (1994), primarily through institutions that promote social stability, conflict resolution and long-term profitability; and they have widespread social benefits.

SSA scholars mostly agree on the tendencies of capitalism and the record of recessions, depressions, and financial crises over successive long waves. They agree that capitalism has been undergoing a series of non-deterministic phases of evolution since at least the 1780s when liberal capitalism began. Differences exist among nations because of uneven development and because, through successive long waves, changes occur among nations and regions as some rise and others fall.[1] Table 5.1 summarizes this broadly accepted periodicity of long waves.

Thus far, there have been four long-wave upswings in the history of capitalism. The first began in the environment of the French and American revolutions of the late 18th century, the second during the gold rushes of the 1850s, the third in the turbulent 1890s, and the fourth after World War II. The first downswing occurred during the time of the European revolutions of 1830 and 1848, the second during the so-called "long contraction" from the 1870s to the 1890s, the third during the Great Depression of the 1930s, and the fourth from the 1970s to the 1990s. Long-wave upswings tend to generate minor recessions and have few banking crises, while downswings are characterized by periodic deep recessions or depressions every decade or so, and major financial crises. One unresolved question is whether we are currently in a long-wave downswing (as argued by Moseley (1997) and Brenner (1998)) or whether a sustained upswing has commenced (as proposed by Lippit (1997) and Yaghmaian (1998).

Table 5.1 Periodicity of Global Long Waves

	Date	Title of Long Wave	Upswing	Down-swing	Technology Style
Long Wave 1	1780s–1840s	Industrial Revolution	1780s–1820s	1830s–1840s	Cotton textiles; iron & steam power; furnace iron smelting; crop rotation
Long Wave 2	1850s–1890s	Large-scale Industry	1850–1860s	1870s–1890s	Steam engine, railways, gold.
Long Wave 3	1890s–1930s	Finance Capital & Imperialism	1890s–1910s	1920s–1930s	Electricity and chemicals.
Long Wave 4	1940s–1990s?	Postwar Global Fordism	1940s–1960s	1970s–1990s	Internal combustion engine, assembly lines, oil.
Long Wave 5?	2000s–2040s?	Globalization & Information Technology?	2000–2020s?	2020s–2040s?	Computers, the internet, and electronics?

In his original formulation of the SSA theory, David Gordon (1980) recognized that a large number of institutions are necessary for sustainable growth, including systems of transport, industrial relations, finance, family formation, material resource supply, infrastructure, labor supply and government. The social requirements for sustained accumulation are multifarious and complex, necessitating widespread structures promoting productivity and demand. Empirical studies of the postwar era by SSA analysts have tended to delimit this analysis somewhat. For instance, Bowles, Gordon and Weisskopf (1990) suggest that the postwar upswing in the United States (and other Western nations) during the 1950s and 1960s was based around four main institutional spheres – Pax Americana, a capital-labor accord, the Keynesian welfare state, and relatively moderate competition. Two other key institutions have been suggested – a system of regulated finance (Wolfson, 1994) and family-household formation (O'Hara, 1995).

The state has impacted all of these. For instance, US hegemony was inextricably linked to military spending and the role of the state in facilitating sustainable growth and accumulation both before and after World War II. The state contributed to the capital-labor accord by facilitating legal and industrial relations outcomes that enhanced agreement.

And the state was implicated in other SSAs through systems of corporate law, financial regulation and family assistance packages. But the main state functions were the Keynesian welfare policies that dominated the 1950s and 1960s in most advanced capitalist economies. This included automatic and discretionary stabilizers; a full package of welfare benefits such as unemployment insurance, pensions and sickness benefits; and an array of military, legal and regulatory arrangements (Bleaney, 1985). Indeed, during the postwar era, the state became the dominant institutional player. Nonetheless, the contribution of companies, unions, and families to governance processes was quite strong (O'Hara, 2000a).

According to SSA arguments, the Keynesian welfare state contributed to this long-wave upswing by enhancing stability, conflict resolution and profitability. Stability was promoted by government spending raising the floor of the business cycle and thereby reducing uncertainty. Conflict resolution was provided by reducing antagonism between capital and labor, finance and industry and national and global economies. And profitability was stimulated by the provision of government contracts with the private sector in areas such as the military, infrastructure and communications.

However, in the late 1960s and early 1970s, the state inhibited long-term accumulation through greater regulations, higher taxes, red tape, long policy lags and incompetence. The Vietnam War contributed to stagflation and declining US hegemony; welfare policies led to a drop in the cost of job loss; the search for higher values questioned the work ethic; and long-term industrial profit was inhibited by higher taxes and regulations. Many non-state institutions contributed to the long-wave downswing as well, according to the SSA argument, including a maturation of systems of technology associated with the product cycle of consumer durables, a reform movement that questioned many of the values of capitalism, and developments in Europe and Asia that challenged US power (Bowles, Gordon & Weisskopf, 1990).

Typically, when a long-wave downswing begins, forces try to maintain long-term growth and accumulation. While some of these are conscious and reasoned responses, many are tantamount to groping in the dark, since the prerequisites of an upswing are by no means obvious and few policy makers recognize the operation of long-wave processes. Central to the struggle for renewed stability and profitability since the 1970s has been an attack on the Keynesian welfare state and a rise of free market ideology. Since the late 1970s, this economic philosophy has had a strong influence on policy in most nations of the world.

Typically, SSA studies have taken a national perspective on the problem. But in the current global age we need to take a more international approach. Since national economies are becoming more open it is critical to explore public-goods functions in a wider context than the national economy. This is not to argue that globalization has destroyed national economies; indeed, the evidence suggests that the global tendency is only partial. Nevertheless, it is no longer desirable to take a purely national view of these matters.[2]

The current neoliberal system of governance

Five dominant trends associated with neoliberal state institutions operate in most nations. First, there is a belief in small government.[3] The neoliberal consensus posits the need to reduce the size of government to a far smaller percentage of GDP than was typical in the postwar era. It seeks to privatize government enterprises, reduce red tape, and increase corporate self-governance. One justification for this is that governance functions can be performed by other institutions such as corporations, non-government organizations, and communities. A second justification is that there has been too much governance, especially during the 1960s and early to mid-1970s, and that a decline in quasi-public goods functions is in order.

Second, all major nations have attempted to sell off public utilities such as gas, water, telecommunications and electricity to the private sector. They have looked to private corporations to administer prisons and created private-sector universities where there were none before. They have also looked to the private sector for cleaning, security, and even research in government departments. Legislation has attempted to reduce red tape; to cut business paperwork and administrative costs required by government for information, regulatory, and policy purposes. And attempts have been made to increase the extent to which private sector corporate watchdogs and corporations themselves administer and oversee company practices concerning auditing, accounting, and financing. This remains true in the early 2000s despite a backlash against this in the light of US corporate scandals such as Enron and Worldcom.

The wave of neoliberal policies enacted from the 1970s to the 1990s attempted to deregulate the domestic financial system through a series of institutional changes. Controls over interest rates on checking accounts, mortgages, and corporate and consumer loans were ended. This was based on the belief that controls hurt those who can least gain access to finance by reducing the overall availability of finance. Monetary authorities also ceased to use variable reserve requirements to control the money supply. Instead, open market operations (the buying and selling of mostly government securities) became the established way of controlling economic activity. Moreover, monetary policy became the main discretionary means used by most governments to affect economic activity in the pursuit of stable prices and GDP growth.

The third plank of neoliberalism has been to deregulate the labor market through reforming industrial relations. Radical, liberal, and conservative economists all believed that during the 1960s and early to mid-1970s workers expanded their dominance over capital, that the wage share of national income had risen to high levels, and that productivity declined markedly. The neoliberal response to this was to try to increase the power of capital by reducing minimum wages, expanding workplace agreements, including privacy clauses in union voting, encouraging non-union and no-strike clauses in labor agreements, and increasing the flexibility of wages and working conditions. The main objective of these policies was to reestablish the power, profitability and viability of individual corporations so as to increase growth and accumulation.[4]

The fourth plank of neoliberalism is to free up international capital so that the global circuit of business can expand. This was done by promoting the free movement of money, production and trade worldwide. In the mid-1990s, the World Trade Organization was established to reduce tariffs and subsidies so that not only products but also services could be traded more freely in the global economy. The protection of intellectual property rights was also enhanced by including China and the former Eastern Block in the system of agreements. And some minimal attempts were made to include underdeveloped nations by putting agricultural reform on the agenda. These multilateral agreements were designed to enhance free trade regionally and globally. Several regional economic alliances were formed as well, including the North American Free Trade Area, the European Union, Asia-Pacific Economic Cooperation, and the fledgling Free Trade Area of the Americas.

Just as critical to the neoliberal agenda has been the freer movement of capital (especially in developed nations) through flexible exchange rates, reduced capital controls, and more uniform taxation at lower rates (especially for corporations). These changes let money capital move more freely to those areas and activities with the highest rate of return and where innovations could be implemented without hindrance. The essence of capitalism is said to be inherent change, dynamic innovation, and a world without barriers to doing business. Only in a system free of restrictions to the movement of money capital could investment enhance global profit and growth. Reduced taxation and greater tax uniformity is consistent with this enhanced free flow of foreign and domestic capital.

A fifth plank of neoliberalism concerns international relations and global development. With the supposed decline of US hegemony in the late 1960s and the 1970s, many believed that global public goods could best be established by military policies and foreign relations aimed at a new global accord. The new policy aims to reestablish US imperial power in the interests of global corporations and finance capital. Hence, in the post-cold-war era Washington and its allies sought to attack (at least verbally) anti-US regimes in Iraq, Iran and North Korea (the "axis of evil"), as well as (in practice) terrorist forces such as the Taliban, al Qaida, and Palestine liberation groups like Hamas (via the Israeli military). Renewed US hegemony is thought to help establish a new pro-corporate global system with stable property rights and greater security. Such a system transcends the United Nations, certain global protocols (such as the Kyoto Agreement on climate change), and the International Criminal Court, in favor of US power and authority.

The same neoliberal principles are imposed on Africa, South and Central America and the underdeveloped areas of Asia. It is thought that development will only occur where flexible markets and free trade are allowed to stimulate the entrepreneurial spirit. No major stimulus is needed to promote development except the freedom of private capital to emerge spontaneously from an environment conducive to private initiative and accumulation. In short, the neoliberal development philosophy is no different than the neoliberal philosophy in general. So, a uniform policy framework is imposed on all nations, regardless of history, government and culture. It is not necessary to understand each nation's experience, so the argument goes, since "one size fits all". A system of individual and corporate property rights is necessary to lay the groundwork for business enterprise. A system of contract, accounting, and private rules and guidelines provides the basis for a spirit of enterprise. Regulations on business need to be dismantled for the bourgeoning business class to emerge and become dominant.

These five planks of neoliberalism form the basis of the policy measures that emerged in the world over the past quarter century. They have been responses to the deteriorating global environment of the 1970s. The question is whether these policies have had a positive impact on the economic performance of national economies. It is also critical to assess the potential of such policies to enhance performance in the future.

The impact of neoliberalism

Because neoliberal policies have been dominant since the late 1970s, we should see some positive impact on the global economy if neoliberalism is an effective governance system. Table 5.2 looks at the global record of economic growth and accumulation from a long-term perspective.

These figures show that the high growth rates in the "golden age" of the 1950s through to the early/mid-1970s were not reestablished during the "neoliberal era" (as Maddison calls it) of the mid-late 1970s onwards through the 1980s and 1990s. Instead, growth has remained subdued since the mid-1970s for the "world", advanced capitalist nations, Latin America, Africa and Eastern Europe (including the Soviet Union/Russia). Moreover, the record of most nations during the 1990s was worse than during the first full decade of neoliberalism in the 1980s. The big change in the 1980s–2000s era is the rising growth of certain newly industrialized Asian nations, due to changes in the

Table 5.2 Growth of GDP Per Capita in the Global Economy

	World	Advanced Capitalist Nations	Latin America	Africa	Eastern Europe	Asia (Excluding Japan)
1950–1973	2.93	3.72	2.52	2.07	3.49	2.92
1973–2001	1.43	1.98*	1.08	–0.38	–1.10*	3.54*
1980–1990	1.43	2.67	–0.77	–1.09	1.60	6.8#
1990–2001	1.13	1.77*	1.64	–0.24	–2.26*	4.2#

Source: Maddison (2000: 126, 129); World Bank (2003); IMF (2002: 172)
Note: * = 1973–2000 or 1990–2000
= Newly industrialized Asian nations only

center-periphery structure of the world-system. However, for the entire global economy there has been no significant improvement since the mid-1970s. The shift in growth from the center to the periphery and the drop in global demand are the basis of the decline in advanced nations and the global economy.[5]

A similar record holds for productivity growth, as Table 5.3 shows. Most major developed nations had higher rates of productivity growth during the 1960s (and 1950s) compared to the years after 1970. The record also supports the conclusion that productivity growth was lower in the 1980s than the 1970s, and lower in the 1990s than the 1980s. Again, these declines for advanced nations occurred in tandem with productivity increases in parts of Asia (see Bloch & Tang, 2004), but the latter expansions have not been large enough to increase average world productivity growth. Thus, there is no evidence that neoliberal policies have been able to improve economic performance and counter the long-wave downswing.[6]

The evidence regarding financial instability is also clear, and fails to support the neoliberal policy agenda. Comparing the upswing of 1945–1971 with the downswing of 1973–1997, banking and currency crises increased markedly. Financial crises became more pronounced in the 1980s than the 1970s, and more pronounced in the 1990s than the 1980s, as Table 5.4 shows.

There was only one *banking* crisis during the long-wave upswing of 1945–1971, but 57 during the downswing of the 1970s–1990s. There were 37 *currency* crises during the upswing, but 113 during downswing. Overall, the probability, number, the output loss, and the recovery time associated with crises were all much greater during the time of

Table 5.3 Productivity Growth in the Manufacturing Sector: 1960–1999 (annual rate of change)

	US*	UK	Japan	Canada	France	**Germany**	Italy
1960–1970	3.7	4.3	17.1	4.5	9.7	7.8	8.7
1970–1980	2.0	2.5	6.8	2.7	5.5	4.8	7.4
1980–1990	1.8	5.7	1.9	2.7	4.0	2.8	4.4
1990–1999	2.0	2.2	3.2	2.1	3.6	2.8	2.2

Source: US Department of Labor, *Monthly Labor Review*, September 2000: 95, 101; June 2001
Note: US data is for the business sector as a whole (which is typically half the value of that for the manufacturing sector)

Table 5.4 Banking and Currency Crises in the World: 1945–1997

	Probability of Crises (% point chance)	Number of Currency Crises	Number of Banking Crises	Twin crises	Output Loss of Crises (% points of growth lost)	Recovery Time (years for output to normalize)
1945–1971	7.04	37	1	1	5.24	1.78
1973–1997	9.68	113	57	27	7.77	2.64
Specified: 1970s				1		
Specified: 1980s				1		
Specified: 1990s				13		

Source: Eichengreen & Bordo (2002)

neoliberalism than beforehand. The real problem is the emergence of twin crises (currency and banking crises), which were only one in number during long-wave upswing, but 27 during the downswing when neoliberalism was strong. Of the 15 twin crises specifically identified by Eichengreen and Bordo, 13 of them occurred during the second full decade of neoliberalism in the 1990s. By this time, both industrialized and emerging nations had in large deregulated their financial system.

Little and Olivei (1999) also document the financial crises of the 1990s being greater in number and intensity than those during the 1980s. Such crises have continued into the new millennium, especially in Argentina, Uruguay and Brazil. During the early 2000s, many nations of the world experienced a deep recession and financial malaise, including the three biggest – the US, Japan and Germany.

One special problem relates to the issue of capital flows. Part of the neoliberal agenda has been to reduce impediments to the free flow of money capital throughout the world. Most nations have followed this policy, often under pressure from the US and the IMF. However, the record of the 1990s shows that this policy became problematic in light of the increasing volatility of capital flows. This is especially the case for "hot" capital (mainly international, short-term bank loans and repayments), which increased the extent of instability and recession in the Mexican crisis of 1994 (Carlson & Hernandez, 2002), the Asian crisis of 1997 (Van Wincoop & Yi, 2000), and the Russian (Poirot, 2001) and Brazilian (Kregel, 1999) crises of 1998. In addition, capital flowing from Asia and elsewhere eventually made its way to the US in the form of loans, portfolio investment and foreign direct investment; and it provided the basis for a speculative bubble in the stock market, and subsequent collapse and recession (O'Hara, 2004a). Hot capital provided an endogenous source of money and credit that contributed to financial crises in the neoliberal age. Since the dominant ideology is that money is exogenously determined by the central bank, policy measures have been unable to reduce such instability. Indeed, neoliberalism has contributed to the endogenous generation of money and credit, especially through off-balance-sheet activities and the freer movement of global money capital, and in this sense it has contributed to greater global risk and uncertainty.

The crises of the 1990s convinced many analysts and policy makers that financial liberalization and innovation generate greater instability through endogenous credit and debt-risk (see Visano, 2004) and that the experience of the 1990s requires greater financial stability in the national and global financial architecture. The Russian collapse of confidence in the 1990s taught many that a "cold turkey" approach to market-based reforms is not sufficient. Rather, markets need to be embedded in a system of suitable institutions, organizations and laws (see Stiglitz, 1999). The IMF has responded to these instabilities and criticism of neoliberal policies by creating poverty relief funds and quasi-international lender of last resort facilities. The poverty relief measures are seen to be necessary because safety nets are critical to maintaining average living standards during crises and contagions.

Reforms have been instituted which resemble, to some degree, the operations of an international lender of last resort; although the IMF cannot create global money (Aglietta, 2001). Two institutional innovations are particularly important – the Supplementary Reserve Facility and the Contingent Credit Line. The Reserve Facility was introduced at the end of 1997 for IMF members already in a financial crisis. It provides (subject to policy conditionality) short-term loans at high interest rates for nations with major balance of payments anomalies due to a large short-term funding need caused by a sudden loss of market confidence. This facility is available immediately if there is a threat of contagion and a likelihood that early help could correct the balance of payments problem. The Contingent Credit Line was introduced in April 1999, and provided funds to countries experiencing contagion.

But these contagion – based funds were never used and hence were officially terminated in 2003. Nevertheless, the Supplementary Reserve Facility served as a useful quasi lender of the last resort for nations in crisis, and such funds have become effective because the IMF has deviated from the neoliberal blueprint and favored a more global form of governance (O'Hara, 2003b). But it is likely that more serious global financial reforms are necessary to embed the economy in society to a greater degree. We need a real international lender of last resort, and a policy that places the onus of adjustment on surplus current account nations (see O'Hara, 2004b).

Last, what is the record for global inequality? This is a very controversial subject, but the basic evidence is fairly clear, as Figure 5.1 shows.

Global inequality has increased significantly during the late 20th century, from a log variance of GDP of under 2.0 (1960) to around 2.4 (1975) to a high of 2.8 (1999). Much of the greater inequality is among nations, as incomes in Africa and (to a lesser extent) Central and South America, have fallen relative to advanced and some emerging nations. Some of this inequality are due to the process of uneven development resulting from neoliberal policies, and some are due to nations falling behind for failing to join the global economy in a substantive fashion. However, inequality has also increased among the highly industrial and emerging nations and among other nations and regions that have put into practice neoliberal-type policies, as shown in Table 5.5, below.

The leading neoliberal nations in the advanced Western world are the US, UK, Australia and New Zealand. The leaders in Latin America have been Brazil and Chile (there is insufficient data for Argentina, another neoliberal nation). Nations of Eastern Europe – along with China – have undertaken substantial privatization and reduction in

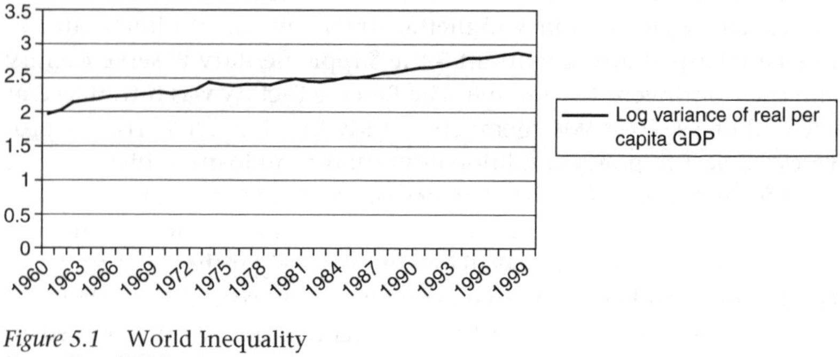

Figure 5.1 World Inequality
Source: Dutt (2004)

Table 5.5 Inequality Under Neoliberal Rule: Gini Coefficient: 1968–1998

	1970s [or 1960s]	1980s	1990s
USA	0.39 [70]	0.40 [80]	0.46 [94]
UK	0.26 [75]	0.29 [85]	0.32 [95]
New Zealand	0.31 [73]	0.34 [82]	0.40 [90]
Australia	0.32 [68]	0.32 [81]	0.35 [94]
Brazil	0.55 [74]	0.56 [87]	0.61 [98]
Chile	0.46 [71]	0.53 [80]	0.57 [98]
Eastern Europe		0.28 [88]	0.35 [97]
China		0.20 [87]	0.28 [95]

Source: King (2003); OECD (2002); Milanovic (1998); Deninger & Squire (2003); Galbraith (2003)

government services that draw inspiration from neoliberal policies. There has been a substantial increase in inequality (increase in Gini Coefficient) for these nations that have embraced neoliberal governance practices over the past one or two decades or more, but usually much less or no greater inequality for those nations that did not fully embrace neoliberalism (particularly Scandinavia) (Galbraith & Kum, 2003). Steven Pressman (2002) explains much of the world's gender inequality as being due to neoliberal policies as well; the failure to assertively assist poor families.

Greater income inequality performs a critical function for neoliberal capitalist economies – by providing a basis for invidious distinctions and demonstration effects. The pressure to "keep up with the Jones's" is a foundational element of the neoliberal age. Conspicuous consumption and display, as well as status and power, inspire those of working age to emulate those higher up in the class system. This is important for keeping consumption spending high through greater debt, as those with lower incomes must spend greater fractions of their income to compete in the fashion and style market.

Neoliberal fiscal and monetary policies

So far we have found that the rise of neoliberalism has not led to a turnaround in economic performance. Now we explore the effectiveness of state-sector governance – fiscal and monetary policy. What impact has the move to privatize government enterprises, cut government programs, balance budgets and reduce red tape had on economic performance? Two main issues are at stake – what influence has a change in fiscal stance had on economic performance, and what type of state programs are likely to enhance investment and economic growth.

Neoliberalism has shifted state spending towards transfer payments and away from the purchase of goods and services. In the US, for instance, the ratio of total government spending to GDP has remained fairly stable at around 32% from the 1950s to the 1990s. But the ratio of government purchases has declined from 32% in the early 1950s to 18% in 1997, while transfer payments have risen from 32% to 46% over the same period (Weber, 2000). A similar pattern emerges for other advanced nations. This change occurred during the 1970 to 1990 period when there has been a marked reduction of GDP growth and greater financial instability. Weber (2000) demonstrates that the two tendencies (changing spending patterns and lower growth) are inextricably related, since the change in government spending accounts for the entire slowdown and more. The change in policy from economic activism to passivism, from actively stimulating economic activity to supplementing income through pensions, subsidies and other benefits, has had a negative impact on growth and accumulation. The wave of privatizations, as well as the decline in public capital, reduced the extent to which government spending expanded GDP, and so contributed to the long-wave decline in growth and accumulation.

Numerous studies from around the globe point to the same conclusion. Research supports a change in policy towards building public capital, such as infrastructure, education, telecommunication, and utilities; towards an activist state with a program of government enterprises that will enhance the capital stock of nations. Using data from the Penn World Tables, Miller & Tsoukis (2001: 1125) found that "on the whole, government investment has been severely suboptimal [recently and]...scope exists for greater productive expenditures by the government sector." In a study of Greece, Ireland, Spain and Portugal, Laopodis (2001) suggests that non-military public spending on education, infrastructure, and health has a net crowding-in effect on private investment and GDP, and that public capital is currently being underprovided. In a study of Malaysia, Ibrahim (2001) concludes that state spending on transport, telecommunications, education and health has a net crowding-in effect on private investment. Ibrahim finds that tax-based financing crowds-out, while debt-based financing tends to crowd-in, private investment.

These and a host of similar studies show that many kinds of government spending increase public capital. They raise serious concerns about the neoliberal project. The 1970s rhetoric about the crowding-out impact of government spending seems to apply only to the low-impact spending priorities typical of a neoliberal program. Overall, the results are fairly clear – if governments are to provide a social structure for accumulation they need to have a solid agenda for building public capital. In addition, deficit spending is usually required to achieve this end – both to provide an autonomous source of demand and to ensure that there is a net expansion of aggregate income (and so reducing deficits in the long run, as growth expands).

Monetary policy under conservative rule also seems to have major limits. Since the late 1970s central bank open market operations have been the main regulator of economic activity in most nations of the world. Central banks change official interest rates by modifying the level of reserves available to banks, consumers and business. Many monetary transmission mechanisms affect economic activity (Iturriago & Lopez, 2000). Interest rates affect consumption and investment directly through changes in the cost of borrowing. More indirect mechanisms include the credit channel, where changes in the level of reserves affect the amount of bank lending, or impact the balance sheet of business firms. Two asset price mechanisms have become especially important during the neoliberalism age. The first is the exchange rate channel, where changes in interest rates impact on the value of the domestic currency, and therefore foreign demand for domestic goods and services. The second is the equity price channel, where changes in interest rates affect the demand for equity.

The equity channel is of special significance for nations following the lead of the (neoliberal) US in emphasizing the equity source of corporate finance more than a credit or bank-based system. Even formerly bank-based systems in Europe, such as France, are moving in the equity direction, while the UK has long followed the equity route. Evidence indicates, however, that the equity-based system of corporate finance and placing more emphasis on the equity channel of monetary policy increases instability and risk in the economy (Arestis, Demetriades & Luintel, 2001). One reason for this is the inability of interest rate changes to moderate speculative bubbles during business cycle upswings, as bank equity returns are ten times more sensitive to decreases than increases in official interest rates (Madura & Schnusenberg, 2000: 435). As Mishkin (2001: 1) said: "targeting asset prices by central banks is likely to lead to worse economic outcomes and might even erode the support for their independence".

This has led to three main developments, according to Binswanger (1999). First, there has been a marked drop in the link between money/credit and inflation during the 1980s and 1990s. Much of the credit created has been used for buying equities, and therefore credit expansion has propelled higher equity prices more than higher prices for investment or consumer goods. This has had an apparently positive effect on the economy by dampening inflationary forces. Second, by reducing inflationary pressures, and limiting interest rate increases, this has led to greater demand for equities, causing speculative bubbles in the economy. Bubbles exist when share prices do not reflect fundamental variables such as long-term dividends or productivity. These bubbles are not sustainable because fundamental variables condition stock prices in the long term. The use of derivates such as options, swaps and futures has reduced the cost of diversification and leverage, and also increased the relative return for equity relative to industry.

This leads to the critical third point. The changing structure and dynamics of the US financial system since the 1970s has increased the conflict between finance and industry, as the real sector has become a sideshow to the main game of capital gains in the equity market. This has had a negative impact on industry and long-term economic growth because it draws funds into equity markets rather than promoting innovation, workmanship and sustainable investment in industry. Thus, during the long-wave upswing, "economists had no trouble in explaining the [1949–1965] persistent bull market by standard valuation models according to which stock prices are determined by market fundamentals. But the [recent, 1984–1995] period is more troublesome" as stock returns have little relationship to fundamentals (Binswanger, 2000: 380).[7]

Broadly speaking, there was a reasonable link between stock prices and production during the long-wave upswing of the 1950s and 1960s. But during the downswing of the 1980s and 1990s stock prices became relatively autonomous from the industrial sector. This autonomy is most likely due to speculative bubbles during the 1980s and 1990s. Linking monetary policy to confidence levels in the stock market, even allowing for some vague recognition by the authorities of bubbles, led to the current crisis of confidence in corporate America and elsewhere where finance is able to dominate industry, leading to financial crises and corporate fraud.

Conclusion

This paper has assessed the current neoliberal system of governance, which has dominated the world since the 1970s. If it constitutes a new, viable SSA it should provide the foundation for a long-wave upswing in national economies. First, we situated the rise of neoliberalism within the framework of tendencies since the 1970s for governments of the world to promote privatization, deregulation, the reestablishment of US hegemony, and a development philosophy of stimulating private initiative. Then we explored the extent to which the recent long-wave downswing has been reversed through neoliberal policies. During the neoliberal era, GDP and productivity growth declined, financial crises were more frequent and intense, and income inequality worsened in both the center and periphery.

Finally, we surveyed the extent to which fiscal and monetary policy have become more effective under neoliberal governments. The conclusions were not good for neoliberalism. Neoliberal policies have increased the crowding-out of private investment through a relative decline in public capital in favor of transfer payments. Most of the decline in GDP could be explained by this shift from capital to current expenditures. Hence fiscal policy needs to be refocused, emphasizing public programs of education, health, infrastructure, transport and communications, and expanding deficits to promote a sufficient supply of reserves in the hands of the private sector.

Monetary policy has also taken a turn for the worse. Greater emphasis on shareholder value has led to a decline in workmanship and industry, and contributed to speculative bubbles and financial crises. Trying to manipulate monetary policy on the back of an overvalued stock market leads to all sorts of problems, especially greater instability, more risk-taking and greater fraud as profitability falters. Hence, current trends in both fiscal and monetary policy are unable to provide a foundation for the creation of a viable state social structure underlying accumulation. Major changes in governance are therefore required to improve long-term economic performance.[8]

Notes

1 One important reason for these differences is that the economic, political, and military power of nations change due to the complexities of socio historical motion and the evolutionary tendencies in process. Western power since the 1960s has declined relative to many Asian nations, which have experienced a dramatic increase in their standard of living defined in traditional terms, such as GDP per capita, and non-traditional terms, such as the Human Development Index (see Wallerstein, 1991; Arrighi, 1994).

2 The question of the global operations of capitalism was a dominant theme in the social sciences in the late 20th century. A critical issue of debate has been how the role of government has changed in the global economy

Some believe that recent changes have little affect on the operation of (at least some) national governments (Helliwell, 2000), while others claim that they have affected some critical state functions (Crotty, Epstein & Kelly, 1998), perhaps great enough to create a "race to the bottom" as states compete for transnational corporate investment (Tonelson, 2000). For an analysis of the debate on how globalization impacts state effectiveness see O'Hara (2004a).

3 Attempts to reduce state spending may not be terribly effective (see O'Hara, 2000b). Although neoliberalism seeks to reduce the size of government, certain critical state expenses and lower economic growth tend to maintain or increase such spending during long-wave downswing. Neoliberalism may thus only lead to changes in the composition of state spending – from productive to less productive activities.

4 Conservative and radical economists had different responses to the perceived increase in the power of labor over capital. Conservative or neoliberal economists wanted to reduce the power of labor, while radicals saw an opportunity to develop an alternative economic policy based on democratic governance programs. For instance, Bowles, Gordon & Weisskopf (1990: 233) proposed policies to reduce corporate waste, expand community knowledge and skills, and promote human rights and democratic participation through the economy. As they say: "We are committed to an economics that would offer sustainable improvements in living standards, strong democracy and community at home and global cooperation abroad, and more extensive economic fairness."

5 These results stem from the main contradiction of neoliberalism – its inability to sustain aggregate demand due to their policy emphasis on supply. Indeed, neoliberal perspectives eschew demand as having no influence on long-run output.

6 In some nations, such as the US, productivity rose sharply in the late 1990s. But the available evidence indicates that this was due to the cyclical upswing, or generally short-term factors. Gordon (2001) argues that productivity growth is unlikely to increase due to the high-tech and computer "revolution" because most of the advances have already taken place, and because computers are a pale imitation of the major technological advances of the past, such as railways, automobiles and steel (at least as far as productivity is concerned). Freeman (2001) paints a similarly dim picture. Even those who are quite optimistic about the computer sector are skeptical about its productivity benefits (Jorgenson & Stiroh, 2000).

7 Binswanger tested for Granger causality between stock returns production growth. He found a temporal link between the two variables leading from stock prices to production for the 1953–1965 period, but not for the 1984–1995 period. The probability that there was no link was very low during 1953–1965 and high during 1984–1995. This led him to conclude that since the mid-1980s "stock returns do not seem to contain significant information about future real activity as before" (Binswanger, 2000: 386).

8 See O'Hara (2006) for a discussion on the type of policies and governance reforms required for a new state SSA.

References

Aglietta, M. (2001) *The International Monetary Fund and the International Financial Architecture*, Centres d'Etudes Perspectives et d'Informations Internationales (CEPII) Working paper.

Arestis, P., Demetriades, P. & Luintel, K. (2001) "Financial Development and Economic Growth: The Role of Stock Markets," *Journal of Money, Credit, and Banking*, 33(1): 16–41.

Arrighi, G. (1994) *The Long Twentieth Century: Money, Power and the Origins of Our Times*, London & New York: Verso.

Binswanger, M. (1999) *Stock Markets, Speculative Bubbles and Economic Growth: New Dimensions in the Co-evolution of Real and Financial Markets*, Cheltenham, UK & Northampton, US: Edward Elgar.

Binswanger, M. (2000) "Stock Returns and Real Activity: Is There Still a Connection?," *Applied Financial Economics*, 10: 379–87.

Bleaney, M. (1985) *The Rise and Fall of Keynesian Economics: An Investigation of its Contribution to Capitalist Development*, Macmillan: London.

Bloch, H. & Tang, S.H.K. (2004) "Recent Performance of the Developing East Asian Economics": in P.A. O'Hara (ed.) *Global Political Economy and the Wealth of Nations: Performance, Institutions, Problems and Policies*. Routledge: London & New York.

Bowles, S., Gordon, D. & Weisskopf, T. (1990) *After the Wasteland: A Democratic Economics for the Year 2000*, Armonk, NY & London: M.E. Sharpe.

Brenner, R. (1998) "The Economics of Global Turbulence," *New Left Review*, No. 229: 1–265.

Carlson, M. & Hernandez, L. (2002) *Determinants and Repercussions of the Composition of Capital Flows*, IMF Working Paper 02/86.

Crotty, J., Epstein, G. & Kelly, P. (1998) "Multinational Corporations in the Neo-Liberal Regime": in D. Baker, G. Epstein & R. Pollin (eds), *Globalization and Progressive Economic Policy*, Cambridge & New York: Cambridge University Press, pp. 117–43.

Dutt, A.K. (2004) "Uneven Development, Convergence and North-South Interaction": in P.A. O'Hara (ed.), *Global Political Economy and the Wealth of Nations*, London and New York: Routledge.

Deininger, K. & Squire, L. (2003) *Measuring Income Inequality: A New Database*. Washington DC: World Bank. http://www.worldbank.org/research.growth/dddeisqu.htm

Eichengreen, B. & Bordo, M.D. (2002) Crises Now and Then: What Lessons from the Last Era of Financial Globalization? National Bureau of Economic Research: Working Paper 8716. http://www.nber.org/papers/w8716.

Freeman, C. (2001) "A Hard Landing for the 'New Economy'? Information Technology and the United States National System of Innovation," *Structural Change and Economic Dynamics*, 12: 115–39.

Galbraith, J.K. & Kum, Hyunsub (2003) *Estimating the Inequality of Household Incomes: Filling Gaps and Correcting Errors in Deininger & Squire*, UTIP Working Paper No 22, LBJ School of Public Affairs, University of Texas, Austin. 3 February.

Galbraith, J.K. (2003) *Manufacturing Wage Inequality in Mexico and China*. LBJ School of Public Affairs, University of Texas, Austin. 3 February.

Gordon, D.M. (1980) "Stages of Accumulation and Long Economic Cycles", in T.K. Hopkins & I. Wallerstein (eds), *Processes of the World System*, New York: Sage Publications, pp. 9–45. Reprinted in David M. Gordon, *Economics and Social Justice: Essays on Power, Labor and Institutional Change*. Edited by Samuel Bowles & Thomas E, Weisskopf. Cheltenham, UK & Northampton, US: Edward Elgar, pp. 93–129.

Gordon, R.J. (2001) Does the "New Economy" Measure Up to the Great Inventions of the Past?," *Journal of Economic Perspectives* 14(4): 49–74.

Helliwell, J.F. (2000) "Balanced Growth: The Scope for National Policies in a Global Economy": in M. Richardson (ed.), *Globalisation and International Trade Liberalisation: Continuity and Change*, Cheltenham, UK & Northampton, US: Edward Elgar, 46–62.

Ibrahim, M. (2001) "The Effects of Government Spending on Private Capital Formation: The Case of Malaysia," *International Economics*, 54(2): 187–201.

IMF (International Monetary Fund) (2002) "Statistical Appendix," *World Economic Outlook*, September, pp. 153–60.

Iturriago, F. & Lopez, J. (2000) "More on the Credit Channel of Monetary Policy Transmission: An International Comparison," *Applied Financial Economics*, 10: 423–34.

Jorgenson, D.W. & Stiroh, K.J. (2000) "Raising the Speed Limit: U.S. Economic Growth in the Information Age," *Brookings Papers on Economic Activity*, (#1): 125–235.

King, W. (2003) *The Functional Distribution, Again*. http://william-king.www.drexel.edu/top/prin/txt/factors/dist7.html

Kregel, J.A. (1999) "Was There an Alternative to the Brazilian Crisis?," *Revista de Economia Politica*. Vol. 19(3): pp. 23–38.

Laopodis, N. (2001) "Effects of Government Spending on Private Investment," *Applied Economics*, 33: 1563–77.

Lippit, V.D. (1997) "The Reconstruction of a Social Structure of Accumulation in the United States," *Review of Radical Political Economics*, 29(3): 11–21.

Little, J.S. & Olivei, G.P. (1999) "Why the Interest in Reforming the International Monetary System," *New England Economic Review*, No 3(September/October): 53–84.

Maddison, A. (2000) *The World Economy: A Millennial Perspective*. (Paris: OECD).

Madura, J. & Schnusenberg, O. (2000) "Effects of Federal Reserve Policies on Bank Equity Returns," *Journal of Financial Research*, 23(4): 421–47.

Milanovic, B. (1998) *Explaining the Growth in Inequality During the Transition*, Washington DC: World Bank. Working Paper.

Miller, N. & Tsoukis C. (2001) "On the Optimality of Public Capital for Long-Term Economic Growth: Evidence from Panel Data," *Applied Economics*, 33: 1117–29.

Mishkin, F. (2001) *The Transmission Mechanism and the Role of Asset Prices in Monetary Policy*, NBER Working Paper No. 8617.

Moseley, F. (1997) "The Rate of Profit and the Future of Capitalism," *Review of Radical Political Economics*, 29 (4): 23–41.

O'Hara, P.A. (1995) "Household Labor, the Family, and Macroeconomic Instability in the United States: 1940s–1990s," *Review of Social Economy*, 52: 89–120.

O'Hara, P.A. (2000a) *Marx, Veblen and Contemporary Institutional Political Economy: Principles and Unstable Dynamics of Capitalism*, Cheltenham, UK & Northampton: Edward Elgar.

O'Hara, P.A. (2000b) "The Evolution of a New 'Neoliberal, Balanced Budget' Social Structure of Accumulation? Emerging Prospects for the United States and World Economies," in H. Bougrine (ed.), *The Economics of Public Spending: Debts, Deficits and Economic Performance*, Cheltenham, UK & Northampton, US: Edward Elgar, pp. 30–56.

O'Hara, P.A. (2003a) "Deep Recession and Financial Instability or a New Long Wave of Economic Growth for U.S. Capitalism? A Regulation School Approach," *Review of Radical Political Economics*, 35(1): 18–43.

O'Hara, P.A. (2003b) "Recent Changes to the IMF, WTO and SPD: Emerging Global Mode of Regulation or Social Structure of Accumulation for Long Wave Upswing?" *Review of International Political Economy*, 10(3): 481–519.

O'Hara, P.A. (ed.) (2004a) *Global Political Economy and the Wealth of Nations: Performance, Institutions, Problems and Policy*, London & New York: Routledge.

O'Hara, P.A. (2004b) *A New Long Wave of Growth and Development in the Global Political Economy? Social Structures of Accumulation and Modes of Regulation*, London & New York: Routledge.

O'Hara, P. (2006) *Growth & Development in the Global Political Economy: Social Structure of Accumulation and Modes of Regulation*, London & New York: Routledge.

Poirot, C.S. (2001) "Financial Integration Under Conditions of Chaotic Hysteresis," *Journal of Post Keynesian Economics*, 23: 485–508.

Pressman, S. (2002) "Explaining the Gender Poverty Gap in Developed and Transitional Economies," *Journal of Economic Issues*, 36(1): 17–40.

Stiglitz, J. (1999) "*Quis Custodiet Ipsos Custodes?*," *Challenge*, 42(6): 26–67.

Tonelson, A. (2000) *The Race to the Bottom: Why a Worldwide Worker Surplus and Uncontrolled Free Trade are Sinking American Living Standards*, Boulder & Oxford: Westview Press.

van Wincoop, E. & Yi, K-M. (2000) "Asia Crisis Postmortem: Where Did the Money Go and Did the United States Benefit?," *Economic Policy Review*, Federal Reserve Bank of New York, September, 51–68.

Visano, S. (2004) "Global Financial Instability, Speculative Bubbles and Financial Crashes": in P.A. O'Hara (ed.), *Global Political Economy and the Wealth of Nations: Performance, Institutions, Problems and Policies*, London & New York: Routledge.

Wallerstein, I. (1991) "The Three Instances of Hegemony in the History of the Capitalist World-Economy": in G.T. Crane & A. Amawi (eds) *The Theoretical Evolution of International Political Economy*, New York & Oxford: Oxford University Press.

Weber, C.E. (2000) "Government Purchases, Government Transfers, and the Post-1970 Slowdown in U.S. Economic Growth," *Contemporary Economic Policy*, 18(1): 107–23.

Wolfson, M.H. (1994) "The Financial System and the Social Structures of Accumulation": in D.M. Kotz, T. McDonough & M. Reich (eds), *Social Structures of Accumulation: The Political Economy of Growth and Crisis*, Cambridge, UK & New York: Cambridge University Press, pp. 133–46.

World Bank (2003) *WDI Online: GDP Per Capita (Constant Prices)* Washington DC: World Bank. http://www.publications.worldbank.org/subscriptions/WDI/
Yaghmaian, B. (1998) "Globalization and the State: The Political Economy of Global Accumulation and Its Emerging Mode of Regulation," *Science and Society*, 62(2): 241–65.

6

A Post Keynesian Theory of the State

Steven Pressman

Introduction

From the end of World War II until the mid-1970s, Keynesian macroeconomics dominated the discipline of economics, and developed economies performed extremely well. On every important measure of economic performance – unemployment, inflation, productivity growth and rising living standards – the 1950s, the 1960s and the early 1970s were a Golden Age of capitalism. Economic life was getting better and Keynesian economics was thought to be responsible for this (see Cornwall, 1994).

Things then started to turn bad. Inflation and unemployment increased at the same time in most developed countries. Productivity growth stagnated and living standards improved very little. In addition, rising budget deficits became an increasing concern. For the Group of Seven (G7) nations, average (unweighted) budget deficits soared from 1% of GDP between 1959 and 1970 to 3.6% of GDP from 1971 to 1981, and then to 4.4% of GDP from 1982 to 1993.

Stagflation called into question the theoretical basis of Keynesian economics and massive budget deficits led economists to question the Keynesian view that government policy should be used to remedy the problems of capitalism. All this opened the door to numerous critiques of the Keynesian view of the state and alternative views regarding the economic role of government. Two alternative viewpoints became particularly prominent. The public choice revolution, stemming from the work of Buchanan, questioned the motivations of economic policy makers, while the Lucas Critique questioned the fundamental assumptions employed in Keynesian macroeconomic models. As Keynes increasingly dropped out of favor in the 1970s, the

1980s, and the 1990s, so did his policy prescriptions to improve economic performance.

This chapter is about the rise and fall of the Keynesian view of the state, and the resurgence of Keynes's insights regarding the state due to the rise of Post Keynesian economics. It proceeds as follows. The next two sections summarize the neoclassical view and the traditional Keynesian view of the state. This will be followed by a section summarizing the main critiques of Keynes and explaining why economists came to hold that fiscal policy was ineffective in remedying macroeconomic problems. We then set out the Post Keynesian response to these critiques and a Post Keynesian view of the state. The latter section contains a discussion of the policy implications of a Post Keynesian theory of the state and a brief evaluation of the Post Keynesian view.

The neoclassical view of the state

Neoclassical economists generally favor a minimal role for the state. Market economies are seen as efficient and are thought to lead to the greatest possible good for its citizens; and any country that allows the market to flourish unhindered will grow and prosper. This conclusion follows logically from the most basic principle of neoclassical theory – non-coercive trade must benefit all parties involved, since parties will only take part in trade if they gain from it.

Going even further, many economists see state involvement in economic affairs as reducing individual freedom (Friedman, 1962; Friedman & Friedman, 1979) and leading down a road to serfdom (Hayek, 1944). Consequently, they strongly support *laissez-faire* policy prescriptions and would prefer that the government stay out of the market economy. This would allow firms and individuals to maximize their profits and utility, respectively; and it would lead to the best of all possible economic outcomes.

Despite these strong leanings against government involvement in economic affairs, neoclassical economics is not entirely opposed to the state and to state actions related to the economy. There are several instances where state action is necessary to support or supplement the market.

First, the state must guarantee property rights and must enforce appropriate rules of conduct. Without such a nightwatchman, making sure that everyone's property is secure, economic activity would not take place since successful entrepreneurs would be left at the mercy of unscrupulous thieves.

Second, government action is justified to reduce the monopoly power of individual firms or to prevent firms from acquiring monopoly power. According to neoclassical theory, trade is beneficial only if it is non-coercive. Firms with market power can extort high prices from consumers, or force workers to accept low pay and dangerous working conditions. Consequently, government must ensure that firms do not acquire such power and that exchange takes place on a level playing field.

Third, government action is warranted in cases with important externalities or spillover effects. When individuals gain or lose, while not taking part in a market transaction, we no longer get the best possible result from free trade. For example, if some production costs can be imposed on third parties via air and water pollution, these goods will sell below their true cost and too many goods will get produced that destroy our environment. On the other hand, too few goods get produced (like public transportation) because producers cannot charge those who benefit from reduced traffic congestion (the people driving to work). In these cases, government must internalize the negative externality (make the polluting firm pay to clean up the environment) or provide the desired goods that firms will *not* produce because they cannot charge everyone who benefits from it.

Finally, government action is warranted when consumers cannot obtain adequate information about goods and services. If consumers cannot understand the most recent medical advances, they can easily become the dupes of someone claiming medical expertise. This is especially so in times of personal medical emergencies, when desperate individuals seek any possible cure for a life-threatening illness. As a result, the state needs to ensure both that medical practitioners are sanctioned by professional experts and that medical treatments are safe before they become widely available.

Keynes and the role of the state

In contrast to the neoclassical view, Keynes saw the state as an integral part of economic activity and a positive force that could and should be used to improve overall economic performance.

The main accomplishment of Keynes (1964 [1936]) was that he gave the state primary responsibility for overall macroeconomic performance. He did this by rejecting the view of a self-adjusting economy that could find full employment equilibrium at low rates of inflation. Instead, Keynes explained how and why an economy could remain permanently stuck at high levels of unemployment, and why it might experience high inflation or other macroeconomic problems that would continue unabated without any action on the part of the state.

Going even further, Keynes argued that the state must employ economic policies to help mitigate these economic problems. In times of high unemployment, deficit spending would be required to expand aggregate demand and put people back to work. This required some sort of tax cut and/or increase in government expenditures. In times of high inflation, tax increases and spending cuts would be needed to reduce those expenditures that contributed to an upward pressure on prices.

This view of the role of the state has important implications regarding the state budget and the national debt. In times of depression or recession, government tax collections inevitably decline as national income falls, and as government spending increases for social programs such as unemployment insurance. This leads to a cyclical budget deficit – government spending exceeding taxes due to the fact that the economy is at the low point of its business cycle.

Any attempt to lessen this deficit by increasing taxes or reducing government spending, Keynes argued, would make the recession worse by reducing demand for goods and thus reducing business sales. Instead, he advocated greater government spending and/or tax cuts – adding a structural budget deficit to the cyclical deficit. This would stimulate spending and help end the recession.

To improve economic performance, it did not really matter how the state spent its money; all that mattered was that the money got spent. But Keynes did have strong preferences about what the state should purchase. In a much-quoted passage, he wrote about the need for more houses, hospitals, schools and roads. But he notes that many people are likely to object to such "wasteful" government expenditures. Another approach was therefore necessary. "If the Treasury were to fill old bottles with banknotes, bury them at suitable depths in disused coal mines which are then filled up to the surface with town rubbish...private enterprise [would] dig the notes up and there need be no more unemployment" (Keynes, 1964: 129).

And in a much-maligned passage, Keynes (1964: 378) called for "a somewhat comprehensive socialization of investment". While many have taken Keynes to be advocating government control of all business investment decisions, what Keynes really advanced was government spending policies to stabilize the aggregate level of investment in the national economy. When private investment was low, he wanted the government to borrow money and engage in public investments such as building new roads and bridges and spending more money on schools and better education. In contrast, when business investment was high due to great optimism about future prospects, the government should stop borrowing and cut back on its public investment. On this view, the state became responsible for stabilizing the economy – increasing investment spending (or doing what firms could not or would not do) when unemployment was high, and reducing their investment spending when unemployment was low and when inflation threatened (see Pressman, 1994).

Two critiques of the Keynesian view of the state

This Keynesian view of the state came under strong attack during the 1970s and the 1980s. The public choice and rational expectations revolutions questioned some of the fundamental assumptions that Keynes made about government policy-making. This, in turn, generated skepticism about the Keynesian policy prescriptions that followed from the Keynesian economic analysis. It also generated skepticism about the large role for the state that came out of Keynes and Keynesian economics. At the same time, poor economic performance throughout the world, beginning in the 1970s, caused economists to search for a new understanding of macroeconomic problems and how they could be mitigated.

A first problem raised about the Keynesian view of the state concerns the motivations of policy makers. Public choice economists pointed out that there was a logical gap between the incentives economic policy makers face and the economic policies that they needed to put into effect.

Buchanan and Wagner (1977) contend that Keynesian economics depends on the assumption that policy makers will act in the public interest rather than in their own self-interest. Their argument is that Keynes fell prey to what Roy Harrod (1951: 192) called "the presuppositions of Harvey Road," a belief that economic policy would be formulated and implemented by bright, enlightened people who will put the good of their country ahead of their own selfish interests. Putting this point another way, Snowden and Vane (2005: 519) point out: "Although Keynes had an extremely low opinion of most politicians, in the context of his era it never really crossed his mind to view the political process as a marketplace for votes."

Keynes saw the economist as providing objective advice and setting forth policy prescriptions based on sound economic analysis. He also saw politicians as willing to accept such advice because it was provided by the best economic knowledge available and because they wanted to improve national economic performance in the most effective way. From this perspective, economic policy was primarily a technical issue devoid of politics. We might disagree about whose taxes to cut or what the government should spend more money on, but there would be little argument about the amounts and directions of change for fiscal policy.

However, as Buchanan has pointed out again and again, policy makers are human too; all have human motives, desires and capacities. They are not benevolent dictators. If policy makers were rational and self-interested, they would pass legislation and develop policies that benefit themselves. But this would *not* likely lead to improved economic performance for the whole nation. Macroeconomic policy would therefore fail to improve economic performance and would likely make things worse.

In addition, Buchanan notes that the people attracted to government service generally prefer a large role for government and are interested in improving social well-being. This will require large budgets. Politicians also need to be reelected periodically. Large budgets enable them to pass out the largesse that improves their chances of reelection. And unelected public employees will recommend and propose large budgets since this gives them more people to supervise and greater incomes. These incentives create a bias towards big government, large budgets and deficits.

Buchanan (1958; Buchanan & Wagner, 1977) argued forcefully against government deficits, contending that public debt has many negative effects. When the government sells bonds to finance its debt, it competes with private sellers of debt and pushes up the cost of borrowing (interest rates). As a result, private investment declines. In the long run, problems are even greater. A rising debt, with rising interest burdens, increases the likelihood of a government default. Furthermore, Buchanan argued that future generations suffer from the deficit because they must pay higher taxes.

Overall, Buchanan, Burton and Wagner (1978) see Keynesian economics "as a disease that over the long run can prove fatal for the survival of democracy". It loosens the moral restraint on politicians to act in morally acceptable fashion and it leads to the false belief that since we owe the money to ourselves, there is nothing wrong with running state deficits.

Rational expectations takes a slightly different approach in its critique of Keynesian economics. Following from the seminal article by Muth

(1961), Robert Lucas brought the standard microeconomic assumptions about individuals into macroeconomic analysis and insisted that all macroeconomic modeling incorporate rational expectations. This meant that individuals are seen as being rational, self-interested, and very smart. These rational economic agents will react quickly to any changes in government economic policy, and they will react in ways that maximize their own utility or well-being.

Because human beings change their behavior in response to changes in the world, and in response to how they view the world, Lucas (1976; Lucas & Sargent, 1978) criticized the Keynesian assumption that all macroeconomic relationships would remain unchanged in the face of policy changes enacted by policy makers. For rational expectations economists, rational individuals who seek to maximize their own well-being should change their behavior in the face of changing economic policy. This, in turn, will change macroeconomic relationships because "a change in policy necessarily alters some of the structural parameters...in a highly complex fashion" (Lucas & Sargent, 1978: 52). Without knowing which economic relationships change, and how they change, an econometric model is of no value in assessing alternative policies. For this reason, according to Lucas, economic policies that follow from Keynesian macroeconomic models are rendered ineffective.

Consider, for example, standard expansionary macroeconomic policies to lower unemployment. When policy makers attempt to stimulate the economy and create jobs, Lucas argues, they will generate expectations of higher inflation among workers. This, in turn, will reduce real wages. But rational workers will not want to work more if their real wages fall, and so employment will not increase. The only impact of stimulative demand policies becomes rising prices.

Another reason expansionary economic policy will fail to lower unemployment, as Barro (1974) points out, concerns the effects of macroeconomic policies on government debt. For Keynes, a tax cut will increase demand for goods and services, and thereby increase hiring. But, as we saw above, tax cuts also lead to larger government deficits. According to rational expectations macroeconomics, smart and logical citizens will realize that these deficits must be paid back in the future and that this will require higher taxes. People will therefore save most of their tax cut so that they can pay their higher taxes in the future. Tax cuts no longer increase consumer spending and employment; instead, savings is stimulated and deficits crowd out consumption. Again, it is the rationality of the forward-looking consumer that ensures that macroeconomic policy will be ineffective.

A Critique of the critiques

Post Keynesians have responded to these two critiques of Keynes. In doing so, they have built upon the insights of Keynes and his followers and have developed a Post Keynesian theory of the state. This theory provides a stronger justification for activist fiscal policies, and argues that interventionist state policy is necessary for good macroeconomic performance. We begin with the public choice school.

Pressman (2004) identifies several key flaws in the public choice perspective. Two are especially relevant here. First, from the public choice perspective no one should ever vote, because the costs of voting (transportation costs of going to the polls, lost time, and in many less-developed countries, the possibility of the loss of life) far exceed the gain from voting – the probability that my vote will determine the outcome of the election (effectively zero) times the benefit to me if my candidate wins the election (extremely small). Yet, voter turnout in developed countries averages more than 70% and reaches 90% in countries such as Australia, Italy and the Netherlands (Dalton, 1995; Powell, 1980). Even public choice economists have recognized that actual voting behavior is a big problem for their approach, an approach that is supposed to explain the political behavior of people (Brennan & Buchanan, 1980: 187, 191; Downs, 1957, ch. 14; Fiorina, 1990: 10; Tullock, 1967).

Voting behavior and politics are the meat and potatoes of public choice; these are the main topics that public choice is supposed to explain. Voting is also the foundation of democracy. It is what gets us a government, which then formulates and enacts economic and social policies in an attempt to improve economic outcomes. If public choice cannot explain simple voting behavior, and if it concludes that voting is not rational and should not occur, there must be something fundamentally wrong with its analysis.

Second, there is good evidence from the political science literature that politicians are not only interested in their own gains and are not just engaged in rent-seeking behavior that leads to bigger and bigger government. Many politicians (for example, Ronald Reagan in the US and Margaret Thatcher in the UK) promised smaller government and won elections on these promises. Then they actually carried out their pledges. Many multimillionaires run for political office, spending huge sums of their own money (recent examples include New York City Mayor Michael Bloomberg and New Jersey Governor John Corzine) in the process. For these individuals, the financial gains from holding public office (no matter how much they rent-seek) will not exceed the huge costs of their campaigns for office and the loss of time and money in running the government if they are elected. And empirical studies of voting behavior of the US Congress find that the political leanings of elected officials matter more than the interests of their districts when they cast actual votes in Congress (Kalt, 1981, ch. 6; Kalt & Zupan, 1984; Kau & Rubin, 1979). This is especially true on important votes that seriously affect the national welfare. All of this real world behavior calls into question the public choice critique of Keynes, and its analysis of the behavior of politicians and their ability to improve economic outcomes.

Finally, on both theoretical and empirical grounds, Post Keynesians have questioned the existence of crowding-out in the real world. Many Post Keynesians (e.g. Davidson, 1994) turned to Keynes's (1937a) finance motive to argue that the funds for investment do not come out of pre-existing savings, but rather come from the finance that is created by banks when they lend out money. Examining whether large budget deficits lead to higher interest rates and less business investment, Eisner (1986) found that deficits tend to increase or "crowd-in" business investment rather than reduce investment. He attributes this to the positive impact of deficits on the willingness of firms to invest. Heilbroner and Bernstein (1989) pointed out that, in the late 20th century, those developed countries experiencing the largest increases in their real government debt do not show any tendency to experience greater increases in real interest rates than countries experiencing small increases in real government debt. In fact, countries experiencing small increases in real government debt tended to have the largest increases in real interest rates. And Pressman (1995) found that government investment spending of the sort advocated by Keynes did not lead to either higher interest rates or to lower private spending of any kind.

We next turn to the Post Keynesian response to rational expectations. From a Post Keynesian perspective, the problem with this critique of Keynesian policy is that it relies on the traditional, but mistaken, assumptions about individual behavior made in standard economic theory. These were the same assumptions that led economists to believe in a full employment equilibrium and that Keynes spent so much time and effort trying to counter. According to rational expectations macroeconomics, individual economic actors are thought to be rational and to have near perfect knowledge about how the economy works. Neither of these assumptions accurately describes the real world.

We noted earlier the substantial empirical evidence that people vote and vote in large numbers, and argued that this is not rational behavior in the economic sense. But there are numerous other problems with the rationality assumption in economics. The prisoner's dilemma, the ultimatum game, the dictator game, and other game theoretical paradoxes (see Selten, 1978) also cast considerable doubt on the logical consistency of assuming rational, self-interested behavior.

In the famous prisoner's dilemma (see Poundstone, 1992), rationality dictates that each prisoner should confess, since each person does better by confessing regardless of what the other prisoner does. Logic and self-interest dictate that one should confess. The dilemma is that each prisoner would do better if they both kept their mouths shut. But this requires that they each trust the other prisoner not to confess.

The prisoner's dilemma rears its ugly head in many real world situations. Issues of public goods provision take the form of a prisoner's dilemma. Issues of nuclear war and nuclear deterrence also take the form of a prisoner's dilemma game. The good news for the human species is that people tend to cooperate when faced with situations like the prisoner's dilemma. This is true even in single-play prisoner's dilemmas, where people have no reason to cooperate in the hopes of influencing their opponent and benefiting from greater cooperation in the future (Frank, 1988: 140ff; Ostrom, Walker & Gardner, 1992). A good part of the reason for this is that the failure to cooperate leads to large losses and so this behavior harms the individual and does not have survival value. It is for this reason that humans have likely developed a genetic disposition to cooperate rather than to act selfishly, especially when cooperation gets reciprocated (Field, 2001).

Kahneman, Knetch and Thaler (1986a) invented two games to study this phenomenon further – the ultimatum game and the dictator game – and had subjects play these games to determine how our sense of fairness affects our behavior.

In the ultimatum game, two people are given a fixed sum of money to divide. The first subject can propose any division of the money that they like; the second subject can only accept or reject that division. If the division is accepted, each person receives the amount of money proposed by the first subject; if the division is rejected, each person receives nothing.

The dictator game is similar to the ultimatum game, but with one key difference. Here there is really no second subject, for the second subject has no power at all. Whatever the first subject, or dictator, decides determines how the money gets divided up.

Kahneman, Knetch and Thaler (1986b) ran a number of experiments where individuals played these games for real stakes. They found that people do not behave as predicted by the rationality assumption employed by economists. In the ultimatum game people chose to make substantial offers to the second subject, when they could have offered close to zero, reasoning that the second subject would not reject even a very small amount of money. Furthermore, most people rejected unfair offers. Similarly, in dictator games, Kahneman found that the dictator did not take all the money, even though they had the (dictatorial) power to do so. Typically, only 20% of dictators keep all the money for themselves. The modal offer is $3 out of $10 (Forsythe, Horowitz, Savin & Sefton, 1994; also see Ledyard, 1995: 121).

Experiments performed all over the world with these games have demonstrated again and again that individual rationality (of the type assumed by economists) does not lead to the most optimal outcomes for all individuals, or to group rationality. Quite the contrary. If individuals follow the path of rational self-interest, the aggregate result will not be optimal from the point of view of each individual and will be sub-optimal for everyone. Defecting players in prisoner's dilemma games are worse off; so are both players in an ultimatum game when a low offer gets rejects and both players wind up with nothing.

Interestingly, this is the same outcome that appears at several places in the *General Theory*. It appears most obviously in the famous paradox of thrift, where savings by one person increases their wealth and security, but when everyone behaves this way it leads to economic stagnation and everyone loses. But the same principle also lies behind Keynes' decision to cast his argument in terms of "wage units" in *The General Theory*. This enabled him to escape from the following sort of prisoner's dilemma.

The usual neoclassical response to high unemployment is to allow the wage rate to fall until the labor market clears. But this ignores the fact that when wages fall, so too does the demand for goods and the demand for labor. It is in the interest of each individual firm to offer lower wages to workers in times of high unemployment and lagging sales. This cuts firm costs, and as long as other firms do not also cut wages, there is no loss in sales. But, when every firm reasons this way and acts this way, everyone loses. Nominal wages are lower (with the resultant negative psychological effects), but real wages do not fall sufficiently to clear the labor market (because costs and prices are lower in the aggregate), and so we are still burdened with high unemployment.

Recent empirical work in psychology provides additional evidence against the rationality assumption as a description of how people actually behave. One well-established result concerns our faulty memory. In large measure, our decisions today depend on what we remember about our past experiences. If our memories about what happened in the past are defective, if we cannot correctly remember what gave us pleasure and pain, it hinders our ability to make good choices now.

Kahneman *et al.* (1993) tested how people remember unpleasant experiences such as undergoing a colonoscopy. When an unpleasant experience was immediately followed by a less unpleasant experience, Kahneman found that it is remembered as less unpleasant. Although adding a less unpleasant experience at the end *increases* total unpleasantness, and increases the time that one is experiencing something unpleasant, people still prefer this to a single very unpleasant experience.

Similarly, a pleasant experience followed by an experience that is not so good is remembered less fondly. For example, lottery winners are less happy after they win than they expected they would be when buying a ticket. Kahneman concludes from this work that, because we have defective memories, people frequently make wrong choices about what will give them pleasure.

A second type of error concerns probability. Probability is important because when we make decisions we do not know the outcome of our choice with certainty. However, if we can make good guesses about the probability of various possible outcomes of our choices, we can choose what is most likely to make us happy. Tversky and Kahneman (1982) found that people are not very good at making probability judgments. One example of this problem is raised by the following description: "Linda is 31 years old, single, outspoken, and very bright. She majored in philosophy. As a student she was deeply concerned with issues of discrimination and social justice, and also participated in anti-nuclear demonstrations." Tversky and Kahneman then asked numerous subjects how likely it is that "Linda is a bank teller" and how likely it is that "Linda is a bank teller and is active in the feminist movement." The laws of probability say the latter *must* be less likely than the former, since it requires that Linda be *both* a bank teller and a feminist. Yet, nearly nine out of ten people said the latter description was more likely to be true, including many people who were trained in statistical analysis.

Kahneman and Tversky (1984); Tversky and Kahneman (1982) also found that people do not understand the relationship between sample size and probability. Their subjects typically assigned similar probabilities to large samples and to small samples, even though the results of large samples are more reliable.

A third problem concerns the issue of framing. Framing exists whenever the presentation of choices affects our actual choices. Tversky and Kahneman (1982, 1986) demonstrated this phenomenon experimentally as follows. Subjects were asked to decide between two public health programs to deal with a life-threatening epidemic on a tiny island village. They were told that one program would save 200 lives, while the other program had a one-third chance of saving all 600 villagers and a two-third chance of saving none. Given these choices, most people preferred the program that would definitely save 200 lives. Subjects were then given an identical version of the two programs, but with a slight wording change – one program was described as leading to 400 deaths, rather than saving 200 lives, while the other program was described as having a two-third chance of saving no one and a one-third chance of saving everyone. In this later formulation, most people preferred the gamble rather than 400 sure deaths. In addition, subjects given the two sets of choices on separate occasions tended to give inconsistent responses, favoring saving 200 lives in the first formulation and the gamble in the second formulation.

Neoclassical economists usually argue that these findings arise because artificial psychological experiments lack the learning incentives present in market activities. However, further empirical work by Tversky and Kahneman (1986) has found that, contrary to neoclassical predictions, greater incentives for rational behavior lead to *less* rational behavior.

Moreover, evidence from financial markets, where enormous sums of money can get made or lost and the incentives to rationality are greatest, supports the psychological literature. There is a great deal of evidence against the rationality of players in financial markets. Shiller (2000) shows that security prices fluctuate based on fashion or mob psychology rather than the rational use of all available information. And Pressman (1998) argued that the prevalence of financial frauds casts doubt on the rationality of investors in financial markets. If the rationality assumption fails to hold in financial markets, where conditions are most favorable, we should not expect it to hold in the political arena, which is not market-like and where the incentives to economic rationality are much weaker.

A Post Keynesian theory of the state

Post Keynesians have not just criticized those who opposed Keynes. They have also used some of their key theoretical ideas to move beyond criticism and thereby develop a Post Keynesian theory of the state.

In doing so, Post Keynesians have focused on real human behavior and its economic consequences. Keynes (1962 [1921]) originally held that people were generally rational, but later came to reject this view when he saw that "people simply lacked the logical ability or rationality to see what was there" (Bateman, 1996: 56). We saw earlier that there was substantial empirical evidence that people are not disposed to act like rational economic man. When individuals have no scientific basic for making rational judgments or forming expectations about the future, or when the future is unknowable and uncertain, people must fall back on habits, instincts and social convention, which are not rational in the economic sense of the term (Keynes, 1979: 294; also see Davis, 1994). But even if people have a good sense of what things were like in the past, there is never a guarantee that the future will be like the past. As Davidson (1982/83, 1991, 1994, 1996) has pointed out, the world is non-ergodic or non-stationary. Things changes and things may change; we cannot count on them always being the same.

When no one has extensive experience in making important decisions, or when the economic world itself seems to be undergoing large changes, we face an uncertain world. For Post Keynesians the existence of fundamental uncertainty undermines the arguments of the rational expectations school and the public choice approach (see Rosser, 2001). If the economic environment is characterized by uncertainty then, contra Buchanan, policy makers will have a great deal of difficulty discerning what is in their self-interest. Should bureaucrats seek to increase their budgets and the number of people they supervise, attempting to build an empire and make more money, or should they seek to cut spending and find ways to spend taxpayer money more efficiently in an attempt to get rewarded and promoted for this behavior? In these circumstances, as pointed out by Keynes ((1964) [1936]: 383), they are likely to follow the dictates of some defunct economist who is currently in fashion. As a result, what is fashionable among economists and politicians becomes important. Similarly, if individual economic actors face an uncertain future, rational expectations cannot render fiscal policy ineffective. Contra Lucas, unemployed workers are not likely to know the inflationary impact of any policy change. And under these conditions, fiscal policy may be more effective if it creates expectations of better economic performance in the future and thereby leads to greater spending in the private sector.

In an uncertain world, rather than following the dictates of rationality assumptions, people generally follow rules of thumb. Workers spend large fractions of their labor income (if not all of it) based on habit and custom (as well as the fact that their pay, habitually, is only enough to cover their basic needs). Firms also follow rules of thumb in pricing (fixed markups or target pricing) rather than setting price equal to marginal cost (Lavoie, 2001).

To be able to navigate in an uncertain world, people also look around and see what others are doing. Faced with uncertainty, Post Keynesians see human behavior as driven by habits, institutions, herd behavior and "animal spirits". In some instances we cannot make any predictions about the consequences of our actions because the future is so uncertain. In other situations we follow the herd, knowing that there is comfort in numbers. Behavior is imitative; we follow the behavior of others, which depends on the behavior of yet other people. Consequently, for Post Keynesians, preferences are not given as traditional economic theory holds. Rather, preferences are formed during the decision-making process because in an uncertain world the consequences of most actions are unknowable so economic agents form expectations via social convention. These preferences then drive spending and also affect economic performance, according to Keynes ((1964)[1936], 1937b, 1979). More importantly, these expectations and behaviors can keep economies from achieving full employment.

This is the key point of Keynes's ((1964) [1936]: 156) famous beauty contest example where people were asked to select not the most beautiful contestant, but the contestant that they thought other people would select as the most beautiful. Keynes argued that investment was like this beauty contest. You won by figuring out what other people would likely do and then just following their lead. So, if you are the only one investing, you will not sell much when your new plant is operational and you will therefore lose money. But when lots of other firms invest also, demand is great and most firms will make money from their new plants and the goods that they produce. This is like the famous prisoner's dilemma. And like the prisoner's dilemma, the solution requires figuring out ways to get everyone not to defect or how to get firms to invest. This opens the door to macroeconomic policies to improve individual or firm decisions and thus improve overall economic outcomes.

Post Keynesians see the state in this light – as a set of institutions working for the public good. It provides public goods and benefits. But most important, the state is an institution that must make sure that the requisite amount of spending takes place, leading to full employment and robust economic growth. If the state does not do this, no one else will do it. And when the state engages in public investment, it makes sense for firms to follow the lead of the government and invest also, rather than losing out during the good times.

It is for this reason that Skidelsky (1989) argues that state policy is justified based on co-ordination failures at the macroeconomic level. If desired savings exceeded desired investment, the economy would contract without state economic policy to increase demand. Institutions also help convert uncertainty into calculable risk for individuals (Giddens, 1991). The state provides laws and sets of regulations. These provide the necessary order for capitalist production to take place. In addition, the state provides for stability and security in life. This includes monetary stability, exchange rate stability, antitrust legislation, welfare benefits, old-age benefits, minimum income floors, health benefits, decent education, etc. All of the modern welfare state seek to reduce uncertainty facing the individual. The welfare state is based on the idea that it is not enough to rely on just the market plus family and social networks. Rather, for individuals to be able to take risks and spend their money (rather than save), they need some kind of guarantee that they will be taken care of during bad economic times.

One important rule concerns the national budget. When unemployment rises, national budgets get squeezed from two sides. First, there are the automatic stabilizers or spending programs that kick in. Unemployment insurance rises, social welfare spending increases, and workers tend to retire if this is possible. All of this increases spending by the state. On the other hand, when unemployment rises, the state collects less revenue through taxes. Both the increase in state spending and the reduction in state revenues cause the state budget to run deeply in the red. One usual response to this is for the state to cut back on its expenditures and raise taxes. What Keynes pointed out was that such actions by the state would only make problems worse. What was needed, instead, was for the state to incur *even greater* deficits when unemployment was high and rising. It needed to stimulate demand through tax cuts and spending increases.

This Post Keynesian view on the role of the state receives some empirical support. History provides a sort of controlled experiment that enables us to test the effectiveness of government policy-making. Before the advent of Keynesian economics governments did not attempt to manage the macroeconomy. Nor did they employ budget deficits as a tool to lower unemployment and stimulate economic growth. After Keynes, it has been regarded as the responsibility of governments to assure that the macroeconomy performs in a satisfactory fashion. Governments that fail inevitably get thrown out of office; governments that succeed generally continue in office.

Christine Roemer (1999) recently compared US business cycles prior to World War I and after World War II. She found that recessions were less frequent (because expansions were greater) in the latter time period and that the business cycle was 15 to 20% less volatile in the 50 years following World War II. Moreover, the output loss in the pre-World War I period was 6% greater than in the post-World War II period. Roemer (1999: 33) concludes these changes are likely due to "the rise of macroeconomic policy after World War II" – the use of monetary policy, discretionary fiscal policy, automatic or built-in stabilizers, and institutional changes like deposit insurance.

For less-developed countries, successful development and growth has been associated with active developmental states (Gerschenkron, 1962; Amsden, 1989; Singh, 1994). In contrast, marketization and other liberalization schemes that keep the government from playing an active role in the economy have had undesirable economic effects (Aslanbeigui, Pressman & Summerfield, 1994). Stiglitz (2002: 54) gives a good real world example of such errors and their egregious consequences. For many years women in a poor Moroccan village received week-old chicks from the government and raised them for both food and sale. Virtually every analyst agreed that the program helped raise the living standard of these villagers. But the World Bank and the IMF told the Moroccan government that it should not be in the business of distributing baby chicks, and it pressured them to stop this practice. As a result, the chicken-raising industry disappeared in Morocco, to the detriment of the poor people living there.

And Pressman (1994, 1995) examined the macroeconomic performance of several developed economies since World War II based upon whether or not they tended to follow the policy advice of Keynes. He found that economic performance has been better whenever governments have run deficits in a manner similar to what Keynes recommended. In contrast, the stagflation of the 1970s and the slow growth of the 1980s were due to a failure to employ Keynesian fiscal policies. During these decades, governments focused more on reducing their budget deficits than on expanding them when economic growth slowed. The 1990s further support this view. As European nations lowered their budget deficits in anticipation of moving to a single currency (the Euro), their unemployment rates remained high. In contrast, the US was under no such pressure and economic growth expanded, leading to large budget surpluses. So there is good empirical evidence supporting the Post Keynesian view of the state as an institution that reduces uncertainty when it generates more spending throughout the economy whenever such actions are necessary.

The other advance made by Post Keynesian economic theory concerns introducing income distribution and class differences into a theory of the state. Keynes himself recognized that income distribution was important in determining economic outcomes. The *General Theory* (Keynes, 1964: 107–110) identified six objective factors affecting the propensity to consume. On the list of these six factors, number five was the distribution of income. Greater income equality puts more money into the hands of people in the lower-income classes. These people have a higher propensity to consume than wealthy individuals. Redistributing income to the lower classes thus increases aggregate consumption. Conversely, the transfer of income from (low income) wage earners to other factors of production is likely to diminish the propensity to consume (Keynes, 1964: 262).

Tax policy also affects income distribution, for it is the distribution of *disposable* income that matters. Keynes, in strong terms, advocated using taxation to equalize incomes. "If fiscal policy is used as a deliberate instrument for the more equal distribution of incomes, its effect in increasing the propensity to consume is, of course, all the greater" (Keynes, 1964: 95). As a result, Keynes advocated high tax rates on unearned income, capital gains, and inheritance, all forms of income that are received disproportionately by the wealthy.

This point about income distribution, consumption and fiscal policy has been ignored by most mainstream interpretations of Keynes as well as by many early followers of Keynes. But it is a point that has been stressed by Post Keynesian economists.

Kalecki (1943) was one of the first Post Keynesians to argue for the importance of class divisions in macroeconomic theory and to make class divisions the heart of macroeconomics. Kalecki argued that government would serve the interests of the capitalist class and deliberately induce recessions to reduce worker bargaining power and wages, and thereby increase profits. But Kalecki did make the important link between distribution and consumption – because much profit income was likely to be saved rather than spent, too much money going to capital would cause the economy to slow down and would cause profits to fall. This analysis opened the door for a full treatment of income distribution in Post Keynesian theory.

Nicholas Kaldor (1956) made the next advance when he provided a non-marginalist theory of distribution, a theory where income distribution did not depend on the marginal returns to capital and labor, but instead depended on demand. Kaldor was able to show that "capitalists get what they spend". Kaldor assumed that workers receive only wages and spend all of their income. Capitalists, on the other hand, will spend some money and save some income. From this he was able to show that capitalist spending (either luxury consumption or investment) generates the profits that are the source of income for capitalists. Capitalist expenditures thus determine aggregate income and the distribution of income between wages and profits.

The next step was to introduce the government. So Post Keynesians analyzed the impact of monetary policy and fiscal policy on distribution; they also showed how changes in distribution impacted the entire economy.

John Kenneth Galbraith (1975) and Kaldor (1982) noted the differential effect of tight monetary policies on the wealthy and the poor. High interest rates benefit the rich, who can lend money and earn high rates at the same time that high rates tend to protect its real wealth from the ravages of inflation. On the other hand, poor and middle-class households are generally borrowers and debtors, and so high interest rates hurt them. Tight monetary policy also favors the strongest parts of the economy (large corporations with plenty of cash and easy access to bond and financial markets) and disfavors the weakest and less-developed parts of the economy – those without ready access to credit at the lowest interest rates and that do not have large cash reserves (Galbraith, 1973: ch. 30). This is why voting and democracy are so important – despite the fact that voting fails the test of neoclassical rationality. Besides giving credibility to the political state, it also provides an opportunity for middle income and poor households to put into place a government that serves the interests of the people rather than the interests of the wealthy and powerful. Galbraith (1960) called the time that people went to the polls to vote "the liberal hour." While this is certainly too optimistic given the large number of conservative governments that have been elected throughout the world at the end of the 20th century and the beginning of the 21st century, Galbraith is certainly right about the potential for politics to trump *laissez-faire* economics in the voting booth.

Post Keynesians have also been concerned with how fiscal policy affects income distribution and how these changes in distribution affect the economy. Galbraith (1958) first raised the issue of poverty alongside plenty in *The Affluent Society*. To redress this imbalance, Galbraith wanted the state to provide more public goods. This means higher taxes, which divert money and resources from private hands, where they buy less-needed commodities, into the public treasury, where they will be used to purchase things needed by the poor.

Taking this analysis further, Pressman (2002–03, 2005, 2007) analyzed the impact of government tax and spending policies on poverty and on the size of the middle class in a number of developed capitalist economies. He found that, absent government fiscal policies, poverty rates would be very high throughout the world. Likewise, without state tax and spending programs, the middle class in most of these countries would be relatively small. Redistributive fiscal policy allows nations to reduce poverty and maintain a large middle class. Here politics in the interest of the many trumps the economic power held by the wealthy.

Nell (1983) argued that government fiscal policy works mainly through redistribution – taking money from those who would not spend it because they are rich and have too much money to spend, and giving it to those with a greater propensity to consume. Brown (2004) and Pressman (1997) provide some empirical support for this view, showing that income distribution does matter for economic performance and government policy is responsible for changes in income distribution.

One usual response to government redistribution policies is that it will have undesirable behavioral effects. Rational individuals will not work if they receive substantial government benefits or they will not work hard if their earnings are heavily taxed. This response has been examined and found wanting. Using the Luxembourg Income Study, an international data base containing income, tax and transfer payment data, plus numerous socio-demographic variables for many developed countries, Pressman (2002–03, 2005) found that greater government redistribution does *not* seem to have any large negative economic consequences in terms of lower work effort (lower productivity growth), lower labor force participation rates, or greater tendencies to be pre-fiscal policy poor. Thus, not only is redistributive fiscal policy an economic and political good, but it has relatively few and relatively minor bad side effects.

Summary and conclusion

The previous sections of this paper argued that people are not as rational as neoclassical theory makes them out to be. They systematically make mistakes as they confront an uncertain world. Post Keynesians see the state as an uncertainty-reducing institution. By reducing uncertainty, the state is able to increase business and consumer confidence, and thereby improve economic performance. In addition, people, including politicians, are not as self-interested as neoclassical economics makes them out to be. Altruism, in the form of not defecting in prisoner's dilemma situations, yields net gains for society. Altruistic behavior thus creates a sort of economic surplus. This classical notion of a surplus cannot be explained within a standard neoclassical framework that relies on the notion of scarcity and individuals making optimal substitutions among scarce resources. But it can be explained within a classical/Post Keynesian framework, where spending determines the size of the surplus, where the state helps determine its distribution, and where this distribution, in turn, determines spending and the size of the surplus.

All this opens the door for the state as an important economic player – one that not only ensures everyone plays by the rules and provides public goods, but also an institution that makes sure people have sufficient incomes and that there is adequate spending and employment in the economy. It also means that for Post Keynesians income effects are more important than substitution effects. For this reason, redistributive tax and spending policy to lower poverty and support the middle class will be important. Income floors (such as basic income guarantees and higher minimum wages) will help to prop up consumption and effective demand, as well as yield a more equal distribution of disposable income. This, in turn, will increase consumer confidence and consumption as well as general business confidence and investment. As such, these fiscal policies will keep firms from deciding not to invest because they do not want to be the only firm investing and suffering large losses as a result of their investment expenditures (essentially they do not want to be the only firm not defecting in a prisoner's dilemma game). It is here too that a progressive tax system both reduces the income going to the very wealthy (who are likely to save a good portion of it) and to keep a futile game of conspicuous consumption from running wild – a game where people drive bigger and bigger cars and live in bigger and bigger houses just to show off to one's neighbors (Frank, 1999).

Correct budgetary policy is also an important uncertainty-reducing institution. It gives business firms the confidence to invest and expand their operations, knowing that the production that ultimately results from this investment will be sold and will generate profits. A healthy economy in the future makes it more likely that firms will adopt an optimistic set of expectations and invest more. Budget policy contributes to this by assuring that demand is increased in bad economic times and reduced in good times.

Post Keynesians also see the state as an error-reducing mechanism. Where people are habitually or genetically disposed to acting in certain ways, and when that behavior leads to mistakes and to bad or undesirable results, the state must alter economic incentives or change the rules of the game or take the lead in spending and hope that others will follow. In these cases, the state can enhance general economic welfare by prohibiting certain choices or by specifying how choices must be presented or framed to individuals. Requiring that workers opt out of pension plans, rather than giving them option of selecting to join a plan (which reduces the likelihood that they will join a plan), provides one good example of how changing frames can lead to better outcomes for workers.

Finally, Post Keynesians see the state as a source of economic power that can counter the power of large business firms. This economic power has benefits as well as costs. As John Kenneth Galbraith (1967, 1973) has pointed out, there are numerous size efficiencies for firms, which is why we have so many large corporations in developed countries. But with size comes economic power – power over workers, power over suppliers, power over the consumer, power over the more competitive parts of the economy, and even power over the state. This power is not mitigated by the market and cannot be controlled unless we break up these corporations. But such actions sacrifice the efficiencies of the large firm. According to Galbraith there is only one possible solution to this dilemma. The state must counter the power of the large firm. If the state does not do this, no one else will.

And when the state acts to counter the power of large firms, voting and democracy become important. When the state counters the power of the large firm, an independent and educated set of public servants are needed who cannot be pressured or coerced by business firms to make decisions in their favor and against the public interest. Voting behavior, although illogical and irrational from the public choice and rational expectations perspectives, keeps us away from the undesirable results of a prisoner's dilemma and generates adequate economic growth that is shared by all citizens.[1]

Notes

1 The author thanks John Davis, Ric Holt, Phil O'Hara and Mark Setterfield for their comments on earlier versions of this paper. The usual caveats apply.

References

Amsden, A. (1989) *Asia's Next Giant: South Korea and Late Industrialization*, Oxford: Oxford University Press.

Aslanbeigui, N., Pressman, S. & Summerfield, G. (1994) *Women in the Age of Economic Transformation*, London & New York: Routledge.

Barro, R. (1974) "Are Government Bonds Net Worth?," *Journal of Political Economy*, 82: 1095–117.

Bateman, B. (1996) *Keynes's Uncertain Revolution*, Ann Arbor: University of Michigan Press.

Brennan, G. & Buchanan, J. (1980) *The Power to Tax: Analytic Foundations of a Fiscal Constitution*, Cambridge: Cambridge University Press.

Brown, C. (2004) "Does Income Distribution Matter for Effective Demand?," *Review of Political Economy*, 16: 291–307.

Buchanan, J. (1958) *Public Principles of Public Debt*, Homewood, IL: Richard D. Irwin.

Buchanan, J. & Wagner, R.E. (1977) *Democracy in Deficit: The_Legacy of Lord Keynes*, New York: Academic Press.

Buchanan, J., Burton, J. & Wagner, R.E. (1978) *The Consequences of Mr. Keynes*, Institute of Economic Affairs.

Cornwall, J. (1994) *Economic Breakdown and Recovery*, Armonk, NY: M.E. Sharpe.

Dalton, R. (1995) *Citizen Politics*, 5th ed., New York: Chatham House.

Davidson, P. (1982/83) "Rational Expectations: A Fallacious Foundation for Studying Crucial Decision-Making Processes," *Journal of Post Keynesian Economics*, 5: 182–97.

Davidson, P. (1991) "Is Probability Theory Relevant for Uncertainty?," *Journal of Economic Perspectives*, 5: 129–43.

Davidson, P. (1994) *Post Keynesian Monetary Theory*, Aldershot, UK: Edward Elgar.

Davidson, P. (1996) "Reality and Economic Theory," *Journal of Post Keynesian Economics*, 18: 479–508.

Davis, J. (1994) *Keynes's Philosophical Development*, Cambridge: Cambridge University Press.

Downs, A. (1957) *An Economic Theory of Democracy*, New York: Harper & Row.

Eisner, R. (1986) *How Real Is the Federal Deficit?*, New York: Free Press.

Field, A. (2001) *Altruistically Inclined?*, Ann Arbor: University of Michigan Press.

Fiorina, M. (1990) "Information and Rationality in Elections," in J.A. Ferejohn & J.J. Kuklinski (eds), *Information and Democratic Processes*, Urbana: University of Illinois Press, pp. 329–342.

Forsythe, R., Horowitz, J., Savin, N.E. & Sefton, M. (1994) "Fairness in Simple Bargaining Games," *Games and Economic Behavior*, 6: 347–69.

Frank, R. (1988) *Passions within Reason*, New York: W.W. Norton.

Frank, R. (1999) *Luxury Fever: Why Money Fails to Satisfy in an Era of Excess*, New York: Free Press.

Friedman, M. (1962) *Capitalism and Freedom*, Chicago: University of Chicago Press.

Friedman, M. & Friedman, R. (1979) *Free to Choose*, New York: Avon Books.

Galbraith, J.K. (1958) *The Affluent Society*, Boston: Houghton Mifflin.

Galbraith, J.K. (1967) *The New Industrial State*, Boston: Houghton Mifflin.

Galbraith, J.K. (1960) *The Liberal Hour*, Boston: Houghton Mifflin.
Galbraith, J.K. (1973) *Economics and the Public Purpose*, Boston: Houghton Mifflin.
Galbraith, J.K. (1975) *Money: Whence It Came, Where It Went*, Boston: Houghton Mifflin.
Gerschenkron, A. (1962) *Economic Backwardness in Historical Perspective*, Cambridge: Harvard University Press.
Giddens, A. (1991) *Modernity and Self-Identity: Self and Society in the Late Modern Age*, Cambridge: Polity Press.
Harrod, R. (1951) *The Life of John Maynard Keynes*, New York: Norton.
Hayek, F. (1944) *The Road to Serfdom*, Chicago: University of Chicago Press.
Heilbroner, R. & Bernstein, P. (1989) *The Debt and the Deficit: False Alarms/Real Possibilities*, New York: W.W. Norton.
Kahneman, D., Fredrickson, B., Schreiber, C. & Redelmeier, D. (1993) "When More Pain is Preferred to Less," *Psychological Science*, 4: 401–5.
Kahneman, D., Knetch, J. & Thaler, R. (1986a) "Fairness as a Constraint on Profit Seeking: Entitlements in the Market," *American Economic Review*, 76: 728–41.
Kahneman, D., Knetch, J. & Thaler, R. (1986b) "Fairness and the Assumptions of Economics," *Journal of Business*, 59: S285–S300.
Kahneman, D. & Tversky, A. (1984) "Choices, Values and Frames," *American Psychologist*, 39: 341–50.
Kaldor, N. (1956) "Alternative Theories of Distribution," *Review of Economic Studies*, 23: 83–100.
Kaldor, N. (1982) *The Scourge of Monetarism*, Oxford: Oxford University Press.
Kalecki, M. (1943) "Political Aspects of Full Employment," *Political Quarterly*, 14: 322–31.
Kalt, J.P. (1981) *The Economics and Politics of Oil Price Regulation*, Cambridge, MA: MIT Press.
Kalt, J.P. & Zupan, M. (1984) "Capture and Ideology – The Economic Theory of Politics," *American Economic Review*, 74: 279–300.
Kau, J.B. & Rubin, P.H. (1979) "Self-Interest Ideology and Logrolling in Congressional Voting," *Journal of Law and Economics*, 22: 365–84.
Keynes, J.M. (1937a) "Alternative Theories of the Rate of Interest," *Economic Journal*, 47: 141–52.
Keynes, J.M. (1937b) "The General Theory of Employment", *Quarterly Journal of Economics*, 51: 209–23.
Keynes, J.M. (1962) [1921] *A Treatise on Probability*, New York: Harper & Row
Keynes, J.M. (1964) [1936] *General Theory of Employment, Interest and Money*, New York: Harcourt, Brace & World.
Keynes, J.M. (1979) *The General Theory and After: Part II, Defense and Development*, Vol. XXIX, *The Collected Writings of John Maynard Keynes*, London: Macmillan.
Lavoie, M. (2001) "Pricing," in R. Holt & S. Pressman (eds) *A New Guide to Post Keynesian Economics*, New York & London: Routledge, pp. 21–31.
Ledyard, J. (1995). Public Goods: A Survey of Experimental Research in: J. Kagel & A. Roth (eds), *The Handbook of Experimental Economics*, Princeton: Princeton University Press, pp. 111–94.

Lucas, R. (1976) "Econometric Policy Evaluation: A Critique," in K. Brunner & A. Meltzer (eds) *The Phillips Curve and Labor Markets*, Amsterdam, North Holland, pp. 19–46.
Lucas, R. & Sargent, T. (1978) "After Keynesian Macroeconomics," in *After the Phillips Curve: Persistence of High Inflation and High Unemployment*, Boston: Federal Reserve Bank of Boston, pp. 49–72.
Muth, J. (1961) "Rational Expectations and the Theory of Price Movements," *Econometrica*, 29: 315–35.
Nell, E. (1983) "On the Concept of the State in Macroeconomic Theory," *Social Research*, 50: 401–28.
Ostrom, E., Walker, J. & Gardner, R. (1992) "Convenent with and without a Sword: Self-Government is Possible," *American Political Science Review*, 86: 404–17.
Poundstone, W. (1992) *Prisoner's Dilemma*, New York: Random House.
Powell, J.B., Jr. (1980) "Voting Turnout in Thirty Democracies: Partisan, Legal and Socio-Economic Influences," in R. Rose (ed.), *Electoral Participation: A Comparative Analysis*, Beverly Hills, CA: Sage, pp. 6–34.
Pressman, S. (1994) "The Composition of Government Spending: Does It Make Any Difference?" *Review of Political Economy*, 6: 221–39.
Pressman, S. (1995) "Deficits, Full Employment and the Use of Fiscal Policy," *Review of Political Economy*, 7: 212–26.
Pressman, S. (1997) "Consumption, Distribution and Taxation: Keynes' Fiscal Policy," *Journal of Income Distribution*, 7: 29–44.
Pressman, S. (1998) "On Financial Frauds and their Causes," *American Journal of Economics and Sociology*, 57: 405–21.
Pressman, S. (2002–03) "Fiscal Policy and Work Incentives – An International Comparison," *Journal of Income Distribution*, 11: 51–69.
Pressman, S. (2004) "What is Wrong with Public Choice," *Journal of Post Keynesian Economics*, 27: 3–18.
Pressman, S. (2005) "Income Guarantees and the Equity-Efficiency Tradeoff," *Journal of Socio-Economics*, 34: 83–100.
Pressman, S. (2007) "The Decline of the Middle Class: An International Perspective," *Journal of Economic Issues*, 41(1).
Roemer, C. (1999) "Changes in Business Cycles: Evidence and Explanations," *Journal of Economic Perspectives*, 23–44.
Rosser, J.B., Jr. (2001) "Uncertainty and Expectations," in R. Holt & S. Pressman (eds) *A New Guide to Post Keynesian Economics*, New York & London: Routledge, pp. 52–64.
Selten, R. (1978) "The Chain Store Paradox," *Theory and Decision*, 9: 127–59.
Shiller, R. (2000) *Irrational Exuberance*, Princeton: Princeton University Press.
Singh, A. (1994) "Openness and the Market-Friendly Approach to Development: Learning the Right Lessons from Development Experience," *World Development*, 22: 1811–23.
Skidelsky, R. (1989) "Keynes and the State," in D. Helm (ed.) *The Economic Borders of the State*, Oxford: Oxford University Press, pp. 144–52.
Snowdon, B. & Vane, H. (2005) *Modern Macroeconomics: Its Origins, Development and Current State*, Aldershot, UK: Edward Elgar.
Stiglitz, J. (2002) *Globalization and Its Discontents*, New York, W.W. Norton.

Tullock, G. (1967) *Towards a Mathematics of Politics*, Ann Arbor: University of Michigan Press.
Tversky, A. & Kahneman, D. (1982) "Judgments of and by Representativeness," in D. Kahneman, P. Slovic & A. Tversky (eds), *Judgment Under Uncertainty: Heuristics and Biases*, New York: Cambridge University Press, pp. 84–98.
Tversky, A. & Kahneman, D. (1986) "Rational Choice and the Framing of Decisions," in R.M. Hogarth & M.W. Reder (eds) *Rational Choice: The Contrast between Economics and Psychology*, Chicago: University of Chicago Press, pp. 67–94.

7
A Feminist View of the State

Ellen Mutari

Progressive economists sometimes view state and market relationships after World War II as relatively ideal, with the state supporting economic activity and helping the market economy thrive. Progressive Era legislation, and the Keynesian macroeconomic policy that emerged during the 1930s Depression, were institutionalized in the post-war period. In many respects, the Keynesian welfare state appears to have enhanced well-being. Most industrialized countries were committed to full employment, and they backed this commitment by using macroeconomic stabilization policy. Growth was maintained via increases in purchasing power and rising consumption levels for the working class. And a variety of income replacement programs for the unemployed, the disabled, and pensioners shielded workers from the harsh vicissitudes of market mechanisms.

Feminist economists are far more ambivalent about state policy, especially the impact of economic policies on gender equity. To the extent that state policies and programs (particularly Keynesian welfare states) incorporated gendered assumptions about the economic roles of men and women, and the value of market versus non-market labor, they reproduced and reinforced gender inequity. Feminists note that economic theory and policy continue to be built on gendered assumptions, even as the world has departed from the norm of a male breadwinner and full-time female homemaker.

A view of the state as merely a tool of capitalist interests, found in some radical economic theory, is similarly oversimplified. In both industrialized and developing countries, feminists have looked to the state for intervention and remediation in response to perceived problems wrought by the interaction of market forces and cultural traditions. Many feminist economists question the efficacy of market mechanisms alone to provision adequately (Folbre, 2001), and see the state as playing an important role in economic processes.

Women and their advocacy organizations in the US, Europe, and other industrialized countries have been key constituencies in the movements for child labor laws, protective labor legislation, anti-poverty and other social welfare programs, equal pay laws, equal employment opportunity and affirmative action programs, comparable worth policies, family and medical leave, and regulations requiring equal treatment for part-time workers. Similarly, in developing countries, women have looked to state programs to moderate the effects of market liberalization and structural adjustment programs. Women have influenced the state in order to assert their rights to property, inheritance, and control over their own bodies. To the extent that they have succeeded, the state has been beneficent.

These two visions of the state and public policy can be reconciled by treating the state as a site for the generation of social practices that can either *reproduce* or *transform* existing gender relations. In fact, government policies have done both. For this reason, a gender analysis of the state needs to be historically specific, grounded in the institutional arrangements of the political economy of a particular time and space. This interpretation of the state derives from a strain of feminist thought called "practice theory."

In practice theory, gender is treated as an organizing principle of social structures rather than a characteristic of individuals (Glenn, 1998: 33; Connell, 1995; Acker, 2000). Society genders people as masculine or feminine, but laws, institutions, and theories can also be gendered. That is, they can be organized to value activities and attributes associated with masculinity (such as breadwinning and competitiveness) over those associated with femininity (such as unpaid caring labor and altruism). Practice theory takes "gender relations into account as both causes and effects of various social, political, economic, and cultural processes and institutions" (Orloff, 1996: 52).

The emphasis on the state as an historically situated *site* rather than as an actor or force marks a shift away from the structural analyses that characterized much feminist thought in the 1970s and early 1980s and toward theories that reassert a role for human agency. The state, like the market and the family, is viewed as a site where notions of masculinity and femininity are contended, constructed, and often naturalized. The state is not simply a lifeboat in the event of market failure, but one of three sites, along with markets and families, where provisioning occurs (Figart, Mutari & Power, 2002: ch. 10).

I begin by presenting a feminist economic perspective that underlies this treatment of the state. I also summarize alternative understandings of gender and their implications for the social sciences. To illustrate how gender can illuminate our understanding of the state, I outline critiques of the gendered public policy promulgated by 20th century Keynesian welfare states. Finally, I turn to the transformative potential of the state, describing controversies among feminists over appropriate employment and social welfare policy.

What is feminist economics?

A feminist framework for analyzing the relationship between the state and the economy must begin by defining a feminist theoretical approach. This is not a simple matter. Feminism lacks the equivalent of a Marx, Veblen, or Keynes as a reference point for founding principles, and feminist economics is of relatively recent vintage. Gillian Hewitson (1999: 5–7) traces usage of the term "feminist economics" back to Marxist feminist writings in the late 1970s and early 1980s. But feminism as an independent research program – rather than the application of neoclassical or Marxist analysis to issues affecting women – did not emerge until the mid-1980s (Hewitson, 1999; Albelda, 1997).

This new school of feminist economics is more than the application of economic analysis to issues specifically affecting women such as labor market discrimination, the cost and benefits of homemaking, or income support for single mothers. Maleness is also a gender, thus men's as well as women's economic outcomes are influenced by their social location (Barker & Kuiper, 2003: 2). Moreover, recent feminist scholarship has sought to deconstruct the androcentric bias within the discipline's theories, conceptual categories, and methodologies. This bias is one source of gender inequity in economic outcomes. In *Beyond Economic Man*, one of the first books presenting feminist economics as a unique theoretical perspective, Marianne Ferber and Julie Nelson (1993: 1) assert: "If we instead recognize that the discipline we call economics has been developed by particular human actors, it is hard to see how it could fail to be critically influenced by ... the social, cultural, economic, and political milieu in which it has been created." Asserting gender bias in economic concepts, theories, and policies is distinct from attributing gender inequity to exogenous, pre-existing social inequality (Bakker, 2001).

Many feminist economists regard the lack of a codified theory and a skeptical attitude toward universal laws as a strength of their approach

(Hewitson, 1999: 220; Peter, 2003: 107). Mainstream microeconomic theory sees the economy as organized according to natural laws, and treats the economy as a found object rather than social institution. For example, macroeconomists have posited a "natural" rate of unemployment, a term that obscures the social context in which unemployment is created, defined, and measured. In contrast, feminists argue that all human knowledge is situated, or filtered through the experience of the observer (Nicholson, 1990).

Nevertheless, the feminist critique of neoclassical theory (Ferber & Nelson, 1993; Strober, 1994; Kuiper & Sap, 1995; Nelson, 1996; Nelson, 2001) has laid the groundwork for an alternative vision of economic processes (Folbre, 1994; Benería, 1999; Figart, Mutari & Power, 2002; Barker & Kuiper, 2003; Ferber & Nelson, 2003). Before exploring feminist economics in more detail, we briefly review its roots in interdisciplinary feminist theory.[1]

The analytical starting point for feminist theory is the concept of gender.[2] The definition of "gender" is nevertheless contentious. Since the 1970s, feminists have used "gender" to signify society's ideas about differences between men and women; it has been used either in place of or in tandem with the concept of patriarchy as a system of male domination. Gender, thus defined, is a social construction. It is more than the bias, prejudice, or stereotypes of individuals (Laslett & Brenner, 1989: 382). Further, socially constructed definitions of masculinity and femininity vary historically, cross-culturally, and even within a given society. Because gender interacts with class, race-ethnicity, and sexuality (constructs that are also socially, not biologically, determined), several modes of gender relations might coexist. For example, the ideal of a full-time homemaker for white, middle-class women in the early 20th century was distinct from the expectation that married black women should work (Jones, 1986; Brewer, 1999; Landry, 2000).

The distinction between sex and gender made in the 1970s and early 1980s was based on the idea that sex itself was biological, thus natural. Social constructionism became associated with a dichotomy between biological sex as a fixed category and gender as fluid. This formulation assumed men/women as an ahistorical and fixed dualism. More recent feminist work suggests that biology itself is shaped and interpreted by its historical context (Lorber, 1994; Foster, 1999; Hewitson, 1999; Squires, 1999). Science and medicine have enforced the biological dualism between men and women surgically, while Western culture naturalized the duality between male and female through designations of sexual deviance.[3] Some poststructuralist theories imply that the contrast between masculine and feminine is wholly ideological; the meaning of each concept derives from the contrast with the other rather than from reference to the material world (Hewitson, 1999: 14).

Most feminist economists have rejected the radical deconstruction of sexual categories associated with postmodernism (Nelson, 1996: 145f.),[4] and use the categories of men and women in empirical research on the labor market, development policies, and the division of household labor (Macdonald, 1995). Also, feminist economists have advocated political agendas based on common interests among women. For Folbre (1994: 38), the "primary goal" of feminist economists is "to explain why individuals of common gender might identify with one another and collectively pursue gender interests." However, feminists have modified social constructionism in response to the destabilization of sex (Foster, 1999). Susan Feiner (1995: 155), for example, discusses "social categories" such as race, gender, class, and ethnicity as "alternative (sometimes complementary, sometimes conflictual) ways of organizing difference" without reference to a biological base. Nelson (1996: 5) focuses on gender as a metaphor, defining it as "the cognitive patterning a culture constructs on the base of actual or perceived differences between males and females." Gendering, then, is a system in which differences are dichotomized and placed in a hierarchy. That which is female is not male and garners less power than that which is male. Such formulations do not assume stable biological identities.

Using these reformulated definitions of gender, feminist economists have examined how gendered dualisms affect the ways dominant economic theorists view the process of provisioning. Because gender has influenced the construction of meaning, social scientists tend to create hierarchical dichotomies tinged with distinctions between what is masculine and what is feminine. Methodologically, economics values reason over emotion, mathematical over verbal, and individual over relational (Nelson, 1996, 2001). Economic theory has centered on the concepts of scarcity, selfishness, and competition. But, as Myra Strober (1994) argues, these three concepts present only half of a series of dichotomies – scarcity/abundance, selfishness/altruism, and competition/cooperation. By excluding abundance, altruism, and cooperation, economic well-being is narrowly conceived.

A feminist standpoint helps illuminate these omissions and inconsistencies, but not because women, including feminist economists, are essentially different from men. Primary responsibility for raising a child, whether experienced by a man or a woman, might lead one to question economic assumptions such as a separate self and selfish utility maximization – not because motives and behavior are necessarily different in families but because they have been socially constructed according to different norms (England, 2003).

How does one reconstruct economics in order to eschew masculine biases? The key is not simply adding omitted spheres of economic activity such as non-market (or caring) labor, but in using these activities to rethink gendered assumptions about economic behavior and economic goals. Overcoming hierarchical dichotomies means incorporating both sides of the dualisms into one's vision of economic actors and economic life.

This methodological critique of neoclassical economics elucidates the need for a gender-sensitive analysis of economic institutions and practices. Feminism is not limited to making generalizations about women or the structure of households. Family and kinship are not the only locus of gender. Indeed, confining gender analysis to a single locus such as the family is itself a form of masculine bias. All institutions, including the state, labor markets, and product markets are structured by gender. Therefore, they can be restructured in a way that recognizes the complexity of human motivations and interactions.

Gendered social practices in welfare states

Feminist research on the welfare state has made an important contribution to political economy by challenging the gender-neutrality of core concepts such as citizenship. Although posed as gender-neutral, this term is embedded with assumptions about the social value of paid versus unpaid labor, and therefore of the men and women who perform these tasks. A similar argument can be made about the macroeconomic functions of the state. Post-war full employment was conceived almost entirely as full employment for white male breadwinners (Bruegel, Figart & Mutari, 1998). The expectation that paid work was a secondary activity for women but not men (or at least for the vast majority of women as distinguished from the vast majority of men) placed white male unemployment at the center of policy debates.

The male breadwinner family as a hegemonic ideal was not new to the Keynesian welfare state. Separation of breadwinning and caregiving dates back to the 19th century, and reflects the social world that evolved with industrial capitalism:

> In this world people were supposed to be organized into heterosexual, male-headed nuclear families, which lived principally from the

> man's labor-market earnings. The male head of the household would be paid a family wage, sufficient to support children and a full-time wife-and-mother, who performed domestic labor without pay. Of course, countless lives never fit this pattern. Still, it provided the normative picture of a proper family (Fraser, 1997: 41).

The citizen-breadwinner of the industrial era gradually replaced the 18th century notion of land as the basis of citizenship (including voting rights) and "gentleman" status. It is interesting to note that US women gained legal property rights in the mid-to-late 19th century as land ceased to be the primary signifier of one's economic and social status. Class and gender were simultaneously redefined in terms of one's relationship to the market.

The evolution of this gender order coincided with the period in which neoclassical economics solidified many of its basic concepts. In fact, the gendered division between market and non-market spheres was incorporated into some core neoclassical concepts. Folbre (1991) traces the gradual disappearance of household labor from Gross Domestic Product. In international statistical publications, the terms "labor force," "economically active population," "economic activity," "gainful employment," and "economic participation" all differentiate those who "work" from those who do not. This division between work and non-work, or more explicitly in many labor economics texts, between work and leisure, is deeply gendered. Because only transactions subject to monetary exchange are counted, housework, and even barter and informal sector work, are defined out of the sphere of economic analysis. The gendered assumptions underlying these basic economic categories appear as natural, or at least eminently rational, to those inside the dominant paradigms (Benería, 1992).

This section explores how the concepts of citizenship and full employment, and the public policies constructed on these concepts, have incorporated androcentric bias. Although this literature includes case studies of many industrialized countries (including Great Britain, Germany, France, Australia, Finland, and Sweden), I focus primarily on the US welfare state.[5]

The gender of citizenship

Feminist research on the concept of citizenship has been framed in response to the power resources school of welfare state theory, which was pioneered by Gøsta Esping-Andersen (1990). Rather than treating welfare capitalism as a unitary concept, he noted that the relationship between the market and the state varied in different institutional and cultural contexts. The generous social welfare polices in Sweden were distinct from the *laissez-faire* model of welfare state capitalism in the US and the UK. Not only did the state take on different forms, but the nature of the market economy was radically different in alternative social and political contexts. Therefore, Esping-Andersen argued, market forces should not be viewed as autonomous and independent of politics.

Esping-Andersen (1990: 48–54) ranked industrialized countries along three dimensions: (1) state-market relations, (2) degrees of stratification, and (3) the degree of "decommodification" of labor through the state providing for economic security pensions, sickness benefits, and unemployment insurance.[6] Each of these empowers workers against market fluctuations. In summarizing the power resources school, Ann Orloff (1993: 307) observes: "Capitalists have greater resources in the market, while workers (because of their numbers) have greater resources in the polity. Wage earners, they argue, will use their political resources to modify market processes and extend social rights." The emancipatory potential of welfare states lies in these social rights of citizenship.

Feminists have praised Esping-Andersen's framework, but they have also criticized it (Williams, 1995). Esping-Andersen biased his definition of "citizenship" by focusing on social rights that compensated for job loss. Because of this, Orloff concludes that, "His citizens are implicitly male workers" (1996: 65). Esping-Andersen's approach has also been criticized for its narrow focus on class conflict in the construction of welfare states. Indeed, Esping-Andersen identifies social classes as "the main agents of change" (1990: 16) and posits that "The central question ... for the entire contemporary debate on the welfare state, is whether, and under what conditions, the class divisions and social inequities produced by capitalism can be undone by parliamentary democracy" (1990: 11). While many welfare state policies do target constituencies based upon their relationship to paid work (see below), others do not. Theda Skocpol (1992) argues that the earliest welfare programs established in the US during the late 19th and early 20th centuries focused on "protecting soldiers and mothers," not workers. A preoccupation with class-based policies has led scholars to underestimate the extent to which the US was functioning as a welfare state prior to the Great Depression and the New Deal.

The power resources framework also ignores how middle-class women social reformers helped develop welfare programs in the US and elsewhere because it focuses only on mainstream political parties (especially labor parties) as arenas for political mobilization.[7] US social welfare programs grew out of reform movements that created institutions such as settlement houses (including the famous Hull House in Chicago), the National Consumers' League, and the Women's Trade Union League in the late 19th century. In fact, US welfare programs were established at the state level early in the 20th century as networks of social reformers (often with women in leadership positions) succeeded in lobbying for mothers' pensions, child labor laws, and minimum wages and maximum hours for working women. Since women could not vote at this time, their participation in the public sphere needed to be based on their private roles. Feminists therefore used the politics of *maternalism* to broaden the scope of political mobilization. That is, they positioned their work to promote maternal and child welfare. Maternalism permitted activists to justify their public roles: "Activist women ... regarded motherhood as empowering, not as a condition of dependence and weakness. They saw the home – domestic and maternal duties – as the locus of their power within the community" (Koven & Michel, 1990: 1091). At the federal level, the Children's Bureau, established in 1912 to administer mothers' pensions and other programs, represented the first institutional commitment to an ongoing welfare state; it was largely staffed by women drawn from these social movements (Gordon, 1994).

Maternalism also provided an ideological basis for state intervention in the market to promote a larger public purpose. Maximum hours laws for women were upheld by a 1908 Supreme Court (*Muller v. Oregon*) decision that ruled there was a large public interest in women's health and safety based on their roles as mothers. This warranted state intervention in labor contracts between employers and employees. Protecting women as mothers thus became the rationale for the first labor legislation in the US. Women gained entitlement to minimum wages not from being workers, but as mothers. Protective legislation was thus a social practice, organized by gender, which reinforced a particular vision of women's appropriate relationship to the economy.[8]

Moving beyond an emphasis on class also entails moving beyond the dyad between the market and the state.[9] By neglecting the role of the family as a site for social reproduction, Esping-Andersen ignores an important institutional pillar of welfare state capitalism. As Jane Lewis (1992: 161) notes, "the worker he [Esping-Andersen] has in mind is male and his mobilization may depend as much on unpaid female household labor as state policies." The ability of male trade unionists and labor party activists to participate in political movements, like their ability to engage in paid labor, is based on their freedom from responsibility for cooking meals, changing diapers, and mopping floors. By including the family as well as the state and the market, feminists have also expanded the types of social policies under discussion. Feminists examined the intersections among markets, the state, and other institutions such as the family, in providing childcare, parental leave, and other services that affect the organization of social reproduction and caring labor.

Linda Gordon (1994) examines the policy debates leading to passage of the US Social Security Act of 1935, particularly Aid to Dependent Children (ADC), a program for single mothers that was established by the Act. Several contending versions of ADC were debated prior to passage, and the program enacted was an historically contingent outcome, subject to the relative strength of various political actors. Gordon underscores the feminist vision implicit in maternalist social policy. By giving women an alternative to dependence on men, ADC improved women's bargaining power and gave them a measure of autonomy. By offering income support for the work of raising children, it also valued women's unpaid caring labor.

However, Gordon argues that the Social Security Act instituted a two-track system of public aid, distinguishing true citizens from those merely receiving institutionalized charity (also see Fraser, 1997). "Deserving" groups such as the elderly and unemployed workers received "entitlements" to social security pensions and unemployment insurance[10] (when the Social Security Act was passed, the term "entitlement" was not a pejorative term). Since the elderly (as former workers and their dependents) and unemployed workers were entitled to their benefits, their participation in these programs was a mark of citizenship. Citizenship was thus implicitly linked to one's relationship to paid labor.

The "undeserving" poor were those outside of paid labor – women and their children. They received "welfare," which was viewed as charity not an entitlement. Benefits were lower than those under other programs and the process of qualifying for benefits was more personally intrusive. Women raising children were "pitied, but not entitled," as Gordon (1994) noted, and therefore not true citizens. Following Esping-Andersen, citizens receive benefits as social rights, not charity.

Some scholars argue that US social welfare policies were limited by a general acceptance of gender difference, even by those reformers advocating on behalf of poor women. The model of a full-time homemaker supported by a male breadwinner fostered the development of social policies such as mothers' pensions designed to replace absent fathers.[11] Sonya Michel (1993) argues that this maternalist mindset precluded support for a widespread federal childcare program. Mothers' pensions, facilitating full-time homemaking in the absence of a male breadwinner, were deemed preferable to programs such as childcare that enabled women to combine paid and unpaid work. Gwendolyn Mink (1995) observes that the maternalist ethos espoused by white middle-class social reformers posited a singular model of mothering as a full-time activity that precluded paid employment. Immigrant and African-American women, who often viewed their paid labor as an equally important contribution to their families, were supposed to be assimilated into this hegemonic gender model.

Welfare states, as well as academic analyses of them, thus suffer from androcentric bias. In particular, US welfare state provisions legitimated and valued paid labor more than the unpaid work of social reproduction. Basing social rights on a record of paid employment distinguishes the US from other industrialized nations, especially the Scandinavian countries, where old age pensions, healthcare, unemployment compensation and other important aspects of provisioning are universally available (Esping-Andersen, 1990). Alice Kessler-Harris (2001: 4) maintains that linking paid work to citizenship in the US became stronger when the scope of the federal government expanded during the New Deal:

> Work, wage work, had long marked a distinction among kinds of citizens: intimately tied to identity, it anchored nineteenth-century claims to political participation. But when the federal government linked wage work to tangible, publicly provided rewards, employment emerged as a boundary line demarking different kinds of citizenship. Casual laborers, the unskilled and untrained, housewives, farms workers, mothers, and domestic servants all found themselves on one side of a barrier not of their own making. Their own benefits not earned but means-tested, classified as relief, not rights, many protested what seemed an artificial division and demanded inclusion. Their voices were quickly stilled.

Social welfare programs presupposed and reinforced the male breadwinner family as the proper organization of society. This was not, however, inevitable. These social practices resulted from a contentious process whereby feminists and others attempted to institutionalize alternative visions (Glenn, 2002).

Current debates over the purpose, structure, and level of benefits of income support for single mothers revisit these contested understandings (or discourses) about the relationship between motherhood and citizenship, this time under different historical circumstances. As the hegemony of the male breadwinner family has slipped, the role of the state as a substitute breadwinner for households with absent fathers has been called into question. Philip Cohen and Suzanne Bianchi (1999: 23) observe that "The Personal Responsibility and Work Opportunity Reconciliation Act is based on a quite different model of motherhood: a 'good mother' locates childcare for her young children and finds a job, perhaps after some additional job training, by means of which she can financially support herself and her children." This "welfare reform" legislation (passed in 1996) treats poor single mothers as potential full-time workers. However, as Cohen and Bianchi document, the majority of *married* mothers with preschool children do not hold full-time, year-round employment, even though a majority are in the labor force. Nor do they support children solely on their wages. Therefore, they pose the question: "To the extent that trends for married women have influenced the welfare debate, is it realistic to expect *single* mothers to combine full-time paid work and childcare?" (Cohen & Bianchi, 1999: 23). Many feminists would argue that we should find ways to value caregiving without requiring one group (women) to specialize in the activity and we should restructure paid employment so that breadwinners can also be caregivers.[12]

The gender of full employment

Restructuring the relationship between the state and the market in industrialized countries during the 20th century involved more than simply providing a social wage to supplement or replace market wages. In addition to the income replacement programs discussed above, public policy was directed toward maintaining paid employment (and thus wages) as the primary means of provisioning. Pensions, unemployment compensation, and support for single mothers were merely substitutes for wage labor. Paid employment was also defined as the basis for macroeconomic growth, especially during the period following World War II. Therefore, Keynesian macroeconomic stabilization policy was institutionalized to maintain full employment as an objective of state policy.

Nevertheless, "full employment" never meant that everyone should engage in paid labor. As William Beveridge (1995: 43) stated in his landmark 1944 report, "Full employment does not mean literally no unemployment; that is to say, it does not mean that every man and woman in the country who is fit and free for work is employed productively on every day of his or her working life." This reasonable caveat, phrased in gender-inclusive language, is followed by further elaboration of what actually constitutes full employment: "Full employment in this Report ... means having always more vacant jobs than unemployed men, not slightly fewer jobs."

This shift in pronouns reveals the gendered assumptions guiding full employment policies in the UK and the US during the post-war period. The employment of men was central to both employment creation and wage policies. The costs of men's job loss were not simply economic, but were intimately tied to the construction of male identity. The association of working-class masculinity with breadwinning dates back to the end of the 19th century, when the growth of heavy industry brought more groups of male workers into wage labor (Connell, 1993). Employers needed male manufacturing workers to sustain their attachment to monotonous, routine jobs; their identity as the family breadwinner facilitated this (Lewchuk, 1993). The breadwinner identity associated with masculinity contributed to economic stability by constructing social relations where being unemployed and unable to fulfill family obligations was worse than being exploited.[13]

Mass production for mass consumption necessitated the coupling of productivity and real wage increases, a set of institutional arrangements that has been labeled "Fordism." Fordism is another gendered concept, since it is defined by the characteristics of male-dominated manufacturing industries and the conditions of work and consumption experienced by white male workers. Within this set of institutional arrangements, the male breadwinner family as a hegemonic gender norm supported macroeconomic stability (McDowell, 1991; O'Hara, 1995; Bakker, 1996; Fraser, 1997). Wage-earning was the bedrock of working-class masculinity and the source of purchasing power to fuel economic growth. The loss of wage-earning capacity generated crises on multiple levels. The Great Depression, for example, was a period in which male unemployment sparked concern over "emasculation" (Humphries, 1976; Storrs, 2000).

Because women were not viewed as breadwinners, their unemployment was not viewed as a problem. This discrepancy was apparent during the Great Depression when employed women were scapegoated for men's unemployment, and laws were passed giving preference to men rather than women in the same household (Humphries, 1976; Scharf, 1980; Kessler-Harris, 1982). Many of these policies, such as bans on married women's employment in particular workplaces, persisted into the post-war period. According to Kessler-Harris (2001: 10f.), the right to work, a tenuous and unenforceable right that nonetheless was considered a basis for democratic citizenship in liberal political theory, was a "deeply rooted gendered prerogative." Until the mid-1960s, she argues, restricting women from paid work was taken as being in the public interest and was reflected in both laws and customs.

Despite the importance of consumption within Keynesian macroeconomics, Beveridge (1995: 44) also informed us that "A person who cannot sell his labor is in effect told that he is of no use." Again, engaging in paid labor rather than social reproduction demonstrates that one is a productive citizen. Amy Koritz and Doug Koritz (2001) assert that devaluing women's work as consumers in the mass production for mass consumption economy represents a relic of neoclassical economics that was only temporarily destabilized when Keynesian theory was first introduced. The post-war neoclassical synthesis reconstituted a gendered hierarchy between production and consumption. Consumers may be citizens, but not in a meaningful sense: "Consumers as citizens or as participants in a culture generate nothing; they only select from the options presented by producers" (Koritz & Koritz, 2001: 57).

Beveridge (1995: 43) focused on attaining an adequate wage as well as a job; full employment "means that the jobs are at fair wages, of such a kind, and so located that the unemployed men can reasonably be expected to take them." A concern with the adequacy of men's wages is also consistent with discourse about the male breadwinner, which influenced regulations such as the Fair Labor Standards Act (FLSA) of 1938 (Figart, Mutari & Power, 2002: ch. 6). In the case of the FLSA, those advocating the first federal minimum wage in the US (especially union leaders), indicated that men's wages and identities were at stake, specifically unorganized, mostly white, male workers.

The limited coverage of the FLSA, when it was first passed, meant that most female-dominated industries, and the two key industries employing African-American men and women (agriculture and domestic labor), were excluded from the federal minimum wage. In the discourse promoted by union leaders, union men who negotiated their wages embodied the hegemonic form of working-class masculinity, while state-protected breadwinners (who needed legislation to ensure a living wage) were subordinate. Those excluded from state protection (black men and women of all races) were subordinated still further. The FLSA thus generated social practices that differentiated wage levels and wage-setting processes by race as well as by gender.

Despite state-generated social practices that promoted the male breadwinner family, women of all ages, races, and marital statuses deepened their labor force attachment during the post-war period (Blackwelder, 1997; Cohen & Bianchi, 1999). Families increased their consumption standards by adding a second earner, as the female-intensive service sector grew. Alternative ways of differentiating gender evolved over time. One was the rise of part-time employment in female-dominated economic sectors, ostensibly offering jobs to married women who were still viewed as secondary labor market participants.

These trends, which have been labeled "post-Fordism," intensified since the 1970s. Likewise, feminist activism in the 1960s and 1970s offered alternative discourses about what it meant to be a woman, while reshaping public policy and other social practices. As a result, the male breadwinner family began to lose its grip on peoples' consciousness.

These changes require rethinking what is meant by full employment (Bruegel, Figart & Mutari, 1998). Unfortunately, not all such attempts are promising. In the late 1970s and early 1980s, some economists blamed the rising Non-Accelerating Inflationary Rate of Unemployment (NAIRU) on increased labor force participation and attachment among women, teens, and racial-ethnic minorities (see Gordon, 1987 for a summary of this literature). For example, in a popular macroeconomics textbook, Robert Gordon (1984) argued that structural shifts in the composition of the labor force from 1955 to 1974 toward groups with higher unemployment rates, specifically adult females and teens, meant that the overall unemployment rate increased even though the adult male unemployment rate was relatively stable. In contrast, David Gordon (1987) argued that the causation should be reversed. Married women's increased labor force participation was partly a response to inflationary pressures and *declining* real wages rather than the cause of these economic problems. Yet even David Gordon treats women's employment as a negative consequence of failed economic policies rather than a transformation of social values.[14]

A return to Keynesian full employment policies, this time with women included, is not a sufficient response. Full employment still presupposes wages as the primary means of provisioning and puts material production over social reproduction. It leaves a critical question unanswered: "Who Pays for the Kids?" (Folbre, 1994; England & Folbre, 1999). In other words, how is social reproduction to be accomplished? If public policy simply seeks to integrate women into the labor force according to the norms established for male workers, will this crowd out other important values and modes of economic behavior (Folbre & Nelson, 2000)? Although some feminists are sanguine about the commodification of social reproduction (notably Bergmann, 1986), many argue that markets cannot meet these needs (Benería, 1999). The next section discusses alternative frameworks for answering these questions in the post-Fordist period.

The state and transformative social practices

The feminist deconstruction of Keynesian welfare states shows that seemingly gender-neutral policies can be based on gendered assumptions and have gendered effects. For this reason, feminists advocate a gender-based analysis of all government policies and programs, not just those with obvious implications for women. This approach was prominent in the Fourth World Conference on Women in Beijing (United Nations, 1996). Since then, the concept of gender mainstreaming has entered the lexicon of policy analysts. The European Union has taken steps to institutionalize gender mainstreaming in all its policy initiatives (see Behning & Pascual, 2001). Canada has also taken a leadership role in gender-based policy analysis. The Canadian government instituted a policy "requiring federal departments and agencies to conduct gender-based analysis of future policies and legislation, where appropriate," as part of a national action plan for achieving gender equity (Status of Women Canada, 1995). A Gender-Based Analysis Directorate has been created to monitor the process. Women's budget initiatives in South Africa and other countries audit government budgets for their impact on women and girls (Bakker, 2001).

Ultimately, feminist economics poses questions about how provisioning might be better organized to ensure the well-being of all the members of society. The unraveling (though not elimination) of the male breadwinner family as a hegemonic social norm provides an opportunity to rethink how public policy can help achieve these ends. Determining the appropriate set of policies and programs to supplant outdated and inequitable ones is not simple, and feminists do not agree on a vision of the proper relationship between markets, families, and the state. The key dilemma, as Gordon (2002: 31) notes, is between "valuing the unpaid caring work still overwhelmingly performed by women, and...enabling women to achieve equality in wage labor and political power."

This issue has been at the core of the equality-versus-difference debate among women activists and feminist theorists since the turn of the 20th century (Kessler-Harris, 1987). The "equality" emphasis in feminism focuses on removing barriers that prevent women from participating in realms of political, economic, and social life that have been defined as male terrain. The rights to vote and hold property, to pursue higher education, to work in non-traditional jobs, and to choose a career-oriented life path are among the goals and achievements of equality feminism. The "difference" strand of feminism is less easy to define. For some, it involves accepting socially constructed differences in men's and women's life paths and focuses on supporting and enabling those activities that fall in women's realms.

The division between feminists pursuing equality initiatives and those advocating policies based on women's special needs was particularly strong following ratification of women's suffrage in the US in 1920. Equality feminists pursued passage of an Equal Rights Amendment, which would have undermined the gender-specific protective legislation passed during the Progressive Era. Many observers have seen a class breakdown to these strategic divisions, as the defenders of working-class immigrant women emphasized protection based on women's social position and lack of bargaining power while the middle-class, educated women who were best positioned to benefit from equal treatment favored equality. During the post-war period, more and more women gained access to education, stayed in the labor force after marriage and children, and defined the scope of their societal contributions beyond the private sphere. In these circumstances policies based on equality, such as the Equal Pay Act of 1963 (mandating equal pay for equal work) and Title VII of the Civil Rights Act of 1964 (covering equal opportunity in employment) took root in fertile soil.

Tensions between these two visions of feminism have resurfaced. The achievements of equality-based feminism in the late 20th century and the withering away of the male breadwinner family have left the issue of the role of caring labor unresolved. Despite US women's greater involvement in the male realm of paid work, unpaid production in the household and caring labor are still largely women's separate sphere. Women perform caring labor not because they are naturally altruistic, but because of historically developed social relations. However, these gendered social norms, preferences, and values have devalued caring labor.

Some caring activities have been commodified, usually into female-dominated parts of the service sector. This commodification process was both a cause and an effect of women's increased labor force attachment. In a market economy, the generation of profits and the act of consumption are the motive force of much economic activity; work is a means rather than an end in itself. As reproductive labor is commodified, society may face a net loss of caring, since it is undervalued within the market paradigm. Markets may be better suited to providing certain types of goods and services than others. Care is rife with externalities and its quality is difficult to monitor. It may not be appropriate to allocate quality care on the basis of ability to pay (Folbre & Nelson, 2000: 136ff.). On the other hand, the coercive nature of traditional gender norms gave women few options besides work in the home. If one assumes skilled caring is a learned activity rather than a natural attribute of one sex, the quality of care might increase if it is performed "more as a matter of choice and less as a matter of necessity" (Folbre & Nelson, 2000: 135).

Public policy can foster alternative approaches to provisioning care while enhancing equity. Nancy Fraser (1997) describes three alternative directions that public policy might take. One is the Universal Breadwinner model, which emphasizes the commodification of caring labor. Whether provided by the market or the state, work would be performed for pay, and jobs at breadwinner wages would be available for all. A commitment to full employment would be degendered, with women working full-time, year-round. Fraser suggests that only a "residual" income replacement programs would remain for those adults truly unable to work.

The US has moved toward the Universal Breadwinner model more than most European industrialized countries. This model was also the implicit vision of the former state socialist regimes. However, we are still a long way from fully commodifying caring labor.

A modified version of the Universal Breadwinner model can be seen in the work of Barbara Bergmann (1986; 1994). Although committed to women's full-time labor force participation, she questions the ability of wages to provide for children's well-being, especially in single-parent households. Therefore, Bergmann (1994: 78) supports the socialization of caregiving activities via state-funded childcare. Although she acknowledges that supplementing wages with childcare subsidies is more costly for taxpayers than generous welfare provision, she argues that it is more consonant with current work-centered values.

A second approach, the Caregiver Parity model, is implicit in the policies and practices of many Western European social democracies. Here the policy objective is to allow women to choose to do the bulk of caring labor for their families, possibly in conjunction with part-time paid employment: "The aim is not to make women's lives the same as men's but, rather, to 'make difference costless'" Fraser (1997: 55). One possibility is caregiver allowances to compensate for socially necessary labor. Fraser also suggests policy initiatives that reduce penalties for labor force intermittency and for choosing part-time employment. This approach would require major structural tax reform to pay for public subsidies. Evaluating these models of gender equity, Fraser (1997: 60) finds that:

> Neither Universal Breadwinner nor Caregiver Parity can actually make good on its promise of gender equity – even under very favorable conditions. Although both are good at preventing women's poverty and exploitation, both are only fair at redressing inequality of respect... Universal Breadwinner fails especially to promote equality of leisure time and to combat androcentrism, while Caregiver Parity fails especially to promote income equality and to prevent women's marginalization.

Most importantly, she argues, neither model asks men to change their lives.

The third option, and the one that Fraser finds most conducive to gender equity, is the Universal Caregiver model. This model rejects the dichotomization of equality-versus-difference policies. The heart of this strategy is to construct new social practices that "*induce men to become more like most women are now*, namely people who do primary carework" (Fraser, 1997: 60). State policies and programs would play an important role in the construction of these transformative social practices.

To implement this vision, public policies would need to eliminate segmented labor markets that differentiate good breadwinner jobs from "mommy track" jobs (Figart, 2002). The social welfare system would need to be restructured to eliminate its dual track nature as well. A shorter work week would enable workers to have time for caregiving activities (Mutari & Figart, 2001). Some employment-enabling services such as childcare would play a role, but employees would not shift all carework to social services. In this scenario, some caring labor would be relocated to civil society, a site that is often overlooked in the tripartite emphasis on markets, states, and families (Bakker, 2001). Fraser (1997: 61) envisions involving childless adults, older people, and others in "democratic, self-managed carework activities."

The fundamental change, according to the Universal Caregiver model, is that breadwinning and caregiving would be viewed as activities, rather than identities. Eliminating the gender-coding of breadwinning and caregiving would, in effect, deconstruct gender itself.

Conclusion

The state, through its policies and programs, is an important site for the development, perpetuation, and transformation of social practices. For this reason, feminists have studied public policy as a form of gendered and racialized social practice. How gender, race-ethnicity, class, and other social categories are structured in a particular time and place reflects the relative dominance of different social interests seeking to establish social practices. During much of the 20th century, public policy and other social practices perpetuated the hegemonic ideal of the male breadwinner family. Social welfare programs and macroeconomic policy were predicated on the separation of market and nonmarket labor and the devaluation of women's unpaid caring labor. Wage labor provided the basis for citizenship and the fuel for economic growth.

Periods of feminist activism were times in which gender structures were intensely questioned and, to some extent, modified. In the latter part of the 20th century, many women rejected their secondary status and fought for access to wage labor as a means of providing for themselves and their families. Most feminists, however, reject the dichotomization of breadwinning and caring. A feminist view of the state, therefore, advocates public policies that permit people to engage in a range of activities. Feminist economists seek to use public policy to de-gender the images of breadwinners and caregivers so that both men and women can make unbiased life choices.

Implementing this vision will not be easy, and many questions remain unresolved. What are the strengths and weaknesses of markets as a means of provisioning? What kinds of caring services should the state provide and to whom? Under what conditions should society continue to offer income support for caregiving in the home? How should childless adults support caring? How can jobs be restructured to accommodate all workers with family responsibilities without stigma or prolonged economic penalties? These are not simply matters of the allocation of resources. They raise fundamental questions about the construction of identity, the development of human capabilities, and the role of the state in contributing to a more fulfilling life.

Notes

1 While I prefer the term "feminist political economy" I will use the more common term "feminist economics."
2 I am grateful to Marilyn Power for suggesting the issue of "starting points" as a fruitful way to delineate a feminist economic perspective.
3 Until recently, psychology reinforced biological categories by labeling gender-inappropriate behavior (especially by women) as a form of deviance. Modern technology is even capable of reshaping biology according to gender norms. For example, children born as hermaphrodites or with genitalia that does not fit into the preconceived distinction between male and female are surgically "fixed.".
4 Hewitson (1999), who favors the postmodern approach, concurs.
5 For a collection of country-specific case studies on the maternalist origins of the welfare state, see Koven & Michel (1993).
6 Esping-Andersen (1990: 3, 36–7) notes that the term "decommodification" was inspired by the work of Karl Polanyi. Polanyi (1957) views the commodification of labor, land, and money as key characteristics of market economies. However, labor is a fictitious commodity because workers lack the ability to withdraw the supply of labor.
7 The lack of a US labor party then becomes part of the explanation for the supposedly non-existent welfare state.
8 For more detail on protective legislation as a gendered (and racialized) social practice, see Figart, Mutari & Power (2002) and Mutari, Power & Figart (2002).
9 Esping-Andersen's more recent work has been informed by the feminist critiques of his earlier work. It argues that the transition away from welfare states toward emerging postindustrial economies is "institutionally path-dependent;" that is, shaped by the legacy of the relationships between state, family, and economy (Esping-Andersen, 1999: 4).
10 Gordon (1994: 288) notes that "entitlement" has become discredited in contemporary usage, now associated with "special interests" rather than "citizenship."
11 War widows were therefore the earliest beneficiaries of mothers' pensions.
12 Such transformative social practices will be discussed in more detail later.
13 Credit for this insight goes to Irene Bruegel.
14 Cohen & Bianchi (1999) provide evidence that it was the opening of opportunities that pulled women into the labor force, rather than "push" factors on the supply side such as declining income of husbands.

References

Acker, J. (2000) "Revisiting Class: Thinking from Gender, Race, and Organizations," *Social Politics*, 7(2): 192–214.

Albelda, R. (1997) *Economics and Feminism: Disturbances in the Field*, New York: Twayne Publishers.

Bakker, I. (ed.) (1996) *Rethinking Restructuring*, Toronto: University of Toronto Press.

Bakker, I. (2001) "Engendering the Economics of Globalization: Sites and Processes": in J. Stanford, L. Taylor & E. Houston (eds) *Power, Employment and Accumulation: Social Structures in Economic Theory and Practice*, pp. 219–37, Armonk, NY: M.E. Sharpe.

Barker, D. & Kuiper, E. (eds) (2003) *Toward a Feminist Philosophy of Economics*, London: Routledge.

Behning, U. & Pascual, A. (2001) *Gender Mainstreaming in the European Employment Strategy*. Brussels: European Trade Union Institute.

Benería, L. (1992) "Accounting for Women's Work: The Progress of Two Decades," *World Development*, 20(11): 1527–60.

Benería, L. (1999) "Globalization, Gender and the Davos Man," *Feminist Economics*, 5(3): 61–83.

Bergmann, B. (1986) *The Economic Emergence of Women*, New York: Basic Books.

Bergmann, B. (1994) "Curing Child Poverty in the United States," *American Economic Review*, 84(2): 76–80.

Beveridge, W. (1995) "Full Employment in a Free Society": in D. Colander & H. Landreth (eds) *Classic Readings in Economics*, pp. 43–6, New Haven, VT: MaxiPress.

Blackwelder, J. (1997) *Now Hiring: The Feminization of Work in the United States, 1900–1995*, College Station, TX: A & M University Press.

Brewer, R. (1999) "Theorizing Race, Class and Gender: The New Scholarship of Black Feminist Intellectuals and Black Women's Labor," *Race, and Gender & Class*, 6(2): 29–47.

Bruegel, I., Figart, D. & Mutari, E. (1998) "A Feminist Perspective on Full Employment and Work Redistribution": in J. Wheelock & J. Vail (eds) *Work and Idleness: The Political Economy of Full Employment*, pp. 69–83, London: Kluwer Academic Publishers.

Cohen, P. & Bianchi, S. (1999) "Marriage, Children, and Women's Employment: What Do We Know?," *Monthly Labor Review*, 122(12): 22–31.

Connell, R. (1993) "The Big Picture: Masculinities in Recent World History," *Theory and Society*, 22: 597–623.

Connell, R. (1995) *Masculinities*, Berkeley: University of California Press.

England, P. (2003) "Separation and Soluble Selves: Dichotomous Thinking in Economics,": in M. Ferber & J. Nelson (eds) *Feminist Economics Today: Beyond Economic Man*, pp. 33–59, Chicago: University of Chicago Press.

England, P. & Folbre, N. (1999) "Who Should Pay for the Kids?," *Annals of the American Academy of Political and Social Science*, 563: 194–207.

Esping-Andersen, G. (1990) *The Three Worlds of Welfare Capitalism*, Princeton: Princeton University Press.

Esping-Andersen, G. (1999) *Social Foundations of Postindustrial Economies*, Oxford: Oxford University Press.

Feiner, S. (1995) "Reading Neoclassical Economics: Toward an Erotic Economy of Sharing": in E. Kuiper & J. Sap (eds) *Out of the Margin: Feminist Perspectives on Economics*, pp. 151–66, London: Routledge.

Ferber, M. & Nelson, J. (eds) (1993) *Beyond Economic Man: Feminist Theory and Economics*, Chicago: University of Chicago Press.

Ferber, M. & Nelson, J. (eds) (2003) *Feminist Economics Today: Beyond Economic Man*, Chicago: University of Chicago Press.

Figart, D. (2002) "Policies to Provide Non-Invidious Employment": in M. Tool & P. Bush (eds) *Institutional Analysis and Economic Policy*, pp. 379–409, Boston: Kluwer.
Figart, D., Mutari, E. & Power, M. (2002) *Living Wages, Equal Wages: Gender and Labor Market Policies in the United States,* New York: Routledge.
Folbre, N. (1991) "The Unproductive Housewife: Her Evolution in Nineteenth-Century Economic Thought," *Signs: Journal of Women in Culture and Society,* 16(3): 463–84.
Folbre, N. (1994) *Who Pays for the Kids? Gender and the Structures of Constraint,* London: Routledge.
Folbre, N. (2001) *The Invisible Heart: Economics and Family Values.* New York: New Press.
Folbre, N. & Nelson, J.A. (2000) "For Love or Money – Or Both?" *Journal of Economic Perspectives,* 14(4): 123–40.
Foster, J. (1999) "An Invitation to Dialogue: Clarifying the Position of Feminist Gender Theory in Relation to Sexual Difference Theory," *Gender & Society,* 13(4): 431–56.
Fraser, N. (1997) *Justice Interruptus: Critical Reflections on the "Postsocialist" Condition,* New York: Routledge.
Glenn, E. (1998) "Gender, Race, and Class: Bridging the Language-Structure Divide," *Social Science History,* 22(1): 29–38.
Glenn, E. (2002) *Unequal Freedom: How Race and Gender Shaped American Citizenship and Labor,* Cambridge, MA: Harvard University Press.
Gordon, D. (1987) "Six-Percent Unemployment Ain't Natural: Demystifying the Idea of a Rising 'Natural Rate of Unemployment'," *Social Research,* 54(2): 223–46.
Gordon, L. (1994) *Pitied But Not Entitled: Single Mothers and the History of Welfare,* New York: The Free Press.
Gordon, L. (2002) "Citizen Jane," *The Nation,* July 22/29: 31–4.
Gordon, R. (1984) *Macroeconomics,* Third Edition, Boston: Little, Brown and Company.
Hewitson, G. (1999) *Feminist Economics: Interrogating the Masculinity of Rational Economic Man,* Cheltenham, UK: Edward Elgar.
Humphries, J. (1976) "Women: Scapegoats and Safety Valves in the Great Depression," *Review of Radical Political Economics,* 8(1): 98–121.
Jones, J. (1986) *Labor of Love, Labor of Sorrow: Black Women, Work, and the Family from Slavery to the Present,* New York: Vintage Books.
Kessler-Harris, A. (1982) *Out to Work,* Oxford: Oxford University Press.
Kessler-Harris, A. (1987) "The Debate Over Equality for Women in the Workplace: Recognizing Differences": in N. Gerstel & H. Gross (eds) *Families and Work,* pp. 520–39, Philadelphia: Temple University Press.
Kessler-Harris, A. (2001) *In Pursuit of Equity: Women, Men, and the Quest for Economic Citizenship in 20th-Century America,* Oxford: Oxford University Press.
Koritz, A. & Koritz, D. (2001) "Checkmating the Consumer: Passive Consumption and the Economic Devaluation of Culture," *Feminist Economics,* 7(1): 45–62.
Koven, S. & Michel, S. (1990) "Womanly Duties: Maternalist Politics and the Origins of Welfare States in France, Germany, Great Britain, and the United States, 1880–1920," *American Historical Review,* 95: 1076–108.

Koven, S. & Michel, S. (eds) (1993) *Mothers of a New World: Maternalist Politics and the Origins of Welfare States*, New York: Routledge.
Kuiper, E. & Sap, J. (eds) (1995) *Out of the Margin: Feminist Perspectives on Economics*, London: Routledge.
Landry, B. (2000) *Black Working Wives: Pioneers of the American Family Revolution*, Berkeley: University of California Press.
Laslett, B. & Brenner, J. (1989) "Gender and Social Reproduction: Historical Perspectives," *Annual Review of Sociology*, 15: 381–404.
Lewchuk, W. A. (1993) "Men and Monotony: Fraternalism as a Managerial Strategy at the Ford Motor Company," *Journal of Economic History*, 53(4): 824–56.
Lewis, J. (1992) "Gender and the Development of Welfare Regimes," *Journal of European Social Policy*, 2(3): 159–73.
Lorber, J. (1994) *Paradoxes of Gender*, New Haven: Yale University Press.
Macdonald, M. (1995) "Feminist Economics: From Theory to Research," *Canadian Journal of Economics*, 28(1): 159–75.
McDowell, L. (1991) "Life Without Father and Ford: The New Gender Order of Post-Fordism," *Transactions of the British Institute of Geographers*, 16: 400–19.
Michel, S. (1993) "The Limits of Maternalism: Policies Toward American Wage-Earning Mothers during the Progressive Era": in S. Koven & S. Michel (eds) *Mothers of a New World: Maternalist Politics and the Origins of Welfare States*, pp. 277–320, New York: Routledge.
Mink, G. (1995) *The Wages of Motherhood: Inequality in the Welfare State, 1917–1942*, Ithaca: Cornell University Press.
Mutari, E. & Figart, D. (2001) "Europe at a Crossroads: Harmonization, Liberalization, and the Gender of Work Time," *Social Politics*, 8(1): 36–64.
Mutari, E., Power, M. & Figart, D. (2002) "Neither Mothers Nor Breadwinners: African American Women's Exclusion from U.S. Minimum Wage Policies, 1912–38," *Feminist Economics*, 8(2): 37–61.
Nelson, J. (1996) *Feminism, Objectivity and Economics*, London: Routledge.
Nelson, J. (2001) "Economic Methodology and Feminist Critiques," *Journal of Economic Methodology*, 8(1): 93–7.
Nicholson, L. (ed.) (1990) *Feminism/Postmodernism*, New York: Routledge.
O'Hara, P. (1995) "Household Labor, the Family, and Macroeconomic Instability in the United States: 1940s–1990s," *Review of Social Economy*, 53(1): 89–120.
Orloff, A. (1993) "Gender and the Social Rights of Citizenship: The Comparative Analysis of Gender Relations and Welfare States," *American Sociological Review*, 58(3): 303–28.
Orloff, A. (1996) "Gender in the Welfare State," *Annual Review of Sociology*, 22: 51–78.
Peter, F. (2003) "Foregrounding Practices: Feminist Philosophy of Economics Beyond Rhetoric and Realism": in D. Barker & E. Kuiper (eds) *Toward A Feminist Philosophy of Economics*, pp. 105–21, London: Routledge.
Polanyi, K. (1957 [1944]) *The Great Transformation: The Political and Economic Origins of Our Time*, Boston: Beacon Press.
Scharf, L. (1980) *To Work and To Wed: Female Employment, Feminism and the Great Depression*, Westport, CT: Greenwood Press.
Skocpol, T. (1992) *Protecting Soldiers and Mothers: The Political Origins of Social Policy in the United States*, Cambridge, MA: Harvard University Press.

Squires, J. (1999) *Gender in Political Theory*, Cambridge, UK: Polity Press.
Status of Women Canada (1995) *Setting the Stage for the Next Century: The Federal Plan for Gender Equality*. Ottawa: Status of Women Canada.
Storrs, L. (2000) *Civilizing Capitalism: The National Consumers' League, Women's Activism, and Labor Standards in the New Deal Era*, Chapel Hill: University of North Carolina Press.
Strober, M. (1994) "Rethinking Economics Through a Feminist Lens," *American Economic Review Papers and Proceedings*, 84(2): 143–7.
United Nations (1996) *Platform for Action and the Beijing Declaration: Fourth World Conference on Women*, New York: United Nations.
Williams, F. (1995) "Race/Ethnicity, Gender, and Class in Welfare States: A Framework for Comparative Analysis," *Social Politics*, 2(2): 127–59.

8

The State and Economic Efficiency: A Behavioral Approach

Morris Altman

Introduction

According to standard neoclassical economic theory, institutions do not matter for understanding the process of economic change or why economies operate inefficiently. In contrast, a behavioral approach lets institutional parameters have a substantive impact on the economy. This paper argues that to understand economic efficiency one must understand the bargaining power of different players in the economic game and that this is critically affected by institutional parameters. Economic efficiency is not the natural product of competitive markets; rather, it is affected by the institutions within which markets operate, including the institutions that establish property and labor rights.

For neoclassical economists, market forces determine the direction of economic change and the level of economic efficiency. Since only efficient economies can survive the test of the market, institutions must evolve to enhance economic efficiency. Institutions might differ across time and space, but they must all contribute to economic efficiency, at least in the long run. Institutional development, therefore, can have neither analytical nor practical interest; and different institutions cannot help explain different levels of economic development. Moreover, at a micro level, different institutions cannot help explain differences in firm productivity. Institutions matter only if they can evolve in a different manner, and only if these different paths can persist in the long run. In this case, institutional change is subject to the choices made by individuals, where such choices are not completely constrained by the market.

Douglass North (1971, 1990, 1994) and Mancur Olson (1996, 2000) explain how institutions have been marginalized by conventional economic theory. Both argue that the neoclassical framework cannot deal with fundamental economic problems, such as persistent differences in economic development, because it ignores institutions. For North and Olson, neoclassical theory is basically price theory. It explains the allocation of scarce resources by rational individuals at a particular moment of time in a frictionless world. But this theory must be revised, they argue, because institutions determine the incentive structure within which economic agents make choices. Because the incentive structure in a particular institutional setting need not yield efficient choices, the incentive structure of institutions matters. Without understanding the evolution and content of this incentive structure we are left with an incomplete understanding of important economic issues.

According to North and Olson, incentive structures that result in inefficiencies can persist over time, and thereby affect economic change. Moreover, the relative bargaining power among different groups of economic agents helps determine the type of institutions that get developed. Those with the greatest bargaining power need not develop institutions that foster economic efficiency.

For North and Olson, efficiency-inducing institutions require private property rights that bring the private rate of return close to the social rate of return. It is this that makes efficient choices profitable. Ultimately, efficient institutions create an incentive structure that mimics what would prevail in a perfectly competitive environment, where no economic agent can affect prices, where there is no rent-seeking, and where all externalities are internalized. Such an institutional setting would also make predatory behavior unprofitable compared to productive economic activities (also see Parente & Prescott, 2000).

I argue below that private property rights alone need not result in an efficient economy. From a behavioral perspective, where work effort and the choice of technologies *can* deviate from some efficient norm, an inefficient economy can exist even when private property rights are secure. Moreover, a competitive environment is no guarantee of economic efficiency, although it can induce more efficiency on the margin. Freer trade, for example, can break the back of local monopolies, but need not result in an economy moving towards more efficient production.

North argues that in a world of positive transaction costs and imperfect competition, groups with the greatest bargaining power will choose an institutional framework that is socially inefficient. They make this choice because it is profitable for them to do so. Olson makes a similar argument. But at the end of the day, we are left with no explanation for these inefficient institutions and no explanation for why institutions do not become more efficient.

I also argue below that institutional change is partly a function of the relative power of economic agents in the labor markets. Increasing the bargaining power of labor creates incentives for socially efficient institutional change. For such change to take place, the right institutional decisions must be made. But this need not be the case. Decision makers will not construct institutions to achieve economic efficiency if this does not maximize their individual wealth and utility.

In our behavioral model, institutional change affects relative factor prices, especially labor costs, as well as the distribution property rights. This, in turn, affects labor costs and the distribution of income. In this scenario, economic efficiency is achieved under the pressure of tight labor markets that both induces investment in the "social capabilities" necessary for economic efficiency and the development of efficient economic enterprises at a micro level. If the state counters the efficiency-inducing effects of tight labor markets, the economy will fall into a low-wage and low-income competitive equilibrium that is inefficient. Market forces alone cannot get the economy out of this inefficient equilibrium; nor can it generate the incentives to make the economy more efficient. The state thus comes to play a vital role in determining whether or not an economy operates efficiently, and whether it develops economically. Understanding that choices exist for the state, and understanding what motivates these choices, provides us with a better understanding of why economic inefficiency has been the norm and how this norm might be changed.

Big bills left on the sidewalk

It is important to appreciate what economic efficiency means. Economic efficiency exists when an economy is on its outermost production possibility frontier or the outermost frontier of its aggregate production function. This frontier represents the maximum level of output that can be realized given factor endowments used at full capacity, prices, transaction costs, and the available technology. In a world of positive transaction costs, that is in the real world, the outermost frontier is one where transaction costs are minimized and property rights are maximized. It is also assumed that all economic agents are working as hard and as best they can. In other words, it is assumed that effort per unit of labor input is maximized and that effort is not a discretionary variable.

Using Harvey Leibenstein's (1966, 1978, 1979, 1987) terminology, the economy is assumed to be x-efficient. X-efficiency in production presumes that firm employees make effort choices involving "co-operation with peers, superiors, and subordinates, in such a way as to maximize their contribution to output" (Leibenstein, 1978: 206). If effort is not maximized, the economy would be x-inefficient and would not be maximizing output per unit of input. The potential existence of x-inefficiency, and its relationship to the institutional setting of an economy, is critical to our analysis of institutional inefficiency.

Effort discretion exists due to incomplete contracts and the different behavioral functions for firm employees and members of the firm hierarchy (Akerlof & Yellen, 1986; Altman, 1996; Miller, 1992; Stiglitz, 1987). By assuming the economy is x-efficient, neoclassical theory presumes that the quality and quantity of effort is not affected by the work environment either at the firm or national level. It assumes that x-efficient behavior is given, and results from either market forces or some moral imperative on the part of individuals (Altman, 1999b; Reder, 1982).

Critics of the neoclassical modeling of institutions, such as North and Olson, see the gap between the economy with the highest per capita output and other economies as a measure of economic inefficiency. The economy with the highest per capita output is on the outermost production possibility frontier, which is also assumed to be the x-efficient frontier. The gap between the outmost frontier and other production possibility frontiers represents bills lying on the sidewalk – an impossible scenario according to conventional economic thinking. This argument is illustrated in Figure 8.1, where XE represents the x-efficient frontier. Frontiers in the interior of XE are a product of inefficient institutions.

From the perspective of North and Olson, secure private property rights and competitive markets take us a long way towards XE. Building on the notion of an x-inefficiency, I argue below that institutional changes related to the work environment are also important in moving the economy to its outermost production possibility frontier. Secure property rights are not the only determinant of economic efficiency. An ideal set of private property rights might move an economy from cd to ab in Figure 8.1; however, additional institutional changes are required to drive the economy towards XE.

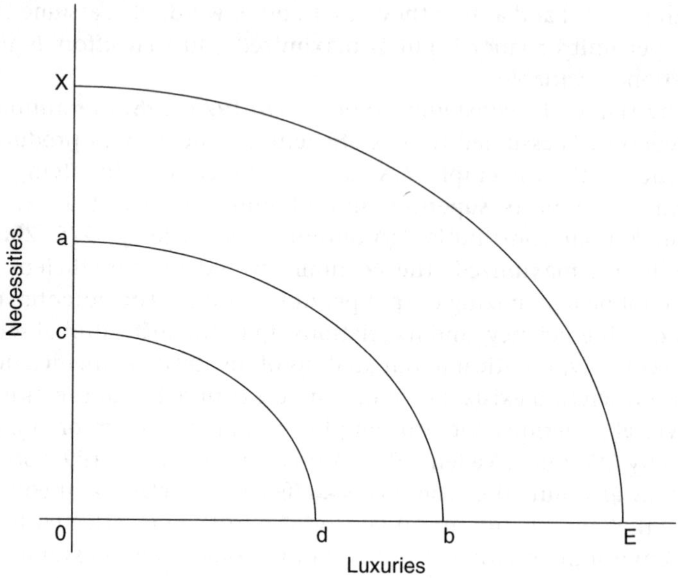

Figure 8.1 Economic Efficiency

Improvements to the level of x-efficiency can be broken down into the contribution of labor productivity and employment to per capita output, as in equation (1):

$$\frac{Q}{P} = \frac{Q}{L} * \frac{L}{P}, \qquad (1)$$

where Q is output, P is population and L is labor input or employment. Per capita output (Q/P) increases as labor productivity (Q/L) increases and as the employment rate (L/P) increases. This drives the production possibility frontier outward. Increasing the level of x-efficiency and introducing more efficient institutions or organizations will increase per capita output by increasing labor productivity, thereby pushing the economy towards its outermost production frontier. Less attention is typically paid to (L/P). However, more efficient institutions can also provide greater employment opportunities to those wanting to work; this too increases per capita output and shifts the production frontier outwards.

Neoclassical theory predicts that market forces will lead to a convergence of per capita output in the world economy. Competitive forces will push the production possibility frontier of every economy towards the most efficient one. Poorer economies will catch up to developed economies through trade and through the migration of capital and labor. The higher rates of labor compensation in wealthier economies will place them at a competitive disadvantage relative to their low-wage and low- output competitors. Any remaining gap (and one would not expect it to be large) would be due to relative differences in productive resources or transaction costs, and not due to unexploited gains from trade.

Unfortunately, the predicted income convergence has not occurred (Altman, 1999a; Baumol, 1986; Baumol & Wolff, 1988; DeLong, 1988; Pritchett, 1997). The extent to which a persistent per capita output gap persists in the world economy can be gleaned from the Heston & Summers (2001) international data set. Table 8.1 presents per capita output estimates for 107 countries. Omitted countries are largely low per capita output economies including Russia, the Ukraine, other formerly Eastern Block economies, and a few African states. Data are presented for 1960, 1973 (the oil crisis), and 1990. Countries are sorted by their 1990 per capita output ranking. If one assumes that the US represents the outermost production possibility frontier, given its number one ranking, the difference between US per capita output and per capita output in other countries represents an output gap; these are unrealized gains from trade or large bills lying on the sidewalk. Given that the omitted countries are relatively low per capita output economies, these output gap estimates are lower-bound.

From 1960 to 1973, the total output gap increased from $19 trillion to $37 trillion in constant 1985 US dollars. It jumped to $62 trillion dollars in 1990. This output gap varied widely in 1990, ranging from less than $1,000 in Canada to almost $18,000 in Chad. The output gap tended to diminish among high-income economies and increase among low-income economies. Per capita GDP increased for most economies even as the output gap increased.

Most striking was the sizable and growing gap between US per capita output and the per capita output in much poorer economies. Taking mainland China as an example, the per capita output gap increased from $9,000 to $14,000 from 1960 to 1973 and to $17,000 in 1990, even as China's per capita GDP more than doubled. India, another populous less-developed economy, witnessed an increase in its per capita gap from about $9,000 to $17,000 between 1960 and 1990, while its per capita GDP increase by about 65%.

To the extent that these enormous output gaps are a product of inefficient institutions, they represent, as Olson (1996) maintains, big

Table 8.1 Real GDP Per Capita and the Output Gap (constant dollars using Chain index in 1985 international prices)

	1960			1973			1990			Per capita GDP 1990/1960
	Per capita GDP	Per capita GDP deficit	Relative per capita GDP	Per capita GDP	Per capita GDP deficit	Relative per capita GDP	Per capita GDP	Per capita GDP deficit	Relative per capita GDP	
		USA=100	USA=100		USA=100	USA=100		USA=100	USA=100	
United States of America	9,895			14,379			18,054			1.82
Canada	7,258	2,637	0.734	11,854	2,525	0.824	17,173	881	0.951	2.37
Switzerland	9,409	486	0.951	13,905	474	0.967	16,505	1,549	0.914	1.75
Luxembourg	7,921	1,974	0.801	11,224	3,155	0.781	16,280	1,774	0.902	2.06
Norway	5,610	4,285	0.567	9,070	5,309	0.631	14,902	3,152	0.825	2.66
Hong Kong	2,247	7,648	0.227	5,758	8,621	0.400	14,849	3,205	0.822	6.61
Sweden	7,592	2,303	0.767	11,363	3,016	0.790	14,762	3,292	0.818	1.94
Australia	7,782	2,113	0.786	11,514	2,865	0.801	14,445	3,609	0.800	1.86
Germany, West	6,570	3,325	0.664	10,315	4,064	0.717	14,341	3,713	0.794	2.18
Japan	2,954	6,941	0.299	8,539	5,840	0.594	14,331	3,723	0.794	4.85
Finland	5,291	4,604	0.535	9,300	5,079	0.647	14,059	3,995	0.779	2.66
Denmark	6,760	3,135	0.683	10,613	3,766	0.738	13,909	4,145	0.770	2.06
France	5,823	4,072	0.588	10,316	4,063	0.717	13,904	4,150	0.770	2.39
Iceland	4,964	4,931	0.502	8,241	6,138	0.573	13,362	4,692	0.740	2.69
Belgium	5,495	4,400	0.555	9,485	4,894	0.660	13,232	4,822	0.733	2.41
United Kingdom	6,823	3,072	0.690	9,605	4,774	0.668	13,217	4,837	0.732	1.94
Netherlands	6,077	3,818	0.614	10,064	4,315	0.700	13,029	5,025	0.722	2.14
Austria	5,143	4,752	0.520	8,669	5,710	0.603	12,695	5,359	0.703	2.47
Italy	4,564	5,331	0.461	8,275	6,104	0.575	12,488	5,566	0.692	2.74
Singapore	1,658	8,237	0.168	4,757	9,622	0.331	11,710	6,344	0.649	7.06
New Zealand	7,960	1,935	0.804	10,631	3,748	0.739	11,513	6,541	0.638	1.45
Spain	3,123	6,772	0.316	6,943	7,436	0.483	9,583	8,471	0.531	3.07

Table 8.1 Real GDP Per Capita and the Output Gap (constant dollars using Chain index in 1985 international prices) – *continued*

	1960			1973			1990			Per capita GDP 1990/1960
	Per capita GDP	Per capita GDP deficit	Relative per capita GDP	Per capita GDP	Per capita GDP deficit	Relative per capita GDP	Per capita GDP	Per capita GDP deficit	Relative per capita GDP	
		USA=100	USA=100		USA=100	USA=100		USA=100	USA=100	
Israel	3,477	6,418	0.351	7,156	7,223	0.498	9,298	8,756	0.515	2.67
Ireland	3,311	6,584	0.335	5,595	8,784	0.389	9,274	8,780	0.514	2.80
Cyprus	2,037	7,858	0.206	4,693	9,686	0.326	8,368	9,686	0.463	4.11
Taiwan	1,256	8,639	0.127	2,914	11,465	0.203	8,063	9,991	0.447	6.42
Trinidad and Tobago	5,627	4,268	0.569	7,670	6,709	0.533	7,764	10,290	0.430	1.38
Portugal	1,869	8,026	0.189	4,459	9,920	0.310	7,478	10,576	0.414	4.00
Greece	2,093	7,802	0.212	5,208	9,171	0.362	6,768	11,286	0.375	3.23
Korea, Rep.	904	8,991	0.091	2,066	12,313	0.144	6,673	11,381	0.370	7.38
Venezuela	6,338	3,557	0.641	7,377	7,002	0.513	6,055	11,999	0.335	0.96
Mauritius	2,862	7,033	0.289	2,584	11,795	0.180	5,838	12,216	0.323	2.04
Mexico	2,836	7,059	0.287	4,609	9,770	0.321	5,827	12,227	0.323	2.05
Hungary	na	na	na	3,910	10,469	0.272	5,357	12,697	0.297	na
Malaysia	1,420	8,475	0.144	2,555	11,824	0.178	5,124	12,930	0.284	3.61
Argentina	4,462	5,433	0.451	5,926	8,453	0.412	4,706	13,348	0.261	1.05
Uruguay	3,968	5,927	0.401	4,098	10,281	0.285	4,602	13,452	0.255	1.16
Yugoslavia	1,921	7,974	0.194	3,669	10,710	0.255	4,548	13,506	0.252	2.37
Chile	2,885	7,010	0.292	3,615	10,764	0.251	4,338	13,716	0.240	1.50
Czechoslovakia	1,603	8,292	0.162	2,906	11,473	0.202	4,095	13,959	0.227	2.55
Brazil	1,784	8,111	0.180	3,228	11,151	0.224	4,042	14,012	0.224	2.27

Table 8.1 Real GDP Per Capita and the Output Gap (constant dollars using Chain index in 1985 international prices) – *continued*

	1960			1973			1990			Per capita GDP 1990/1960
	Per capita GDP	Per capita GDP deficit	Relative per capita GDP	Per capita GDP	Per capita GDP deficit	Relative per capita GDP	Per capita GDP	Per capita GDP deficit	Relative per capita GDP	
		USA=100	USA=100		USA=100	USA=100		USA=100	USA=100	
Fiji	2,108	7,787	0.213	3,183	11,196	0.221	4,007	14,047	0.222	1.90
Seychelles	1,258	8,637	0.127	1,821	12,558	0.127	3,973	14,081	0.220	3.16
Gabon	1,789	8,106	0.181	4,179	10,200	0.291	3,958	14,096	0.219	2.21
Syria	1,575	8,320	0.159	2,540	11,839	0.177	3,897	14,157	0.216	2.47
Poland	na	na	na	3,859	10,520	0.268	3,820	14,234	0.212	na
Turkey	1,622	8,273	0.164	2,471	11,908	0.172	3,741	14,313	0.207	2.31
Thailand	943	8,952	0.095	1,648	12,731	0.115	3,580	14,474	0.198	3.80
Costa Rica	2,096	7,799	0.212	3,232	11,147	0.225	3,499	14,555	0.194	1.67
Iran	2,946	6,949	0.298	5,780	8,599	0.402	3,392	14,662	0.188	1.15
Colombia	1,684	8,211	0.170	2,440	11,939	0.170	3,300	14,754	0.183	1.96
South Africa	2,191	7,704	0.221	3,408	10,971	0.237	3,248	14,806	0.180	1.48
Jordan	1,162	8,733	0.117	2,054	12,325	0.143	2,919	15,135	0.162	2.51
Tunisia	1,101	8,794	0.111	1,805	12,574	0.126	2,910	15,144	0.161	2.64
Panama	1,575	8,320	0.159	2,903	11,476	0.202	2,888	15,166	0.160	1.83
Namibia	1,790	8,105	0.181	3,595	10,784	0.250	2,854	15,200	0.158	1.59
Algeria	1,723	8,172	0.174	2,012	12,367	0.140	2,777	15,277	0.154	1.61
Ecuador	1,461	8,434	0.148	2,241	12,138	0.156	2,755	15,299	0.153	1.89
Jamaica	1,773	8,122	0.179	2,838	11,541	0.197	2,545	15,509	0.141	1.44
Congo	1,123	8,772	0.113	1,710	12,669	0.119	2,211	15,843	0.122	1.97
Peru	2,019	7,876	0.204	2,928	11,451	0.204	2,188	15,866	0.121	1.08
Dominican Rep.	1,195	8,700	0.121	1,916	12,463	0.133	2,166	15,888	0.120	1.81
Morocco	815	9,080	0.082	1,384	12,995	0.096	2,151	15,903	0.119	2.64

Table 8.1 Real GDP Per Capita and the Output Gap (constant dollars using Chain index in 1985 international prices) – *continued*

	1960			1973			1990			Per capita GDP 1990/1960
	Per capita GDP	Per capita GDP deficit	Relative per capita GDP	Per capita GDP	Per capita GDP deficit	Relative per capita GDP	Per capita GDP	Per capita GDP deficit	Relative per capita GDP	
		USA=100	USA=100		USA=100	USA=100		USA=100	USA=100	
Paraguay	1,177	8,718	0.119	1,522	12,857	0.106	2,128	15,926	0.118	1.81
Guatemala	1,660	8,235	0.168	2,193	12,186	0.153	2,127	15,927	0.118	1.28
Sri Lanka	1,259	8,636	0.127	1,253	13,126	0.087	2,096	15,958	0.116	1.66
Indonesia	638	9,257	0.064	831	13,548	0.058	1,974	16,080	0.109	3.09
Egypt	809	9,086	0.082	1,182	13,197	0.082	1,912	16,142	0.106	2.36
El Salvador	1,427	8,468	0.144	1,957	12,422	0.136	1,824	16,230	0.101	1.28
Philippines	1,133	8,762	0.115	1,532	12,847	0.107	1,763	16,291	0.098	1.56
Bolivia	1,148	8,747	0.116	1,803	12,576	0.125	1,658	16,396	0.092	1.44
Papua New Guinea	1,235	8,660	0.125	1,903	12,476	0.132	1,425	16,629	0.079	1.15
Pakistan	638	9,257	0.064	907	13,472	0.063	1,394	16,660	0.077	2.18
Bangladesh	952	8,943	0.096	756	13,623	0.053	1,390	16,664	0.077	1.46
Honduras	1,039	8,856	0.105	1,320	13,059	0.092	1,377	16,677	0.076	1.33
China	567	9,328	0.057	740	13,639	0.051	1,324	16,730	0.073	2.34
Nicaragua	1,606	8,289	0.162	2,357	12,022	0.164	1,294	16,760	0.072	0.81
India	766	9,129	0.077	786	13,593	0.055	1,264	16,790	0.070	1.65
Cameroon	641	9,254	0.065	830	13,549	0.058	1,226	16,828	0.068	1.91
Ivory Coast	1,120	8,775	0.113	1,694	12,685	0.118	1,213	16,841	0.067	1.08
Zimbabwe	989	8,906	0.100	1,203	13,176	0.084	1,182	16,872	0.065	1.20
Senegal	1,047	8,848	0.106	1,062	13,317	0.074	1,145	16,909	0.063	1.09
Guyana	1,596	8,299	0.161	1,998	12,381	0.139	1,094	16,960	0.061	0.69

Table 8.1 Real GDP Per Capita and the Output Gap (constant dollars using Chain index in 1985 international prices)
– continued

	1960			1973			1990			Per capita GDP 1990/1960
	Per capita GDP	Per capita GDP deficit	Relative per capita GDP	Per capita GDP	Per capita GDP deficit	Relative per capita GDP	Per capita GDP	Per capita GDP deficit	Relative per capita GDP	
		USA=100	USA=100		USA=100	USA=100		USA=100	USA=100	
Cape Verde Island	469	9,426	0.047	531	13,848	0.037	1,058	16,996	0.059	2.26
Nigeria	567	9,328	0.057	1,068	13,311	0.074	995	17,059	0.055	1.75
Lesotho	313	9,582	0.032	640	13,739	0.045	972	17,082	0.054	3.11
Benin	1,100	8,795	0.111	1,149	13,230	0.080	920	17,134	0.051	0.84
Kenya	659	9,236	0.067	804	13,575	0.056	911	17,143	0.050	1.38
Ghana	894	9,001	0.090	973	13,406	0.068	902	17,152	0.050	1.01
Sierra Leone	na	na	na	1,184	13,195	0.082	901	17,153	0.050	na
Gambia	602	9,293	0.061	869	13,510	0.060	799	17,255	0.044	1.33
Mauritania	780	9,115	0.079	850	13,529	0.059	791	17,263	0.044	1.01
Guinea	559	9,336	0.056	573	13,806	0.040	767	17,287	0.042	1.37
Mozambique	1,153	8,742	0.117	1,681	12,698	0.117	760	17,294	0.042	0.66
Sudan	na	na	na	705	13,674	0.049	757	17,297	0.042	na
Rwanda	537	9,358	0.054	621	13,758	0.043	756	17,298	0.042	1.41
Guinea-Bissau	503	9,392	0.051	856	13,523	0.060	689	17,365	0.038	1.37
Zambia	965	8,930	0.098	1,163	13,216	0.081	689	17,365	0.038	0.71
Madagascar	1,191	8,704	0.120	1,069	13,310	0.074	675	17,379	0.037	0.57
Togo	367	9,528	0.037	601	13,778	0.042	641	17,413	0.036	1.75
Central African Republic	704	9,191	0.071	731	13,648	0.051	579	17,475	0.032	0.82

Table 8.1 Real GDP Per Capita and the Output Gap (constant dollars using Chain index in 1985 international prices)
– continued

	1960			1973			1990			Per capita GDP 1990/1960
	Per capita GDP	Per capita GDP deficit	Relative per capita GDP	Per capita GDP	Per capita GDP deficit	Relative per capita GDP	Per capita GDP	Per capita GDP deficit	Relative per capita GDP	
		USA=100	USA=100		USA=100	USA=100		USA=100	USA=100	
Comoros	543	9,352	0.055	743	13,636	0.052	564	17,490	0.031	1.04
Uganda	598	9,297	0.060	634	13,745	0.044	554	17,500	0.031	0.93
Burundi	640	9,255	0.065	447	13,932	0.031	550	17,504	0.030	0.86
Mali	535	9,360	0.054	424	13,955	0.029	531	17,523	0.029	0.99
Malawi	380	9,515	0.038	479	13,900	0.033	519	17,535	0.029	1.37
Burkina Faso	456	9,439	0.046	376	14,003	0.026	511	17,543	0.028	1.12
Chad	756	9,139	0.076	722	13,657	0.050	399	17,655	0.022	0.53
Per capita average weighted GDP/USA per capita GDP		0.179			0.238			0.240		
Per capita average unweighted deficit		7,184			10,597			12,993		
Per capita average weighted deficit		8,127			10,952			13,723		
Total Bills on the sidewalk (000)		19,060,185,608			36,587,181,132			61,839,345,606		

Source: Derived from the data contained in the Penn State Tables, Heston and Summers (2001)

bills on the sidewalk just waiting to be picked up through the introduction of wise economic policy. The trillion dollar question becomes: what makes institutions inefficient and what drives institutional change?

A behavioral model of institutional inefficiency

Institutions are inefficient when an economy is inefficient. These inefficient institutions can exist at the firm level, or at the macro level where bad policy creates incentives affecting the choices at the firm level. North refers to macro institutions as fundamental institutions, whereas the firm is a secondary institution. The former are more difficult to change, especially if they are embodied in law. Secondary institutions (organizations) can change if there are changes in the fundamental institutions. These original changes, North points out, can also force changes in the fundamental institutions, either towards a more efficient or a less efficient economy (North & Thomas, 1970; North, 1990: chs 1, 2).

For our purposes, what is important is that macro institutions establish the rules of the game within which economic agents and organizations engage in decision-making – an argument quite similar to that of Hayek (1944). These decisions are not completely constrained by the fundamental organizations in society such as government policy or the law. In turn, decisions at the firm level or in the labor market can affect government policy and the legal infrastructure of society.

The issue of institutional or organizational inefficiency can be examined at various levels. We examine this at the firm level, through the lenses of a behavioral model, building on the x-efficiency and efficiency wage literature. A key proposition here is that the quantity and quality of effort, and technological change, are choice variables in the production function. Effort inputs and technical change affect productivity and output per capita. A society where effort levels are higher and technological change is greater (i.e., more productive technology is employed) is a society with higher per capita output. It can realize higher levels of socio-economic well-being such as lower mortality and morbidity rates, higher rates of life expectancy, and higher rates of education. Such a society is closest to the outermost production possibility frontier – the neoclassical ideal. In the behavioral model developed below, firms not only fail to realize the ideal level of output, but such inefficiency is also compatible with competitive markets and rational choice among firm decision makers. This possibility is denied not only by neoclassical theory, but also in the critical work of Leibenstein, North, Olson, and Parente & Prescotte.

Ceteris paribus, assuming constant technology, less effort per unit of labor input translates into higher average product costs. This point is clear from the following equations where, for simplicity, it is assumed that labor is the only factor input:

$$AC = \frac{wL}{Q}, \tag{2}$$

where AC is average cost, w is the wage rate, Q is output, and L is labor input.
This equation can be transformed into equation (3):

$$AC = \frac{w}{\frac{Q}{L}} \tag{3}$$

where average cost (AC) is a product of the weighted input costs deflated by the weighted average productivity of factor inputs. As effort increases, so does Q, yielding a higher level of labor productivity and a lower AC. Reducing effort, on the other hand, reduces labor productivity, thereby increasing the average cost of production. In a competitive product market, relatively x-inefficient firms (those with lower levels of effort) will fall by the wayside or be forced to into performing x-efficiently. Leibenstein (1966, 1979) argues that x-inefficiency tends to subside as product markets become more competitive.

But x-inefficient firms need not be swept aside, nor need they be forced into becoming more efficient once non-market variables that affect the level of x-efficiency are brought into the analysis. In the behavioral model, work culture and firm organizational structure, which includes the rates of labor compensation as well as the system of industrial relations embodied in the firm, determines the level of x-efficiency achieved by the firm. It is now well-recognized that this is the case (Altman, 2001: ch. 9; Ichniowski, Kochan, Levine, Olson & Strauss, 1996; Gordon, 1998; Levine & Tyson, 1990).

Increasing firm efficiency imposes costs on the firm in terms of increased wages, improved working conditions, more investment in physical capital, and an altered power structure within the firm. It might also involve reducing the percentage of the firm members at the top of the firm hierarchy, reducing their relative rate of compensation, or increasing their work effort. Therefore, changes in the level of x-efficiency are associated with both benefits and costs. There is no reason to expect that more x-inefficiency yields higher unit costs or that less x-inefficiency yields lower unit costs. In terms of equations (2) and (3), assuming that *w* is a proxy for all costs incurred in altering the firm's level of x-inefficiency, changes in the level of x-inefficiency, by affecting the level of labor productivity (*Q/L*), will not change average costs if labor costs (*w*) change sufficiently to negate the impact which changes in the level of x-inefficiency would otherwise have on unit costs. In this case, it would be possible for one level of average cost to be associated with an array of labor costs, up to the point that one enters into the realm of diminishing returns and increasing labor costs can no longer be compensated by increasing the firm's level of x-efficiency.

In Figure 8.2, unit costs (0a) do not change as labor costs change up to point b. Thereafter, unit costs increase with higher labor costs and benefits, and improved working conditions. In this scenario, both x-efficient and x-inefficient firms can co-exist in competitive product market equilibrium. Making an economy more competitive need not result in firms becoming more x-efficient since relative x-inefficiency need not generate higher unit production costs. In this case, reducing

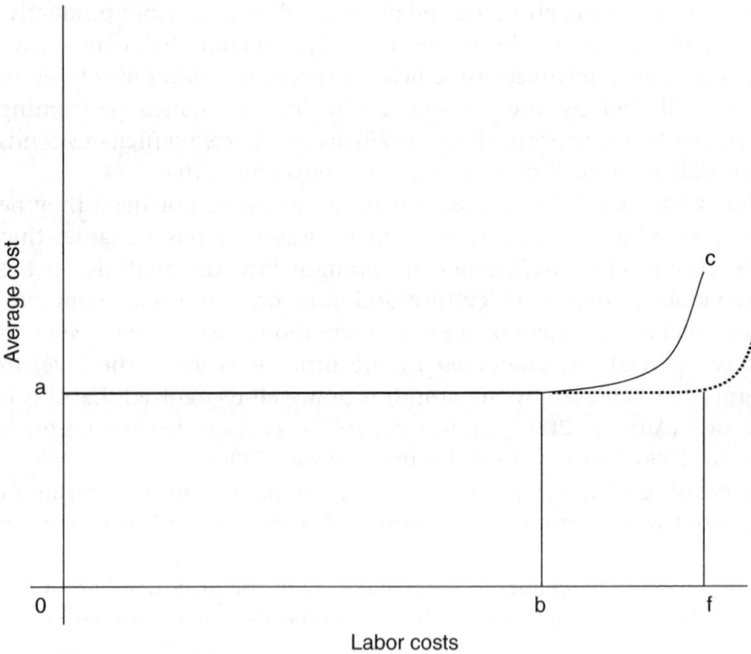

Figure 8.2 Unit Production Costs and X-Efficiency

labor costs need not make a firm more competitive and increasing labor costs need not make a firm less competitive, since changes in labor costs are causally related to the level of x-efficiency achieved by the firm.

In contemporary market economies many firms fail to employ more x-efficient work organizations or cultures (Altman, 2001: ch. 9; Levine & Tyson, 1990). This is true despite the fact that increasing the level of x-efficiency benefits society as a whole through its impact on labor productivity and per capita output. Workers stand to benefit most from more x-efficient work organizations. However, in a typical multi-person firm, the cost and benefits from making the firm more efficient are not shared equally by all economic agents. For simplicity, we may divide firm members into two groups, workers and the firm hierarchy, where the latter group makes key decisions in the firm. Assuming that members of the firm hierarchy are rational (calculating and forward-looking), they will not choose a more efficient organizational form if it is not utility maximizing from their perspective to do so, given the binding constraint that their firm must remain cost competitive. To the extent that more x-efficiency in the firm benefits workers (which will be true unless the firm hierarchy internalizes all the benefits realized by more efficient workers), there is no reason for members of the firm hierarchy to choose a more efficient organizational structure. In addition, many members of the firm hierarchy will not be receptive to power-sharing with workers and many managers believe that they will be disadvantaged by a shift away from the traditional work culture. Also there are considerable short-run costs to adopting and developing a more efficient work organization, while benefits generally appear in the more distant future. Such long-run returns can be problematic because the institutional environment supports large short-run returns that can be more easily realized in the traditional work culture.

Given these constraints, it is rational and utility maximizing for the firm hierarchy to reject more efficient systems of work organization – despite the social costs of such a decision. Picking up big bills does not occur without a cost. When those who make the decisions about whether or not to pick up the big bills see little benefit for themselves in hunting and gathering them on the sidewalk, big bills will remain there and society will fall short of its outermost production possibility frontier. Self-interest speaks against x-efficient choices being made. Nevertheless, many firms have adopted more efficient organizational forms across an array of different macro-institutional environments.

From the perspective of the behavioral model, the work culture of a firm depends on pressures placed on the firm hierarchy to adopt more efficient organizations in terms of labor costs, the macro-institutional environment that affects the costs of introducing new organizational forms, and the preferences of the firm hierarchy. Where the latter incorporates the utility of workers, the probability that the firm hierarchy will choose a more efficient work culture or organization increases if such a choice does not damage the firm's competitive position. In the behavioral model, competitive market forces cannot, by themselves, pressure firms into adopting more efficient work cultures or organizational structures when both the efficient and the inefficient work environment are cost competitive. Moreover, competitive pressure is not even a necessary condition for more efficient organizational structures to be adopted. Changing preferences by the firm hierarchy, or changing constraints imposed by the state, can lead to more efficient organizational forms. However, given competitive conditions, hierarchical preferences, and state imposed constraints, labor market pressure on the firm is a key determinant of whether or not the firm's organization or work culture is relatively x-efficient.

This argument can be extended to the realm of technical change; that is, whether or not a firm adopts an available technology. Technical change must be at the forefront of any explanation of different levels of labor productivity. Our behavioral model suggests that different levels of x-efficiency can also be an important explanatory variable. Technical change shifts the production possibility frontier outwards through its impact of labor productivity as seen in equation (3). If firms that produce similar goods and services adopt technologies with different productivities, different levels of per capita output will characterize these firms. Altman (1998; 2001: chs 2, 6) shows how technical change may differ across firms and economies, with many economic entities making rational choices (from the perspective of decision makers) that result in firms and economies falling inside the outermost production possibility frontier.

The behavioral model assumes that technological change is a function of relative production costs. This relates to the theory of induced technical change (Hayami & Ruttan, 1971; Ruttan, 1997) and to the role of effort discretion in determining technological change (Leibenstein, 1973). Therefore, technological change is not exogenously determined, nor is it simply a function of investments in human capital or research and development (Aghion & Howitt, 1998; Romer, 1990, 1994). In the behavioral model, high-wage firms are induced to adopt more productive technologies. These firms may also find it worthwhile to innovate, and to invest in research and development. Low-wage firms will not adopt new technology if they can compete on the basis of low wages. Moreover, in low-wage regimes, labor may be too x-inefficient for new technology to be cost-effective. If the new technology were to be adopted by all firms, it must be cost effective in the sense of lowering unit costs to all firms, even to low-wage firms. In this case, any firm not adopting the new technology will lose their competitive edge. When new technology yields such a threshold effect, the production function shifts out for all firms (Rosenberg, 1982: 3–33). Unless new technology has such a threshold effect, it is possible that an array of technologies will be used by firms producing an identical output, and that the most productive technology will be used by firms with the highest labor costs. Moreover, in this scenario, the more productive technology need not generate lower unit costs than the less productive technology since the higher productivity yielded by the more productive technology compensates the firm for its higher labor costs. Therefore, competitive pressures alone cannot force convergence in the use of technology.

More productive technologies, however, make it economically viable to increase wages and improve working conditions without compromising the competitive position of the firm. In terms of Figure 8.2, technological change shifts the cost curve from ac to ad, allowing labor costs to increase from 0b to 0f; but it will not increase average costs. Without technical change, increasing labor costs beyond 0b raises average costs, since improvements in the level of x-efficiency are exhausted.

One can generalize from the firm level to the economy-wide level. To the extent that an economy consists of x-inefficient firms, it can remain x-inefficient, even in the face of competition from relatively x-efficient firms, as long as their x-efficient competitors cannot produce at relatively lower unit costs. Moreover, in this scenario, where x-efficiency is causally related to higher wages and better working conditions, there is no reason to expect convergence between the relatively x-efficient and x-inefficient economies, or between low-output and high-output economies. Since different levels of x-efficiency mean different work cultures, there is no reason to expect that competition will induce convergence in firm organization towards x-efficient production. However, increased efficiency in the firm can be induced by changes in labor costs, which in turn can be affected by macroeconomic variables. Higher labor costs pressure firms to become more efficient and more technologically advanced. In the absence of increased efficiency and technological progress, unit costs will rise. Alternatively, lower labor costs allow firms to remain x-inefficient and technological laggards. Changes in the level of efficiency can also result from preference changes by decision makers within the firm for more x-efficient organizational forms.

The behavioral model helps explain how inefficient institutions can persist over time, even in the face of competitive pressures. Neoclassical theory dismisses institutional analysis by assuming that market forces will push institutions to become efficient. It argues that economic development will precede *post haste* with the removal of trade barriers and other obstacles to the competitive process. Such reasoning is not far removed from the critiques of neoclassical theory by North and Olson. However, they both emphasize the role of government in constructing efficient institutions.

The behavioral model suggests that competitive pressures need not result in efficient institutions, even if private property rights are guaranteed over the short run and the long run. Economic inefficiency can persist as long as inefficient firms remain competitive. On the other hand, given the level of product market competition, the level of economic efficiency can be elevated by labor market pressures that induce the firm hierarchy to develop more efficient organizational structures. Thus, the behavioral model suggests that a key to understanding institutional efficiency is to understand the causes of x-inefficiency and induced technical change. An understanding of markets and private property rights remain an important part of the causal story, but it is only one part of the story.

Bargaining power and induced institutional change

In the behavioral model, as in North's analytical framework, bargaining power is important in determining the extent to which institutions are efficient. North argues that institutions are not designed to be socially efficient. Rather, they are designed to serve the interests of those with decision-making power (North, 1990: 6, 79, 86; 1994: 361). For North (1990: 9, 67), the critical dimension of bargaining power is the capacity of entrepreneurs and power-brokers to exploit their positions of power and to secure economic gain on their own behalf. These activities are a product of a society's institutional setting, and are considered to be rational and efficient from the perspective of these individuals; but they are not socially efficient. In such a society, individuals become privately efficient and socially inefficient. These activities are, in effect, predatory, or economically unproductive, knowingly leaving many large bills on the sidewalk and imposing significant deadweight losses on society (see Olson, 2000: chs 1, 2). Such behavior is largely attributed to the lack of competitive pressures and insecure private property rights. Institutions that increase labor power, such as unions and minimum wages, are viewed as inefficiency-inducing institutions, which is consistent with the neoclassical worldview (Altman, 1999b).[1]

In contrast to this line of argument, the behavioral model suggests that strengthening the bargaining power of labor induces firms to engage in efficiency-enhancing behavior, and to adopt and develop an efficient organization. Greater bargaining power for labor increases labor costs and makes firms less competitive unless they adjust to this new constraint by becoming more productive, either by increasing the level of x-efficiency or by introducing more productive technology.[2] In other words, increasing the bargaining power of labor can pressure firms into becoming more productive. The enhanced bargaining power of labor can result from a variety of factors including unionization, minimum wages, tight labor markets that are a product of demographic change relative to the availability of jobs or macroeconomic policy, and social security. Greater bargaining power for labor filters upwards to transform the macroeconomic institutions and pressures the firm to engage in efficiency-enhancing behavior if it is to survive. At the macro level, this might involve investment in economic infrastructure or rewriting laws and legislation, thereby making macro-institutions more efficient. As North (1990) argues, dynamic changes at the micro-level can trigger the necessary macro-institutional changes.[3]

But various alternatives to becoming more efficient are available to the firm when labor costs rise. The firm can invest in instruments that protect it from competitive pressures. It can lobby the government to provide protection to products produced by the firm. Such protection serves to redistribute income to the firm as its prices rise to cover increased labor costs. The firm can also invest in instruments that reduce the bargaining power of labor. This can take the form of lobbying government to ban or reduce the power of unions, reduce or abolish minimum wages, and weaken or abandon the social security network such as unemployment insurance, socialized healthcare, and welfare. But such advocacy must pass the political litmus test and filter of democratic politics. Overthrowing democracy is another alternative, and many market economies remain undemocratic with limited labor and related human rights. In the distant past, weakening the bargaining power of labor took the form of landlords lobbying the state to weaken the bargaining power of the peasant population by introducing organizational forms such as serfdom or slavery (Blum, 1957; Brenner, 1985; Domar, 1970). When successful in constraining the power of labor, economic decision makers were capable of producing competitively, albeit inefficiently. Big bills were left on the sidewalk, but economic decision makers did not have an incentive to hunt and gather big bills when they could do quite well in an inefficient economy with poorly compensated labor.

In the behavioral model, factor price changes (as mediated through the labor market) play a key role in affecting institutional change. Efficient institutional change at the micro and macro levels is induced by factors that enhance the bargaining power of labor. Therefore, whether or not efficient institutional change takes place depends on the state. The state can encourage and facilitate greater bargaining power for labor. Or, state policy can have the opposite effect. For this reason, understanding the direction of institutional change requires understanding how the state might respond to changes in factor prices. Only a state interested in improving the socio-economic position of labor, in the context of an economy that allows for and encourages firms to respond efficiently to increasing labor costs, can behave in a fashion that will enhance efficiency in the economy. Therefore, one cannot predict the direction of institutional change simply by understanding the impact of market forces on the bargaining power of labor. Such bargaining power is mediated by the state. How the state reacts to such pressure by affecting the bargaining power of labor will determine the direction of institution change. However, one can expect a positive relationship between the extent of labor market pressures, and the extent of economic efficiency and the level of socio-economic well-being.

The democratic state

A democratic state can facilitate efficiency in production given existing labor market pressures. In a democracy, where representatives of the public set the macro rules of the game, labor can be better represented than in an undemocratic state, where such representation is unlikely and where labor rights are not guaranteed by law. Democracy can guarantee labor rights so that firms will have an incentive to become economically efficient. This is possible because, in a democracy, labor has the right to vote for candidates it believes represent its best interests. Also, in a democracy labor has some voice in both corporate and public governance, even when this voice does not always have legislative representation. Moreover, this voice has a higher probability of being supplemented by transparency in both levels of governance.[4] A democracy that develops an efficient economic framework is one where workers, broadly defined, reap significant benefits from the process of economic growth without impairing the private property and contract incentives required to generate growth in a market economy. These benefits contribute to the process of economic growth and thus to efficient and effective big bill production, hunting, and gathering.[5]

There is no guarantee that democracy will establish rules of the games to maximize economic efficiency from a social perspective. Much depends on who gets elected and whose interest they represent. Much also depends on the models that elected representatives use to evaluate proposed policy changes. With incorrect models of the economy, elected officials will pursue socially suboptimal and inefficient policies. Such policies may serve the economic interests of particular groups at the expense of the entire society. For example, if politicians think that unions and labor rights are bad for the economy, they will support legislation to weaken unions and labor rights. But this will make the economy less efficient and will reduce the economic well-being of workers. A necessary condition for a democracy to be efficient is, therefore, that the models individuals use to evaluate and interpret the economy are brought into line with correct models that accurately reflect the workings of the economy (North, 1990: 109).[6]

To the extent that good models are in place, the probability of democracy generating efficiency-enhancing rules of the game increases when the elected group represents a larger percentage of the total population. The probability of predatory behavior diminishes as the group in power is more representative. The same can be said for efficiency-enhancing policy. Democracy increases the probability that groups in power have a greater stake in current and future losses and gains to society generated by their economic policy.

Both North and Olson focus on democracy as a necessary institution for sustained economic growth because of its capacity to nurture and sustain private property rights. For example, Olson (2000: 42) argues that "the only societies where individual rights to property and contract are confidently expected to last across generations are securely democratic societies. In an autocracy, the autocrat often has a short time horizon, and the absence of an independent power to assure an orderly legal succession means that there is always substantial uncertainty about what will happen when the current autocrat is gone." But North and Olson pay no heed to labor rights which, according to neoclassical wisdom, are seen as creating inefficiencies.

Given the importance of democracy for securing private property and contract rights, and thus economic efficiency, the behavioral model suggests that there is another dimension to the story of the construction of efficient economies. Labor rights and power represent another set of necessary conditions for the realization of economic efficiency. Democracy increases the probability that labor rights and powers will be realized, irrespective of the state of the market. It induces firms to perform in a more x-efficient and technologically beneficial fashion. Secure private property and contract rights alone will not lead to efficient behavior because, absent secure labor rights and power, the x-inefficient route to production becomes a cost-competitive and profitable option.

Conclusion

To the extent that institutional change is induced by changes in the bargaining power of labor, whether efficient institutional change takes place depends on whether the political-institutional framework allows labor to increase its bargaining power. This, in turn, depends on the role taken by the state. Typically, the bargaining power of labor has been suppressed by forms of serfdom or autocratic restrictions on labor bargaining rights and mobility (as under Communist, Fascist and other totalitarian regimes) that yielded benefits to small unrepresentative groups while generating inefficient results. In contemporary democratic market economies labor power is affected by macroeconomic employment policy and by government regulatory policy with respect to unions, unemployment insurance, and minimum wages. Economic theory cannot predict whether government will support or hinder the bargaining power of labor.

The behavioral model suggests that enhancing the bargaining power of labor, and then letting firms respond to higher labor costs, will promote economic efficiency and technological progress. In terms of public policy, this implies that private property rights and competitive markets, by themselves, are no guarantee of economic prosperity. Inefficient economic behavior can take place within such an institutional context. Labor rights are also required for an economy to move towards its outermost production possibility frontier, allowing laggard economies to catch up with the leaders. Labor rights can therefore be viewed as a component of a human rights bundle (Ignatieff, 2001) critical to democratic governance. Economic theory, however, cannot specify the micro-details of such labor rights, which are context dependent.

The neoclassical view that enhancing labor rights and bargaining power is antithetical to economic success is found seriously wanting from the perspective of the behavioral model. Moreover, policy that flows out of this perspective, such as restricting labor rights and the ability to organize, only serves to reduce economic efficiency. Since both inefficient and efficient economies can be cost competitive and provide utility-maximizing income to key decision makers, there is no guarantee that macro-institutional changes will maximize a society's efficiency.

What is in the private interest of the few need not be socially optimal, since the utility of decision makers does not incorporate the utility of the many unless altruism enters into decision makers' utility function or decision makers are forced to do so by dint of labor rights and labor power. Democracy, by allowing the economic interests of more groups to be represented, increases the odds that macro rules of the game will be designed to enhance efficiency. But much depends on how voters and their representatives understand the economic implications of public policy.[7]

Notes

1. Whether or not income redistribution, *ceteris paribus*, enhances or diminishes economic efficiency depends on what is done with this income. Neoclassical theory assumes that income redistribution is at best a zero-sum game where there is always a loser, and sees income redistribution as increasing inefficiency. Olson (2000: Ch. 1) recognizes that the state can use its redistributive power to enhance an economy's productivity. But this would only be the case when the agents of the state can secure a large fraction of any increase in productivity or when it represents individuals who do the same. In general, redistribution is viewed as enhancing inefficiency. This is especially true of any sort of monopolistic behavior (apart from natural monopolies). However, as Lane (1958, 1975) argues, much depends on what is done with the transferred income. Is it used to build productive infrastructure, for war, or for conspicuous consumption? (Also see Baran, 1969.) The behavioral model suggests that the state can be induced to spend its income in an efficiency-enhancing manner in the context of relatively tight labor markets to facilitate an economy's competitiveness as labor costs increase. For a critique of the conventional perspective of income redistribution see Aghion, Caroli & García-Peñalosa (1999) and Altman (2000).
2. Habbakkuk (1962) argues that the key to US industrial dynamism in the 19th century, compared to Britain's relatively laggard economic performance, was the tight labor market in the US, which generated high wages and forced firms to become relatively more productive and technologically progressive.
3. See Abramovitz (1986) on the significance of developing the necessary social capacity for economic development to proceed.

4. Stiglitz (1999) emphasizes the importance of voice, participation, and openness in both the corporate and public domains. These variables facilitate and contribute to the process of both long-run and short-run economic growth. Sen (1999, 2000) emphasizes the importance of democratic governance as a positive "good" with no opportunity costs for growth and with positive implications for the level of socio-economic well-being.
5. The view that democracy negatively impacts the growth process, especially for less-developed economies, has been challenged by Sen (1999, 2000) and Stiglitz (1999). (See also the UNDP, 2002.) The empirical work of Shen (2002) strongly suggests that there is a positive causal relationship between democratic forms of governance and economic growth, but the met-analysis of Przeworski & Limongi (1993) suggests no clear empirical relationship between democracy and growth.
6. This speaks to the importance of institutions, including educational institutions and the media, which affect how individuals construct models of the economy to inform their decision-making.
7. This paper was originally presented at the Eastern Economic Association meetings in New York, February 22–25, 2001. Thanks to Louise Lamontagne as well as to Christine Rider, my discussant, for their helpful comments and suggestions.

References

Abramovitz, M. (1986) "Catching Up, Forging Ahead, and Falling Behind," *Journal of Economic History*, 46: 385–406.

Aghion, P., Caroli, E. & García-Peñalosa, C. (1999) "Inequality and Economic Growth: The Perspective of the New Growth Theories," *Journal of Economic Literature*, 37: 1615–60.

Aghion, P. & Howitt, P. (1998) *Endogeneous Growth Theory*. Cambridge: MIT Press.

Akerlof, G.A. & Yellen, J. (eds) (1986) *Efficiency Wage Models of the Labor Market*, Cambridge, UK & New York: Cambridge University Press.

Altman, M. (1996) *Human Agency and Material Welfare: Revisions in Microeconomics and their Implications for Public Policy*, Boston: Kluwer Academic Publishers.

Altman, M. (1998) "A High Wage Path to Economic Growth and Development," *Challenge*, 41: 91–104.

Altman, M. (1999a) "Social Capacity and Convergence," in P. O'Hara (ed.) *Encyclopedia of Political Economy*, London: Routledge, pp. 1033–5.

Altman, M. (1999b) "The Methodology of Economics and the Survivor Principle Revisited and Revised: Some Welfare and Public Policy Implications of Modeling the Economic Agent," *Review of Social Economics*, 57: 427–9.

Altman, M. (2000) "A Behavioral Theory of Economic Welfare and Economic Justice: A Smithian Alternative to Pareto Optimality," *International Journal of Social Economics*, 27: 1098–131.

Altman, M. (2001) *Worker Satisfaction and Economic Performance: The Microfoundations of Economic Success and Failure*, Armonk, New York: M.E. Sharpe.

Baran, P. (1969) [1953] "Economic Progress and Economic Surplus," in J. O'Neill (ed.) *Paul A. Baran, The Longer View: Essay Toward a Critique of Political Economy*, New York & London: Monthly Review Press, pp. 271–307.

Baumol, W. (1986) "Productivity Growth, Convergence, and Welfare: What the Long-Run Data Show," *American Economic Review*, 76: 1072–85.
Baumol, W. & E.N. Wolff (1988) "Productivity Growth, Convergence, and Welfare: Reply," *American Economic Review*, 78: 1155–9.
Blum, J. (1957) "The Rise of Serfdom in Eastern Europe," *American Historical Review*, 62: 807–36.
Brenner, R. (1985) "Agrarian Class Structure and Economic Development in Pre-Industrial Europe," in T.H. Aston & C.H.E. Philpin (eds) *The Brenner Debate: Agrarian Class Structure and Economic Development in Pre-Industrial Europe*, Cambridge: Cambridge University Press, pp. 10–63.
DeLong, B.J. (1988) "Productivity Growth, Convergence, and Welfare: Comment," *American Economic Review*, 78: 1138–54.
Domar, E.D. (1970) "The Causes of Slavery or Serfdom: A Hypothesis," *Journal of Economic History*, 30: 18–32.
Gordon, D.M. (1998) "Conflict and Cooperation: An Empirical Glimpse of the Imperatives of Efficiency and Redistribution," in S. Bowles & H. Gintis (eds) *Recasting Egalitarianism: New Rules for Communities, States and Markets*, London: Verso, pp. 181–207.
Habbakkuk, H.J. (1962) *American and British Technology in the Nineteenth Century: The Search for Labour-Saving Inventions*, Cambridge: Cambridge University Press.
Hayami, Y. & Ruttan, V.W. (1971) *Agricultural Development: An International Perspective*, Baltimore: Johns Hopkins University Press.
Hayek, F.A. (1944) *The Road to Serfdom*, Chicago: University of Chicago Press.
Heston, A. & Summers, R. (2001) The Penn World Tables (Mark 5.6), http://datacentre.chass.utoronto.ca:5680/pwt/index.html.
Ichniowski, C., Kochan, T.A., Levine, D., Olson, C. & Strauss, G. (1996) "What Works at Work: Overview and Assessment," *Industrial Relations*, 35: 299–333.
Ignatieff, M. (2001) *Human Rights as Politics and Idolatry*, Princeton: Princeton University Press.
Lane, F.C. (1958) "The Economic Consequences of Organized Violence," *Journal of Economic History*, 18: 401–17.
Lane, F.C. (1975) "The Role of Governments in Economic Growth in Early Modern Times," *Journal of Economic History*, 35: 8–17.
Leibenstein, H. (1966) "Allocative Efficiency vs. 'X-Efficiency'," *American Economic Review*, 56: 392–415.
Leibenstein, H. (1973) "Notes on X-Efficiency and Technical Change." In E.B. Ayal (ed.) *Micro-Aspects of Development*. New York: Praeger, pp. 18–38.
Leibenstein, H. (1978) "X-Inefficiency Xists – Reply to an Xorcist," *American Economic Review*, 68(1): 203–11.
Leibenstein, H. (1979) "A Branch of Economics is Missing: Micro-Micro Theory," *Journal of Economic Literature*, 17(2). 477–502.
Leibenstein, H. (1987) *Inside the Firm: The Inefficiencies of Hierarchy*, Cambridge & London: Harvard University Press.
Levine, D.I. & Tyson, L. (1990) "Participation, Productivity, and the Firm's Environment," in A. Blinder (ed.) *Paying for Productivity: A Look at the Evidence*, Washington, D.C.: Brookings Institute, pp. 183–237.
Miller, G. (1992) *Managerial Dilemmas: The Political Economy of Hierarchy*, New York: Cambridge University Press.

North, D.C. & Thomas, R.B. (1970) "An Economic Theory of the Growth of the Western World," *Economic History Review*, 23: 1–17.
North, D.C. (1971) "Institutional Change and Economic Growth," *Journal of Economic History*, 31: 118–25.
North, D.C. (1990) *Institutions, Institutional Change and Economic Performance*, New York: Cambridge University Press.
North, D.C. (1994) "Economic Performance Through Time," *American Economic Review*, 84: 359–68.
Olson, M. (1996) "Big Bills Left on the Sidewalk: Why Some Nations are Rich, and Others Poor," *Journal of Economic Perspectives*, 10: 3–24.
Olson, M. (2000) *Power and Prosperity: Outgrowing Communist and Capitalist Dictatorships*, New York: Basic Books.
Parente, L. & Prescott, E.C. (2000) *Barriers to Riches*, Cambridge & London: MIT Press.
Przeworski, A. & Limongi, F. (1993) "Political Regimes and Economic Growth," *Journal of Economic Perspectives*, 7: 51–69.
Pritchett, L. (1997) "Divergence, Big Time," *Journal of Economic Perspectives*, 11: 3–17.
Reder, M.W. (1982) "Chicago Economics: Permanence and Change," *Journal of Economic Literature*, 20: 1–38.
Romer, P.M. (1990) "Endogenous Technical Change," *Journal of Political Economy*, 98: S71–S102.
Romer, P.M. (1994) "The Origins of Endogenous Growth," *Journal of Economic Perspectives*, 8: 3–22.
Rosenberg, N. (1982) *Inside the Black Box: Technology and Economics*. Cambridge, UK: Cambridge University Press.
Ruttan, V.W. (1997) "Induced Innovation, Evolutionary Theory and Path Dependence: Sources of Technical Change," *Economic Journal*, 107: 1520–9.
Sen, A.K. (1999) "Democracy as a Universal Value," *Journal of Democracy*, 10: 3–17
Sen, A.K. (2000) *Development as Freedom*. New York: Anchor Books.
Shen, J.G. (2002) "Democracy and Growth: An Alternative Empirical Approach," Discussion Paper, 13, Bank of Finland, Institute for Economies in Transition, BOFIT.
Stiglitz, J.E. (1987) "The Causes and Consequences of the Dependence of Quantity on Price," *Journal of Economic Literature*, 25: 1–48.
Stiglitz, J. E. (1999) "The Role of Participation in Development," Development Outreach, The World Bank Group: *Http://www1.worldbank.org/devoutreach/summer99/article.asp?id=5*.
UNDP (2002) *Human Development Report 2002: Deepening Democracy in a Fragmented World*, New York & Oxford: Oxford University Press.

9

Making the Menu: Russia's Recipe for Calculating Political-economy Constraints

Peter J. Boettke and Bridget I. Butkevich

Introduction

When the Berlin Wall fell in 1989, Western economists were asked for advice on how to manage the transition from a state-controlled economy to a market economy. This task has proven more difficult than first imagined. One source of difficulty is that the transition to the market is less a process to be managed and more a process to be observed.[1] Nonetheless, the standard advice was straightforward. If consumers suffered under the old state-administered economy from a shortage of consumer goods, then reform would allow prices to fluctuate equilibrating supply and demand.[2] If the system suffered from production inefficiencies due to perverse incentives caused by state ownership of enterprise, then reform would privatize enterprises.[3] Finally, if the system had macroeconomic imbalances due to the soft-budget constraints needed to subsidize inefficient firms and maintain a cradle-to-grave social safety net, then reform would harden those budget constraints and restructure the social safety net.[4]

In short, the conception of the role of the state in economic life had to be radically transformed, moving the economy from state-control to a more *laissez-faire* system. Changing the public's conception of the state involves changing the public's expectations of the economic role that the government plays. This paper examines the evolution of economic expectations held by Russians about their government and the evolution of the government's relationship with the market and the public.

During the 1917 transition in Soviet history, the state was viewed as the mid-wife of the revolution. The "dictatorship of the proletariat," represented by the Bolshevik party vanguard, would usher in a new order through the use of state power; the state would then wither away. In the more recent transition period, the state was also expected to wither away as the power of the market replaced state power in the exchange and production of goods and services.[5] Just as those responsible for the first transition period underestimated the problems of bureaucracy and the interest group dynamics that would prevent the state from withering away under mature socialism, those responsible for the second transition period underestimated the institutional context required for the satisfactory workings of the market economy.[6]

Formulating new institutions is the transition problem that our chapter examines. We first examine the debate over the conception of the state in political economy. Then, we turn our attention to whether the conception of the state in political economy in post-communist Russia is moving towards a stable equilibrium.

Conceptions of the state and economy

Debate over the economic role of government can be traced to the very beginning of economics. If we date the systematic study of political economy to Adam Smith's *Wealth of Nations* ((1976) [1776]) we can see that the birth of the discipline is intimately connected to the question of comparative conceptions of the role of government in the economy.[7] Smith contested the ideologies of the mercantilist system. Within mercantilism the state played a significant role as an economic player in foreign as well as domestic transactions. Domestic regulation and foreign protectionism aimed to promote the interests of certain domestic producers (see Smith, 1976 [1776]: Book IV). As Smith concluded, under mercantilism "the interest of the consumer is almost constantly sacrificed to that of the producer; and it seems to consider production, and not consumption, as the ultimate end and object of all industry and commerce" (1976: 625). Such a system of "conspicuous production" ought to be replaced, according to Smith, by a system based on an unregulated domestic economy and free international trade. The economic role of government was to shift from protecting the interests of producers to the limited (albeit essential) role of establishing the basic laws of justice to govern trade. Smith's system of "natural liberty" limited the state to the basic functions of the administration of justice, defense against foreign invasion, and the production of certain public goods which a market system will not have the appropriate incentives to supply in appropriate quantities.[8] But there should be little doubt of the great benefits Smith saw for a society that transformed itself from a mercantilist system to a market economy. As Smith ((1976) [1776]: xliii) put it in his 1750–51 lectures, which were later incorporated into *The Wealth of Nations*: "Little else is requisite to carry a state to the highest degree of opulence from the lowest form of barbarism, but peace, easy taxes, and a tolerable administration of justice; all the rest being brought about by the natural course of things. All governments which thwart this natural course, which force things into another channel or which endeavor to arrest the progress of society at a particular point, are unnatural, and to support themselves are obliged to be oppressive and tyrannical."

Compared to the classical liberal view, which perceives the state as a referee of the game of economic life, mercantilism sees the state as a player within the economic game.[9] Its chief aim was to maintain policies that would generate a favorable balance of trade and regulate the balance of payments. Above all, mercantilism is an interventionist policy. "The essence of the system (of mercantilism) lies not in some doctrine of money, or the balance of trade...not in tariff barriers, protected duties, or navigation laws; but in something far greater:- namely in the total transformation of society and its organisation, as well as of the state and its institutions, in the replacing of a local and territorial economic policy by that of the national state."[10]

When the state is viewed as a player within the economic game, there is really no autonomous economic sector apart from the political sector. However, if the state is viewed as a referee of the economic game, then economic decisions are separate from political decisions.[11] The state is there to define and enforce the rules, but its officials do not get involved in determining the outcome of the game. Who wins or loses the game ought not be the concern of the state; rather, the concern is limited to ensuring that the economic game is played according to the rules.[12]

Ultimately, most political economy positions fall into either one or the other camp – to intervene into the market or not to intervene. After the fall of communism, it was not easy for advocates of reform to work with these distinctions. The communist system required the state to play an active role in economic life, reform required the "destatization" of economic life and the establishment of the state as the enforcer of contracts. Since they were not working from a *tabula raza* (scorched earth) this was easier said than done. All that is entailed in defining and enforcing contracts is a consequence of an intricate mix of formal institutions and informal norms which compliment and reinforce one another.[13] One clear lesson from the post-communist experience is that "getting the prices right" is a lot more difficult then simply withdrawing the restrictions that previously existed on the pricing of goods and services.

As this complicated mix of formal and informal rules which govern economic life became the focus of scholars and political actors, the role of civil society in a working political economy moved to the forefront. Our view contrasts Civil Society with the State. Throughout East and Central Europe this way of viewing the matter should be natural given their long history of dissident culture, which forced a schism between private and public existence. The totalitarian systems threatened to squelch the development of civil society, but instead they pushed it underground. Of course, this submerged form of civil society is truncated compared to what it would be capable of if given an above ground existence. Communism failed to eliminate civil society, although it did threaten and distort it. This was one of the great ironies of Communism, an idea that sought to eliminate the private autonomous struggle with public consciousness inadvertently led to a social system where a genuine public life disappeared. A genuine public life can only emerge within a system that insures an autonomous private life. The communist reality of having to "live the lie" is but one manifestation of this irony (see Kuran, 1995).

The literature on civil society emerging in the wake of the fall of Communism understood that a vibrant civil society was necessary for establishing a working democratic state.[14] Throughout the emerging societies in East and Central Europe and the former Soviet Union, the state and civil society was often contrasted with the profit motive of the market. The story went that the market runs on the principle of everything for sale, while civil society was based on norms and codes of behavior outside of the profit motive. The conception of the State versus the Market changed to a more complicated relationship, the State vs. Market dichotomy, because it did not seem to recognize the informal norms which underlie democratic life on the one hand, and economic behavior on the other. In light of these criticisms, the terms of the debate contrasted either the STATE versus CIVIL SOCIETY, or STATE (including civil society) versus the MARKET.

The view which conceives of civil society as the foundation for an effective State is flawed on several grounds. Contrasting the market with civil society commits two errors of commission and one error of omission. First, it underestimates the coercive nature of state action. The state, as Max Weber emphasized, has a geographic monopoly on coercion. The state is a powerful instrument through which some parties can gain by exploiting others. Second, it underestimates the role of civil society as an opposition force of self-governance against the coercive power of the State. This role for civil society was evident in the *samizdat* culture of underground civil society under Communism. But it was also evident in the 19th century America that captured the imagination of Alex de Tocqueville. Tocqueville saw self-governance as opposed to reliance on the formal structures of state action as a defining characterization of American society. Self-governance was seen as an alternative to the state, not as a prerequisite for a working state sector. Third, the contemporary juxtaposition omits a discussion of the importance of the self-enforcing norms and bonds of trust which must be in existence for a market economy to operate effectively.[15] Formal contracts and various less formal alternative institutional facilitators of voluntary cooperation are at work in the day-to-day operation of a market society. Economic actors must build a reputation for trustworthiness, craftsmanship, and reliability in order to be successful in the market due to the discipline of repeated dealings. It is true, as Adam Smith stressed, that it is due to the powerful force of self-interest that we expect our dinner from the butcher, the baker and the brewer and not due to their benevolence. But it is also true that the self-interest of the butcher, the baker and the brewer is best served by their taking into account the desires and demands of others with whom they must deal in the market. Without a certain background of institutions (formal and informal rules) markets will not operate effectively to coordinate production and exchange. In short, market activity is embedded within a larger context of rule-governed behavior (formal institutions) and social behavior (unwritten institutions).

We suggest that in lieu of a distinction that sees the profit motive as contrasted with civil society, a more appropriate contrast would be STATE vs. CIVIL SOCIETY, where Civil Society is divided into Non-market and Market activity. This contrast is built on a recognition of the coercive nature of state action and the voluntary nature of civil society. In the arena of civil society, whether at the local bridge club or the grocery store, interactions are based on mutually beneficial voluntary interaction. State activity, on the other hand, is built on the foundation of force – the ability of one entity to dictate to another the terms of their interaction.

These distinctions have mainly been developed by Western scholars studying transition issues and not the participants in the process or the people who populate the reforming economies. The dominant conception of the state and its relation to the economy in actual practice in the post-Soviet period has been one which sees the STATE and CIVIL SOCIETY as wedded together as a buffer against the uncertainties of economic freedom of the MARKET. Ironically, we come full circle back to where Adam Smith started – a modern form of mercantilism. The modern post-Soviet state protects certain key participants from the rigor of competition rather than promoting competition among participants as a more market-oriented outlook would.

The metamorphosis of the State in the past decade from rent-seeking under state socialism to rent-seeking under state capitalism was not a consequence of implementing new ideas, but of the realities of the existing political actors and the institutions which constrained the changes in political structure.[16] Given this audience of stake-holders, economists have been long on specifics of public policy, but short on the precise structure and scope of the State.

However, the biggest problem has been redefining the structure and scope of the State since the collapse of the Soviet system. James Buchanan (1975) has argued that we can usefully distinguish between (1) the protective state, (2) the productive state, and (3) the redistributive state. The protective state engages in those activities that could not be provided through the market mechanism, but yet are essential for the maintenance of civil order – police, courts and national defense. The productive state captures the capacity of the government to engage in activities that also could not be provided through the market mechanism, yet raise the productivity of society (for example, roads, bridges and certain public works projects). The redistributive state employs the coercive powers of the state to benefit one party by exploiting another. The key for steering the path between anarchy and Leviathan, according to Buchanan, is to find an appropriate mechanism that enables the protective and productive state, but constrains the redistributive state. If the redistributive state is unbounded, it will undermine the effectiveness of the protective and productive state and the Leviathan alternative will prove to be the only viable equilibrium to the process. This led Buchanan to advocate the somewhat strained notion of a "*strong minimal state.*" One of the main problems with post-communist political economy, Buchanan warned, is that many market-oriented thinkers by concentrating on reducing the role of government in economic life tend to overlook the crucial role the state must play in a vibrant market economy (Buchanan, 1997: 93–107, 151–9). In short, by working so hard to figure out how to constrain the redistributive state, we also may constrain the protective and productive state.

Throughout the post-Soviet nations, a strong minimal state has proven to be illusive in practice and curtailed in theory. The classic paradox of governance (articulated by James Madison in *Federalist #10*) that because men are not angels we need to simultaneously empower and constrain the state, haunts the post-Soviet reform effort. This is highlighted in the tension that a strong leader may be needed in order to constrain the government. However, a government strong enough to bind its own hands is by definition strong enough to break those bonds.[17]

Issues of credibility and commitment in the political economy of reform move to the center of attention in an analysis that recognizes Buchanan's essential point about rules in political economy (see Boettke, 2001). Government's commitments must be structured to increase credibility. When broken promises are punished and kept promises rewarded, under either outcome the state may maintain its credibility with society. However, when promises are broken without punishment, its credibility diminishes in society's eyes. This is what happened under the Yeltsin regime, which waffled on both forming the structure of the state and implementing reforms. In addition to the difficulties of establishing effective constraints on the structure and scope of the State, we contend that there is a basic equilibrium logic between conceptions of the state and beliefs economists hold about their role in society.

Belief and behavior equilibrium

We argued earlier that political economists are faced with two choices regarding the basic conception of the state – either government is viewed as a player in the economic game, or as the referee. These positions are mutually exclusive by definition. We would also like to consider the beliefs that economists hold of economics as a discipline. We postulate a situation of multiple-equilibria between these two dimensions of belief and behavior. The following matrix illustrates the possible combinations: (see Figure 9.1)

If the role of the economist is to be a student of society, the mutually compatible position would be for the state to be viewed as the referee in economic life. In that situation, the economist is expected to study society and teach others about the general principles that govern economic life. But the economist has no role in dictating the operation of

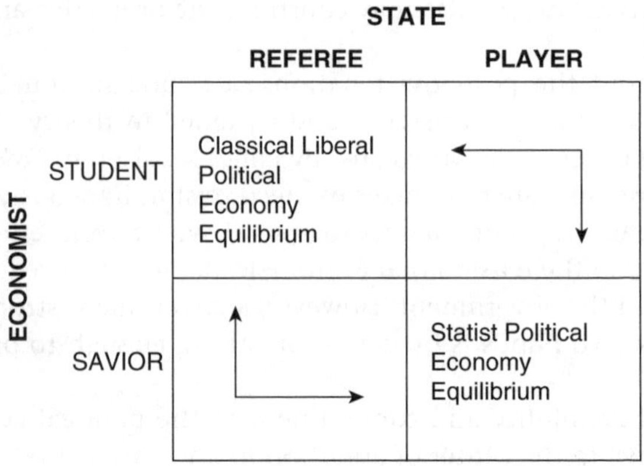

Figure 9.1 The State and the Economist

those principles. If economists disappeared from the planet, the principles of economic life would still operate in the same way. The equilibrium between the belief of economists as students and the non-activist state is self-enforcing because the state does not need any experts to play the economic game as no government official is to intervene in the workings of the economy. There is no strong incentive for economists to perceive themselves as the saviors of society. Instead, their role is restricted to that of either student or critic.

On the other hand, if the state is as an active player in economic life, and the discipline of economics was content with a self-image as student, then the state would demand the services of other scientists who could serve as players within the game. The economists who stayed above the fray by restricting their role to student or critic would lose out in terms of prestige and financial remuneration to those disciplines that believe themselves to be expert enough to aid the state in its activist role. Thus, the equilibrium position is one of an activist government and the belief of economics as a discipline as social engineers who can offer their expert advice to salvage society from its ills.

We need, then, to examine both the ongoing debate over the changing conception of the state in the post-Soviet situation and the changing beliefs about the role of the economist in society. Although there are four possibilities in our diagram, only two of them provide sustainable paths – the player-savior quadrant and the referee-student quadrant. The other two quadrants are inherently unstable and bound to collapse in the short run, since the roles played by the state and the economist are incompatible. If the state chooses to be a player in the market, then it needs an economist to advise how to play and is not just willing to examine the market without giving forecasting schemes. Moreover, if the state only wants to be a referee, setting and enforcing the rules of the market, then it has no interest in any specific outcomes of the market and no need for a savior-economist to forecast what the government ought to do.

When the state is viewed as a referee, but the economist is viewed as a savior to lead society to the promised land, we have an unstable position – the position the post-Soviet situation thrust upon the societies of East, Central Europe and the former Soviet Union. It is an empirical question which direction beliefs and conceptions of the state will go, but logic suggests that it will either be state as referee/economist as student, or state as player/economist as savior. We examine the evidence to see if we can glean an answer to the empirical trend currently being played out in Russia. Russia is an ideal case to examine, since from 1991 until 2001, the conception of the role for government and the role of the economist changed repeatedly, both in Russia and in the Western advisory community. Scholars and policy makers are still searching for the right political economy balance.

We contend that the equilibrium of the state as player/economist as savior produces a low-growth equilibrium, while the equilibrium of state as referee/economist as student produces a high-growth equilibrium. Societies can be trapped in the low-growth equilibrium.[18] Some societies can sustain a low-growth equilibrium for a period of time by consuming accumulated surpluses from an earlier time of high-growth equilibrium. Nonetheless, even rich societies cannot maintain (or increase) living standards once they find themselves in a low-growth equilibrium. The move from a poor developing economy to a developed economy, and from a developed economy to a wealthy economy, is one that can only be accomplished when a society finds itself in a high-growth equilibrium. The argument we are offering gives modern meaning to the above quote from Adam Smith to the effect that all that is required to transition from the poorest of countries to the wealthiest is peace, easy taxes and the administration of justice. The state need not engage in any other activities except to provide for domestic and foreign peace through the definition and enforcement of a rule of contract. Reforming Russia must confront these issues to avoid the low-growth equilibrium trap. Russia is still in flux and therefore allows us to examine the cost and benefits of the player-savior quadrant, the player-student quadrant, the referee-student quadrant, and the referee-savior quadrant. It was the referee-savior quadrant that Western advisors rushed towards, trying to keep politicians from infringing on civil liberties but leaving economists free to interfere and redirect market outcomes. Throughout the Yeltsin regime, it wound up looking more like the player-student quadrant, where the politicians acted, but the hands of economists were tied. As classical liberals, we fear the player-savior quadrant most, and it is the one which most resembles the Soviet era. Hope lies in the referee-student quadrant, which holds the promise of prosperity and liberty.

Path I: Putin's paternalism; dangers of the *player-savior quadrant*

During the rule of Catherine the Great, false fronts were put up in villages throughout the Russian empire to give the elite foreign and domestic visitors passing through the Russian countryside the illusion of better living standards.[19] The mastermind behind these false fronts was Grigory Potemkin, so the towns became known as "Potemkin villages." These are places that could only be thought as beautiful if you were quickly passing through. Putin may be creating a Potemkin paternalism, where once you look beneath the surface of his policies their meaning changes completely. Paternalism on the surface is the state joined with the common man (the non-market part of civil society) against the onslaught from the market (which is a part of civil society). Once the state inhibits the market (under the guise of protecting citizens from negative phenomena associated with the market, such as unemployment, high prices, instability, etc.), it creates deeper economic problems (i.e., inhibiting innovation, creating shortages, increasing poverty, etc.) and may next move to inhibit citizens' political freedom.[20] Thus, paternalism may be a Trojan horse; once opened, it becomes more destructive than constructive. This is a worst-case scenario, but nonetheless a possibility that must be considered. Better to forecast the death of civil liberty in Russia too soon than to write its eulogy too late.

Putin suggests, "Paternalistic sentiments have struck deep roots in Russian society...Russians are used to connect [sic] improvements in their own conditions more with the aid and support of the state than with their own efforts."[21] He then proceeds to say that such Russian values are not to be judged as good or bad: they are simply the Russian way. These traditional values may change over time, but so, they will change slowly. While tapping into the desire for stability after a time of upheavals, Putin reestablished the importance of the role of a strong state.[22] This first major speech as leader of Russia has a little something for everyone; thus it has many contradictions. The speech illustrates two possibilities: state (with the public) against the market and state (with the market) against the public. Another, more desirable path for Russia, which cannot be found in the aforementioned words by Putin, is that of a civil society strengthened and a state that withers away. There is some evidence to support this last and best-case scenario, but this section examines the most probable case: the state against the market.

One notorious case of Putin's regime attacking the market is his campaign against the oligarchs. "Oligarch" has come to mean someone to be resented for their wealth during difficult economic times. Undoubtably, these "oligarchs" have benefited from their connections to the Yeltsin regime, which put them in a better position than most to take advantage of many opportunities during Russia's initial reforms, particularly privatization. Although much of the public resents the advantages gained by oligarchs in the transition, some are also aware that attacking the them may be a harbinger of an attack on others' civil rights.[23] The catch-word which provides an excuse for going after individuals in Russia is *corruption*.[24] This is something they are likely guilty of, since the laws are so convoluted as to pull all citizens into this possible trap.[25] The oligarchs are not like the average Russian citizen; mostly what they are guilty of is exploiting personal connections, and profiting from a pre-existing (and transition created) political structure that was intertwined with most major economic opportunities. The danger that is ever present is the arbitrary discretion to go after some and not others. One reason for this, aside from the massive gulf between the *de jure* and *de facto*, is the conflicting laws between the federal and regional governments. Putin boasted of bringing two-thirds of the regional laws into accord with federal laws. This still leaves 30% of regional laws in conflict with the federal laws.[26] So the question is whether or not to break a law; rather, the question is which law to break and which will be enforced. The move against the oligarchs is only the start of Putin's bringing order.

Resentment against the oligarchs does have a basis in reality. They are broadly viewed as having hijacked the political process and being responsible for the 1996 reelection of Yeltsin.[27] Thanks to oligarchs' bank-rolling of the campaign, and especially the support of their media outlets (which was more important and useful than the money they contributed), Yeltsin was seen as beholden to their wishes. Their wishes included insider advantages gained during some of the most lucrative privatizations. Whatever influence the oligarchs had on the Kremlin, it did drive out other domestic as well as foreign investment. Oligarchs possessed much of the relational capital, which helped them both gain property and enforce their property rights in a climate of hazy lines between *de facto* and *de jure* rights. Thus, by the end of the Yeltsin regime, the notion of Kremlin cronyism, as exemplified by the widely loathed Kremlin "family," which consisted of Yeltsin's family members (especially his daughter Tatyana), certain oligarchs (especially Berezovsky), and reformers (Anatoli Chubais[28]), was abhorrent to nearly every Russian. This gave Putin a perfect setting if he desired to use government to "clean up corruption."[29]

There are examples of government intruding on the market in both a destructive and creative fashions. Destructively, the government attacks any businessmen foolish enough to show a profit despite the 13% flat-income tax recently implemented by the Putin administration, any business that paid all of its taxes would pay up to 70% of its profits.[30] Creatively, the government supports enterprises and households that would fail if left to the market. This is the benefit sought from paternalism, so it is worth examining what the market is being given up for.

The priorities of a politician may be mapped out by where he chooses to visit. The day after his election, Putin chose to visit Snezhinsk, a closed nuclear city in a region dominated by the defense sector. During Soviet times, the consumer sector suffered greatly due to the preferences shown to the military enterprises.[31] This is not a uniquely Russian problem – even Western economies have suffered inefficiencies by giving defense production a priority over commercial production.[32] This is not to say that Russia should not invest in arms or other defense products; it is the government's interference with the products that brings on the inefficiencies, not the type of product itself. Arms exports or other scientific products could be a great economic engine for Russia's economy in the future, as long as the government does not try to steer the train. Making the government part of the production process distorts the function of the market price as a value signal. Due to the inherent information asymmetry between state and non-state actors, given the hierarchy or coercive power, the costs and benefits of any economic endeavor will never be clear.

The above analysis shows that a Soviet-state is not the only method that politicians and economists (qua saviors) may use to interfere with the market and individuals lives. Although the USSR will not be reconstituted, that does not mean that the liberties gained since its collapse are guaranteed. Being within the player-savior quadrant will always leave individual liberties vulnerable to attack by the state.

Path II: Pinochet possibility; myths of the *player-student quadrant*

This is the primary view of Putin's path in many Russian and Western press circles, so it is worth seeing what all the fuss is about. Entering the names Putin and Pinochet into the FBIS (Foreign Broadcast Information Service) search engine retrieved articles 198 articles.[33] This gives some sense to the extent of how seriously this possible track for Putin is taken in Russian domestic and international circles. It is not terribly important for our purposes to discover who General Pinochet really was or the exact nature of Chile's political economy.[34] Our purpose is rather what commentators, pundits, and policy makers believe him to be when they bandy him around as a model for Putin.

The Pinochet model means that the market will be protected from civil society by the state, within the player-student quadrant. If he chooses this course, Putin will stop the pensioners, labor unions, and unemployed from hampering the development of firms. Some of Putin's words support this view, such as his recognition that government control of the economy results in distortions which place, "a ban...on the initiative and entrepreneurship of enterprises and their personnel...the result of our [the government's] own mistakes, miscalculation and lack of experience" (Putin, 2000). This is music to a free-marketer's ears. The problem is that everything else in his speech contradicts this analysis. However, he is not to be judged just by what he says, but also by whom he associates with. The number one reason for the liberal hopes placed on Putin is his economic advisor, Andrei Illarionov. Using Illarionov as a key, we might be able to unlock the mystery of which course Putin will take.

Illarionov himself, an admirer of the Russian-American liberal icon Ayn Rand, is not as clear-cut a figure as some pundits suggest.[35] He first built up liberal credentials in St. Petersburg as an economist working under Yegor Gaidar and German Gref, helping to found the Center for

Strategic Studies and conducting his own groundbreaking research into the meaning of Russian GDP statistics.[36] He concluded that even the low estimates of GDP were inflated, and he placed the blame for stunted economic growth squarely on the shoulders of government interference with the market. This all sounds liberal so far. However, like his current boss, Putin, he has given lip-service to two views (libertarian and statist) which are completely contradictory. As with Putin, the question arises as to which of Illarionov's words does *he* believe and which will he try to implement as policy.

The majority of his words before joining the Putin administration are on the libertarian side, so it is worthwhile to examine his recent statist views. During an interview on the problems of the Russian economy, Illarionov pointed to an odd mix of nations as models of economic growth. The list included Chile, Taiwan, Hong Kong on the liberal side, along with South Korea and China on the statist side. His support of China as an economic model pre-dates his association with Putin, so this suggests that his statist leanings are not merely the means of keeping his influence with Putin, but rather part of his economic perspective.[37] He has not become a "yes-man" and has been one of the few advisors to publicly challenge the government thus far. Nonetheless, these challenges have not translated into any clear policy changes or increased influence, and he has even backtracked on challenges made publicly.[38] Much of our analysis on Illarionov comes from watching this rising star economist for the past few years, while some of it comes from a well-detailed FBIS (Foreign Broadcast Information Service) report. That report's title is "Putin Advisor Pushes Authoritarian Development," but the report itself paints a more balanced and nuanced picture.[39] Taking the report's meaning by the title would be as big a mistake as taking Illarionov on only part of his words. We have yet to see which words will dictate his policy actions.

Despite the evidence supporting the Pinochet-path, including all the notable scholars and journalists who support this perspective, the possibility of this model coming to fruition falls short in a variety of ways. First, it assumes that Russia has become a market economy and Putin's talk about stability means he will protect the economic advances made over the past decade.[40] However, Russia has not become a market economy, although some declared victory as early as 1995. Also, he is concerned with stability, but this means keeping firms afloat that should be allowed to sink. That is not the market and that is not Pinochet's path; it is paternalism.

There is still a large portion of society which works directly for the Russian government – as of 1999 a total of 38.3% of the labor force. This figure does not include municipal workers or those that work at enterprises with a mixed private-public ownership. The vast ties between the government and the market does not lend any credence to the notion that the government is moving out of the economy.[41]

Thus, the player-student quadrant does not exist in Russia. If this quadrant does arise at times, the contradictions between politicians' powers and economist's (qua students) constraints will make it unsustainable. Giving individuals economic liberty will induce the desire for political liberty, as surely as night follows day.

Path III: The great liberal hope; who wants to be in the *referee-student quadrant*?

The option of a smaller role for the state has some roots in Russian history. Whether or not it is likely is another matter. *Perestroika* was one example of civil society joining together (market and nonmarket elements; dissidents and businessmen, environmentalists and nationalists; etc.) for a smaller role of the state.[42] The spirit of *perestroika* did survive in the Yeltsin administration, but not for long. *Perestroika* itself means to rebuild, and this era was ushered in from the top (Gorbachev) down. However, the changes got out of the leaders' hands and the *perestroika* era, along with the Soviet Union itself, ended from the bottom (civil society) up. This civil society was composed of some strange bedfellows, as civil societies usually are. The *perestroika* civil society included Soviet dissidents and human rights advocates (Andrei Sakharov, Yelena Bonner, Ludmila Alexeeva, and many more), disgruntled coal miners from the Far North to Siberia (Vorkuta and the Kuzbass), Russian nationalists (Alexander Solzhenitsyn, Valentin Rasputin), enterprise managers and bootleggers, and many more individuals one would not expect to get along if put in the same room. Yet they shared a common cause: to get the government out of their lives.

Once some of their goals were realized, they all faced the problems of the wreckage remaining from the Soviet state. Some have continued to champion the cause of individual liberty, while others (quite reasonably) have sought shelter from the economic storm and political tumult. Predictably, with the Soviet state, the common enemy, gone, their fragile grouping fractured. Along with independence came new freedoms and new (although not newly created) hardships. Suddenly one can criticize the government and most citizens are free to travel for the first time. However, with economic guarantees gone, so went the stability, guaranteed wages, and much of the available cash.[43] Each individual is facing a different crisis, and various groups have supported differing models of what the state ought to become. The different directions taken by the Russian people will hopefully steer the course of events.

Looking at how the population fits into our political-economy matrix, whether they see economists as saviors or students, and whether they see the government as a referee or a player, will tell us what type of Putin they will support and what type of government they will undermine. As rough and problematic as polls are, they do give a sense of the direction that public attitudes are taking.

Path IV: Western-advisors' wishes turned into Russian wishes; *referee-savior quadrant*

Without conducting our own polls into how much government interaction with the market the public wants (whether they are more inclined towards the player-savior quadrant or towards the referee-student quadrant), we may look at public opinion polls already taken. The results are striking. Russian preferences lean towards the referee-student quadrant. Russian citizens trust the market (as they have known it) less than they trust the government; they see the role of the government more as a guarantor of outcomes than as a referee. However, the opinion polls seem to hang on the hope that control of the market will not translate into control over recently acquired civil liberties. Russians want to keep the freedoms they have gained since the collapse of the USSR. The public hopes that the government will be only a referee setting the rules of their daily lives, but that the government (via economists qua saviors) will constrain the market and change the distribution of winners and losers.

The distinction between an actual market economy and a quasi-market economy (the virtual economy[44]) is important. The market in Russia did not have an "invisible hand" in the 1990s. Instead, Russia ended up with certain aspects of the market that remained distorted. This is what drives public opinion. Opinions are not based on disillusionment with the laws of supply and demand, but disillusionment with the economic havoc of their existence. So the variables, which are not market variables but distorted quasi-market variables that we will examine to see the population's outlook, are: privatization, corruption, bankruptcy, and poverty.[45]

Privatization did not fare well in the public's eyes. To the question of whether or not it should be reviewed, 51% answered it should be reviewed, only 21% thought it should be left as is, and 21% could not answer either way. The results of privatization fared even worse. Asked about the overall results of privatization, 59% responded that it brought more harm than good! Only 8% answered that it brought more positive than negative results, with 25% thinking it had a balance of positive and negative results (8% could not answer).

As proof that Russians are not adverse to the market economy, 88.5% of those polled answered that competition facilitates development and would be good for the growth of the Russian economy. However, their attitudes towards the market display even greater complexity when it comes to how the state should handle "losers." When asked what the state should do when a *private enterprise* fails, 43% would nationalize it and only 7% would leave to its current owner (unfortunately the question does not get into whether owners should be held liable for the outstanding debts). Only 30% of respondents would have it sold to a new owner and 20% were unsure of what to answer.

Russians were unsure of how to answer questions regarding corruption. First, 38.6% claim to never have encountered corruption. Albeit shocked, perhaps even skeptical, we may be happy for this privileged minority. This figure means 61.4% have encountered some form of corruption since everyone responded to the corruption question.[46] There was a difference within this group as to the amount of corruption, but it was unquestionably a presence in their lives. Of those answering that they had encountered corruption, 20.4% came across various forms of corruption on a regular basis, 21.3% encountered it several times in their lives, and 17.8% answered that they encountered corruption, but only on rare occasions. The only economic variable left that we examine, which indicates the level of desperation throughout society, are questions on poverty.

The poverty measures we are looking at are not figures on living standards, but perceptions of how citizens cope with the economic problems they face.[47] Based on a survey conducted in August 2000, 66.5% knew of friends, coworkers, or relatives who at least once stole food to feed their families. Even more dramatically, 86.4% knew of someone who has stopped paying rent for a portion of time, due to chronic liquidity constraints (lack of hard-currency wages). Also, 65% know of people who admit to stealing from work in order to re-sell the items. Although all of the aforementioned statistics are compelling, the most dramatic has to be that 48.8% of respondents know of someone committing suicide due to financial problems.[48] This shows the problems with the economy, but nothing shows the direction of what the public expects from the government as clearly as opinions on Putin.

The honeymoon may be over, but the public still places a great deal of their hope for Russia's future on Putin's shoulders (as a player, not a referee). Their opinion on his main governmental action to date, dividing the country into seven federal districts, is highly favorable. Forty-eight percent of Russians think the presidential representative in the regions will increase law and order, and 42% believe that five of the seven representatives being former military or KGB officers is positive. They are even willing to give up some electoral power for great order, since 63% support the right of Putin to fire the governors they elect and 51% even think that it would help the nation if Putin gained full control over the elected legislature.[49] This tends more towards a player-savior role than a referee-student role for the government. However, these poll results are not an indictment of Russia's path, merely an indicator of the course Russia is on.

Conclusion: Beliefs as a basis for behavior

There are words like Liberty
That almost make me cry.
If you had known what I knew
You would know why.

"Refugee in America," Langston Hughes (1990)

Hughes' call for liberty is a call for opportunity. His poem was written during the Jim Crow era, when institutions limited opportunities for blacks in America. Conditions of poverty are dispiriting, but the lack of prospects to move out of poverty are utterly debilitating. Luckily, in the US today we enjoy equity of opportunity which is unprecedented in world history. Unfortunately, today many countries, including Russia, suffer not merely from endemic poverty, but from the lack of choices that could lead them out of such poverty. Hope must be served to the world's developing nations through a change in their institutions. The institutions are the rules that decide which belief quadrant the politicians and economists will be placed in; this impacts the nation's chance to grow.

We have gone through the four-belief quadrants as possible paths for Russia. However, as the Russian case shows, while our ideal path (referee-student) or the path we most fear (player-savior) may be the only sustainable options, the political and economic conditions on the ground may pull nations into the other two quadrants, albeit temporarily. The political establishment will have stake-holders, who will try to keep their hierarchical position if they cannot cash out their relational capital. Given previous state intervention into the market, there will be individuals relying on continued subsidies. These political and economic stakeholders need to be brought out of their roles, for the good of the whole society. Only a nation that guarantees freedom of voluntary mutually beneficial transactions will be able to promise prosperity.

Notes

1 A core difference between the different schools of economic thought may be found in the differing advice given to transition economies. Keynesians and Neo-Keynesians are advocates of managing fiscal levers and even monetary levers of control. Monetarists and Neo-Classical economists tend to favor the government being restricted to manipulating monetary levers of control. However, the Austrian school looks at the market as a process which tends towards an equilibrium, where the point is not achieved by any government intervention. Rather, equilibrium is only approached when individual actors in the market place are free to choose whether to enter into transactions.

2 The price liberalization was theoretically the simplest aspect, to stop trying to predict the consumers demand and thus eliminate the information gathering burden. One less job for the government. Finally, the prices would act as signals of value and convey information. This did not happen for multiple reasons. First, there were still some price controls and state production, which was not guided by market demand forces. Also, personal relationships still govern much economic activity and limit the extent of the market. Plus, there are still monetary and non monetary prices on goods, so the calculation of costs and benefits from trade are still not given by prices. See Hayek (1935) and Stigler (1966), for more of information prices convey and the informational value.

3 For more on the privatization process by some of the designers, see Boycko, Shleifer & Vishny (1996).

4 Kornai (1990). These soft budget constraints persist in a variety of forms. Given direct subsidies were cut, indirect subsidies were created in a variety of forms. Energy given without payment was a major subsidy given to households and inefficient firms alike. See Yergin (1991), Yergin & Gustavson (1993), and Gaddy & Ickes (1998).

5 For more on the *perestroika* period and Gorbachev's reforms, see Hewett & Winston (1991) and Lewin (1991).

6 There were also plenty of bureaucratic and interest group problems that had a stake in preserving soviet hierarchical system. For more on interest-group problems and the dilemmas of getting the stake-holders to go along with a transition of power, see Tullock (1975) and McChesney (1987).

7 Of course, our choice of *Wealth of Nations* is not a blindly arbitrary one. For more on the growth of political economy in France, and the reason it emerged in a coherent form of Smith's handiwork from the Scottish highlands, see Waterman (2001).
8 Smith's notions of natural liberty were not as bold as David Hume. Smith still held a broader role for the government, but there was a good deal of interaction of letters and ideas between Smith and his precursor. See Hume (1948) and Robbins (1998).
9 For more on mercantilism, see the pamphleteers, Malynes [1622], Misselden [1622], and Mun [1664].
10 von Schmoller (1902: 51). Heckscher (1935) also found that mercantilism is primarily concerned with nation building.
11 For more on the separate stages of creating the rules and playing by the rules, see North (1990) and Buchanan (1971).
12 For more on institutions being the rules of the game and organizations as players, see North (1990).
13 If the informal and formal institutions do not reinforce one another, then they undermine one another. One example is the corruption that existed in soviet enterprises, which has carried over to many post-soviet enterprises. There is an informal rule that allows for a certain amount of theft. However, there is a distinction between stealing for the firm and from the firm. Stealing for the firm is an informal slack to make up for formal rigidities in supplies. Whereas, stealing from the firm will undermine its longevity. For more on this distinction see Latynina (2000).
14 See Putnam (1993). Putnam distinguishes between Northern Italy's strong institutions and weak interpersonal connections and Southern Italy's weak institutions and strong interpersonal connections.
15 For more on the role of trust in society, see Fukuyama (1995).
16 This of course is what Public Choice theory would predict. Political actors are rational actors, so if there are rents to be had they will expend energy to gain the rents as long as the benefits exceed the costs of rent-seeking. For a little more on the Public Choice theory, see Buchanan (1969, 1971) and Tullock (1965).
17 This is the basis of hopes and fears of Putin that we examine later in our article.
18 A burgeoning field of macroeconomics is growth. There is a question as to whether or not there is convergence to multiple equilibria. For more on growth, see Barro & Sala i Martin (1999), Landes (1999), and Diamond (1997).
19 See Riasanovky (1984: 266). The infamous journey was in 1787 taken by Emperor Joseph II of Austria, Polish king Stanislaw Poniatowski, and Catherine the Great. The nature of Catherine's relationship with Potemkin is questioned by historians, but it is certain she showed him great favor and they shared much information with one another. For more on Catherine, see Madariaga (1990).
20 Although economic freedom improved with the collapse of the Soviet Union, Russia did not become a market. Some economic reforms that have advanced are: price liberalization, privatization, increase in the ability to enter and exit the market, a hardening of budget constraints, and an overall

movement bringing the *de jure* closer to the *de facto*. Some places to look for indicators on economic freedom are: United Nations Development Program, the World Bank, and the Heritage Foundation, to name a few.

21 This is a quote from Putin's first speech as President of the Russian Federation, given on New Year's Day of the Millennium. It may be found in English at his website, http://www.government.gov.ru/english/statVP_engl_1.html.

22 During one of Putin's most recent speeches he remarked, "We are only strong with an integral state. Another process has begun – the process of consolidation. It is on the basis of strengthening statehood that the progress toward consolidation has been made." Mikhail Kozhokin, *Izvesitia*, March 22, 2001, pp. 1, 3, as found online at www.izevstia.ru and as translated by WPS monitoring Agency, www.wps.ru/e_index.html.

23 Surely, the split between political and economic power has positive repercussions. It was the continued state-monopoly of major economic opportunities which soured the public on many aspects of the 1990s transition and reforms.

The greatest imminent danger of Putin's actions of going after the "oligarchs" is in his selection of whom to attack. So far he has gone after Berezovsky and Gusinsky, *the only two of the "oligarchs" with mass media holdings*. If the prosecution was on purely corruption grounds, he has at least as much reason to go after Potanin and Abramovich. Interestingly enough, just as of February 2001, Abramovich (Putin's favored oligarch) acquired Berezovsky's shares in television channel ORT. Putin also took Gusinsky's shares of the television channel NTV to give over to Gazprom, a company that the government has shares in. Thus, much of the attacks on the "oligarchs" thus far have only diminished the amount of free press, while not severing the ties between the locus of political and economic power.

Feelings on the importance of freedom of the press are unclear. One poll shows 38% of Russians believing in the need for an independent press that may by an impartial critic of Putin, whereas 34% answered that the media should fully support the Russian president. This poll was conducted on October 31, 2000, a little over one month after the Kursk disaster. See Interfax, November 9, 2000. We will revisit the implications on the attacks on the media further in this paper.

There are multiple cases of regional governments' attacks on the freedom of the press and the federal government not reigning in the regional administrations for the protection of the freedom of the press. For a recent case of this, see Pryanishnikov (2001: 14).

24 There is an interesting twist on the notion of corruption provided by a Russian government official. The Russian Interior Minister stated in response to accusation of government officials corruption that, "only those who have links with organized criminal gangs can be regarded as corrupt officials. *Do not mistake bribe-taking for corruption*." (Our emphasis.) RIA (2001).

25 This is not to imply that corruption is not a problem facing the government. Rather, it is an institution (à la Douglass North) which has both costs and benefits for the government. The cost of corruption is money lost, particularly taxes. The benefit of corruption is to have a ready-made excuse to interfere with citizens rights and property. For more on institutionalism, see

North (1990) and Israel (1989). For more on corruption in Russia and the Soviet period, see Grossman (1977) and Hewett (1988).

26 Kozhokin (2001), as found online at www.izevstia.ru and as translated by WPS monitoring Agency, www.wps.ru/e_index.html.

27 Not only did some Russian politicians learn from the Western use of charismatic campaigning, but they picked up on the American-style deep-pockets campaign financing. The Communist Party had the organizational network developed, but they lacked the mega-financing available to Yeltsin.

28 As an insult to this politician, reformer, and businessman, it became a common joke in the late 1990s to name one's cat Chubais in order to "order Chubais around." This is the anecdotal evidence, but one of this article's coauthors personally knows of three cats and one goldfish named Chubais.

29 The term "cleaners" is illustrative of some of the dangers of the reigning in corruption possibly going too far. This is a term used by some of the neo-fascist groups sprouting up around Russia, particularly in the North Caucusus region. They see it as their mission to clear out anyone who goes against the motherland or their version of the "Russian idea." For more on the rise of fascism in Russia, see Shenfield (2001), and for more on the activities of various hate-groups throughout Russia and the former Soviet Union, see UCSJ (2001). For a movie depicting the activities and roots of a small clandestine neo-fascist group in Moscow, see *Luna Park*.

30 Noviy Kompanon, February 27, 2001, as found through East-West Institute, *Russian Regional Report*, Vol. 6, no. 11, March 21, 2001.

31 See O'Prey (1995) and Gaddy (1996) for more on defense sector economics in the Soviet Union.

32 For a great work on the automotive sector from the point of view of an auto worker, see Hamper (1991). This book gives good insights into what happens when military orders and commercial orders are produced on the same line, and the negative impact this has on quality.

33 Although this is from mostly Russian sources (newspapers, journals, radio, and television networks), this also includes periodicals from Africa, Asia, Europe, Latin America, and the Middle East. The search was last conducted April 17, 2001, covering sources from January 1, 1999 through November 1, 2001.

34 For more on Chile's economy, see Birdsall, Graham & Sabot (1998).

35 Admiring Ayn Rand and following her recommendations are two different matters. Alan Greenspan, Chairman of the Federal Reserve, is also an admirer and was even a friend of Ms. Rand's. Nonetheless, he leads an institution that her libertarian values would suggest should not exist (see Woodward, 2000). This draws the distinction between words and actions, which is something that must be drawn with all political figures. Libertarian words plus statist actions do not add up to a libertarian policy. For more on Illarionov's admiration of Rand, see News Conference transcript, National Press Institute (Federal News Service, April 25, 2000).

36 Illarionov presented this insightful work at the CATO Institute, January 1999. It is also published in *Ekspert*, no. 8 (2000), available online at www.ekspert.ru, and *Voprosy Ekonomiky*, nos. 1 & 4 (1998).

37 For more on Illarionov's early support of the Chinese economic model, see "Secrets of the Chinese Economic Miracle," *Voprosy Ekonomiky*, no. 4

(1998). For his support of various nations as economic models see, *Trud*, October 24, 2000, available online at: www.trud.ru, and *Voprosy Ekonomiky*, no. 4 (2000).

38 Illarionov must be respected for his outspokenness when he does not agree with the administration. For a selection of his critiques of recent government policy see: *Vedomosti*, December 18, 2000, *Polit.ru*, December 20, 2000, *Segodnya*, January 2000, *Kommersant*, January 2000, and his criticisms of government policy were even carried by the government run daily, *Rossiyskaya gazeta*, January 24, 2000, but the article's criticisms must have caught the Kremlin's attention before the paper went to press, because Illarionov went onto the government-run TV channel, ORT (January 22, 2000) reversing his position on the Paris Club debt that he had taken in *Rossiyskaya gazeta*.

39 "FBIS Media Analysis: Putin Advisor Pushes Authoritarianism," January 25, 2001, Document ID: CEF20010125000438.

40 For more on our views on how Russia deviated from the market and distorted incentives given to entrepreneurs see Boettke & Butkevich (2001).

41 This portion of the labor force in the public sector remained remarkably steady throughout the late 1990s. While the portions of the labor working in the private sector (albeit loosely defined as such) was a mere 17.3% in 1990, it jumped to a dramatic 57.9% by 1995. Subsequently, it only slowly progressed to 61.7% of the workforce being in the private sector by 1999. This illustrates the slowdown in privatization efforts and the inability of new private firms to develop. Goskomstat, *Rossiyskiy Yezhgodnik, 2000* (Moscow: Goskomstat, 2000), p. 14.

42 For more on *perestroika* see Hewett & Winston (1991) and Lewin (1991).

43 For a comprehensive look at the decline of the ruble and the rise of barter, see Woodruff (2000).

44 The theory of Russia's economy as a "virtual economy" was developed by Clifford G. Gaddy and Barry W. Ickes. This perspective on the economy has been heralded in Russian and Western circles, including by Andrei Illarionov. For more on this theory see the issue *Post-Soviet Geography and Economics* (Volume 40, number 2, 1999), which includes an article by Gaddy and Ickes along with articles by other scholars on their theory.

45 The poll sources are two online Russian sources, FOM (Public Opinion Fund, at: www.fom.ru) and ROMIR Consulting and Public Relations (Russian Public Opinion and Market Research, at: www.romir.ru). The original Russian data was found at these sites after consulting the always helpful FBIS reports. See "Russian Public Opinion Monitor – Social and Economic Issues," FBIS, January 18, 2001, Document ID: CEP20010118000307.

46 *Ibid*. The FBIS report lists that, "'Almost no one,' said they could not answer the question." We checked the websites, and found similar wording used for other survey questions, but rarely.

47 Living standards, by the Russian government measure, have declined dramatically throughout the 1990s. One of the great dropping points was the August 1998 devaluation of the ruble, after which there was a bit of a leveling off and a rise in the payments of wage arrears. For more current economic statistics on Russia, see: Interfax, *Interfax Statistical Report*, published weekly, or RET, Russian Economic Trends.

48 *Ibid*. For more on the demographic catastrophe of Russia's rising suicide rates and simultaneously plummeting life expectancy amongst males, see Feshbach & Friendly (1991). His ongoing research is available through the Woodrow Wilson Center's website: www.wwisc.gov. The demographic crisis is so bad that Russia's death rate is currently the highest in Europe (15.3 per 1,000 people) and is the highest in Russia since the end of World War II. Also see *Moscow Times* (July 17, 2001).

49 Interfax, May 31, 2000, results of a poll taken immediately after Putin adopted the seven super-regions plan.

References

Barro, R.J. & Sala i Martin, X. (1999) *Economic Growth*, Cambridge: MIT Press.

Birdsall, N., Graham, C. & Sabot, R.H. (1998) *Beyond Tradeoffs: Market Reform and Equitable Growth in Latin America,* Washington, DC: Brookings/IDB.

Boettke, P.J. (2001) *Calculation and Coordination: Essays on Socialism and Transitional Political Economy*, New York: Routledge.

Boettke, P.J. & Butkevich, B.I. (2001) "Entry and Entrepreneurship: The Case of Post-Communist Russia," *Journal des Economistes et des Etudes Humaines*, 11: 91–114.

Boycko, M., Shleifer, A. & Vishny, R. (1996) *Privatizing Russia,* Cambridge: MIT Press.

Buchanan, J.M. (1969) *Cost and Choice: An Inquiry in Economic Theory*, Chicago: Markham Publishing Company.

Buchanan, J.M. (1971) *The Bases for Collective Action*, New York: General Learning Press.

Buchanan, J.M. (1975) *The Limits of Liberty: Between Anarchy and Leviathan*, Chicago: University of Chicago Press.

Buchanan, J.M. (1997) *Post-Socialist Political Economy*, Aldershot: Edward Elgar.

Diamond, J. (1997) *Guns, Germs, and Steel: The Fates of Human Societies*, New York: W.W. Norton.

Feshbach, M. & Friendly, A. Jr. (1991) *Ecocide in the USSR: Health and Nature Under Siege*, New York: Basic Books.

Fukuyama, F. (1995) *Trust: The Social Virtues and the Creation of Prosperity*, New York: Free Press.

Gaddy, C.G. (1996) *The Price of the Past: Russia's Struggle with the Legacy of a Militarized Economy,* Washington, DC: Brookings Institution.

Gaddy, C.G. & Ickes, B.W. (1998) "Russia's Virtual Economy," *Foreign Affairs*, 77: 53–67.

Grossman, G. (1977) "The 'Second Economy' of the USSR," *Problems of Communism*, 26: 25–40.

Hamper, B. (1991) *Rivethead: Tales from the Assembly Line*, New York: Warner Books.

Hayek, F.A. (1935) *Prices and Production*. 2nd edition, London: Routledge & Kegan Paul.

Heckscher, E.F. (1935) *Mercantilism*, trans. Mendel Shapiro, London: George Allen & Unwin.

Hewett, E.A. (1988) *Reforming the Soviet Economy: Equality versus Efficiency*, Washington, DC: Brookings Institution.

Hewett, E.A. & Winston, V.H. (1991) *Milestones in Glasnost and Perestroika: Politics and People*, Washington DC: Brookings Institution.

Hughes, L. (1990) *Selected Poems of Langston Hughes*, New York: Vintage Books.

Hume, D. (1948) *Dialogues Concerning Natural Religion*, H.D. Aiken (ed.), New York: Hafner.

Interfax, *Interfax Weekly Report*, November 9, 2000, available online at http://www.interfax-news.com/

Israel, A. (1989) *Institutional Development: Incentives to Performance*, Washington, DC: World Bank.

Kornai, J. (1990) *The Road to a Free Economy: Shifting from a Socialist System: The Example of Hungary*, London: W.W. Norton.

Kozhokin, M. (2001) "The President Speaks," *Izvesitia*. March 22, pp. 1, 3, as found online at www.izevstia.ru and as translated by WPS monitoring Agency, www.wps.ru/e_index.html.

Kuran, T. (1995) *Private Truths, Public Lies: The Social Consequences of Preference Falsification*, Cambridge: Harvard University Press.

Landes, D. (1999) *The Wealth and Poverty of Nations: Why Some are so Rich and Some are so Poor*, New York: W.W. Norton.

Latynina, Y. (2000) "Inside Russia: FSB Grounds a Good Business," *Moscow Times*, October 4.

Lewin, M. (1991) *The Gorbachev Phenomenon: A Historical Interpretation*, Berkeley: University of California Press.

Madariaga, I. de. (1990) *Catherine the Great*, New Haven: Yale University Press.

Malynes, G. de. [1622] *The Maintenance of Free Trade*, New York: Augustus M. Kelley, 1971.

McChesney, F. (1987) "Rent Extraction and Rent Creation in the Economic Theory of Regulation," *Journal of Legal Studies*, 16: 101–18.

Misselden, E. [1622] *Free Trade; or The Meanes to Make Trade Flourish Wherein the Causes of the Decay of Trade in this Kingdom are Discovered*, New York: Augustus M. Kelley, 1971.

Mun, T. [1664] *England's Treasure by Foreign Trade*, Oxford: Basil Blackwell, 1928.

North, D.C. (1990) *Institutions, Institutional Change and Economic Performance*, Cambridge: Cambridge University Press.

O'Prey, K. (1995) *A Farewell to Arms? Russia's Struggle with Defense Conversion*, New York: Twentieth Century Fund Press.

Pryanishnikov, P. (2001) "The Lipetsk Bug," *Versiya*, (January 16), p. 14.

Putin, V. (2000) "Russia at the Turn of the Millennium," (January 1) as found online at, http://www.government.gov.ru/english/statVP_engl_1.html.

Putnam, R. (1993) *Making Democracy Work*, Princeton: Princeton University Press.

Riasanovky, N.V. (1984) *A History of Russia*, 4th edition, Oxford: Oxford University Press.

Robbins, L. (1998) *A History of Economic Thought: The LSE Lectures*, ed. S.G. Medema & W.J. Samuels, Princeton: Princeton University Press.

RIA (Russian Information Agency), "Russian Interior Minister Believes Bribe Taking is Not Corruption," *RIA-Novosti*, March 13, 2001.

Shenfield, S.D. (2001) *Russian Fascism: Traditions, Tendencies, Movements*, Armonk, New York: M.E. Sharpe.
Smith, A. (1976) [1776] *An Inquiry into the Nature and Causes of the Wealth of Nations*, Oxford: Clarendon Press, 1976.
Stigler, G.J. (1966) *Theory of Price*. 3rd edition, New York: Macmillan.
Tullock, G. (1965) *The Politics of Bureaucracy*, Washington, DC: Public Affairs Press, 1965.
Tullock, G. (1975) "The Transitional Gains Trap," *Bell Journal of Economics*, 6: 671–8.
Union of Councils for Soviet Jews (UCSJ) (2001) *Antisemitism, Xenophobia and Religious Persecution in Russia's Regions: 1999–2000*, ed. N. Butkevich, Washington, DC: Union of Councils for Soviet Jews.
von Schmoller, G. (1902) *The Mercantile System and Its Historical Significance: Illustrated Chiefly from Prussian History*, New York: Macmillan.
Waterman, A.M.C. (2001) "Why was Adam Smith Not a Frenchman? Why 'Classical Political Economy' Was Born in England," presented at Summer Institute for the Preservation of the Study of the History of Economics, George Mason University.
Woodruff, D. (2000) *Money Unmade: Barter and the Fate of Russian Capitalism*, Ithaca: Cornell University Press.
Woodward, B. (2000) *Maestro: Greenspan's Fed and the American Boom*, New York: Simon & Schuster.
Yergin, D. (1991) *The Prize: The Epic Quest for Oil, Money, and Power*, New York: Simon & Schuster.
Yergin, D. & Gustavson, T. (1993) *Russia 2010: And What it Means for the World*, New York: Random House.

Index